HUGH LENOX SCOTT, 1853-1934

HUGH LENOX SCOTT
1853–1934

Reluctant Warrior

ARMAND S. La POTIN

UNIVERSITY OF OKLAHOMA PRESS : NORMAN

This book is published with the
generous assistance of the Kerr Foundation, Inc.

Library of Congress Cataloging-in-Publication Data

Names: La Potin, Armand Shelby, 1940– author.
Title: Hugh Lenox Scott, 1853–1934 : reluctant warrior / Armand S. La Potin.
Description: Norman : University of Oklahoma Press, [2021] | Includes bibliographical references and index. | Summary: "Biography of Hugh Lenox Scott (1853–1934), U.S. Army Chief of Staff, whose most notable achievements include the study of Indian sign language and development of ethnographies of Great Plains peoples, and how his work with the Indians influenced his service in both Cuba and the Philippines following the Spanish American War"—Provided by publisher.
Identifiers: LCCN 2021010715 | ISBN 978-0-8061-7574-4 (hardcover)
ISBN 978-0-8061-9203-1 (paper)
Subjects: LCSH: Scott, Hugh Lenox, 1853–1934. | Generals—United States—Biography. | Indians of North America—Government relations. | United States. Army—Officers—Biography. | United States. Army—Military life.
Classification: LCC E181 .L27 2021 | DDC 355.0092 [B]—dc23
LC record available at https://lccn.loc.gov/2021010715

The paper in this book meets the guidelines for permanence and durability of the Committee on Production Guidelines for Book Longevity of the Council on Library Resources, Inc. ∞

Copyright © 2021 by the University of Oklahoma Press, Norman, Publishing Division of the University. Paperback published 2023. Manufactured in the U.S.A.

All rights reserved. No part of this publication may be reproduced, stored in a retrieval system, or transmitted, in any form or by any means, electronic, mechanical, photocopying, recording, or otherwise—except as permitted under Section 107 or 108 of the United States Copyright Act—without the prior written permission of the University of Oklahoma Press. To request permission to reproduce selections from this book, write to Permissions, University of Oklahoma Press, 2800 Venture Drive, Norman OK 73069, or email rights.oupress@ou.edu.

To Carolyn for everything

▼ ▼ ▼

CONTENTS

List of Maps ♦ ix

Preface ♦ xi

INTRODUCTION ♦ 1

CHAPTER 1
The Beginnings: Starting a Life of Adventure ♦ 7

CHAPTER 2
The Making of a Frontier Diplomat ♦ 22

CHAPTER 3
The Fort Sill Years and Beyond: Advocacy and Its Limitations ♦ 53

CHAPTER 4
A Peacekeeper's Dilemma: The Challenge of Military Advancement ♦ 105

CHAPTER 5
Up the Administrative Ladder: A Star at Last ♦ 147

CHAPTER 6
A Full and Enriched Retirement: Tribal Groups First and Foremost ♦ 168

CONCLUSION
The Legacy of a Reluctant Warrior ♦ 197

Notes ♦ 205

Bibliography ♦ 247

Index ♦ 259

▼ ▼ ▼
MAPS

The Great Plains and the Border Lands, 1868–1890 ♦ 25

Moro Province in the Southern Philippines ♦ 127

Places in Mexico that Pancho Villa visited or occupied during
the Border War, 1914–1916 ♦ 156

▼ ▼ ▼
PREFACE

When I began my research on the life and professional career of Hugh Lenox Scott in 1983 as a result of a National Endowment for the Humanities (NEH) grant, my intention was to write a standard military biography addressing Scott's contribution to the solution of what U.S. officials in the late nineteenth and early twentieth centuries referred to as "the Indian problem." The demands of college administration caused me to delay the project until my retirement. As a result of my long hiatus from further research and writing, as well as my own intellectual growth through college teaching, this analysis of Scott's life is not only very different than the one I originally intended to write but, I hope, markedly improved.

Although historians have long abandoned the premise that the frontier army played no positive role in assisting American Indians in the transition to reservation life, cultural anthropologists, ethnologists, and sociologists, among others, have joined with more traditional historians in broadening the discussion of the government's dynamic and multifaceted relationship with indigenous peoples.[1] More recent scholarship has taken two directions that shed light on the evolution of tribal societies and attempts at assimilation. Initially, ethnohistorians and cultural anthropologists undertook full-length tribal studies that often utilized nontraditional oral and pictorial source material drawn from a spiritual orientation addressing questions of race, gender roles, and lifestyles among American Indians on the western frontier. Many of these studies document traumatic changes to their societies as a consequence of Euro-American contact and penetration, what some define as "imperialistic practices."[2] More specifically and as examples, differences in the meaning of spatial relationships and tangible objects such as the buffalo are used by scholars to document the cultural infringement on tribal societies.³ Another and more macro approach to the question of cultural assimilation addresses the issue from the perspective of federal policies and procedures. Such studies compare the U.S. government's treatment of Cubans and Filipinos at the dawn of America's imperialistic endeavors to its initial involvement with indigenous American Indians.⁴

In writing a history that addresses pluralist cultural issues, the use of names to identify certain groups takes on added significance and often, unfortunately, added confusion. I have used the term *American Indian* to refer to indigenous groups on the American continent. I have referred to individual tribes by their specific names where possible and use terms such as *tribal groups* or *tribal peoples* to differentiate other American Indians who no longer resided on reservations. I have also used the term *indigenous peoples* to describe the Moros of the Muslim faith who occupy the province of Mindanao in the southern Philippines.

Imprecision exists when defining phrases like *white settlers* to describe the groups of more recent origin that came to the shores of and penetrated the North American continent. However, this phrase is commonly applied to studies that address contrasting cultures, and this frequency justifies its usage in this narrative. For variety, although no less imprecise, I have used such phrases as *Anglos*, *Anglo-Americans*, and *Euro-Americans* to refer to more recent settlers of the North American continent who interacted with older inhabitants of the region.

In a broad sense, any historical narrative of an event, a movement, or of an individual's life is a collaborative effort, and this study is no exception. As previously noted, the topic itself came about because of an NEH award to college professors of history. It enabled me and other potential scholars to attend colleges and universities often far from our traditional campuses during the summer months to acquire an understanding in a subfield that we could ultimately teach to our students. In the summer of 1981, I was a fortunate to be selected by Roger Nichols, the NEH program director at the University of Arizona and a scholar in nineteenth-century Native American history, to attend his seminar. One consequence of my selection was the opportunity to offer my students at the State University of New York College at Oneonta a course, The Indian in American History, in both lecture and seminar format for a twenty-year period prior to my retirement in 2003. Another was the opportunity to learn of and write about the life of Gen. Hugh Lenox Scott (1853–1934), a nineteenth-century U.S. Cavalry officer. Scott's tenure on the frontier and throughout his military career and beyond, including the application of the Indian sign language, was both unique and significant. Through the challenges incurred as a result of the army's transformation from a predominantly frontier constabulary to an overseas military force, he rose to be its chief of staff prior to his retirement in 1917, at the beginning of America's involvement in World War I.

Many individuals have assisted me in furthering my research on Scott's life over the last twenty-five years. Research stipends from the State University of New York, including but not limited to the Maynard Redfield Fund, paid for the necessary trips that I took to Washington, D.C., to work at the Library of Congress, where the Scott Family Papers are housed; the National Archives, where Scott's official papers are located; and the National Anthropological Archives of the Smithsonian Institution, where Scott's treatises on tribal lore, investigative studies of the Plains Indian sign language, and his numerous reports as a commissioner of Indian Affairs are located. Like thousands of other researchers, I am indebted to librarian-archivists at these institutions, such as Ryan Brubacher, C. Fred Coker, Paul T. Heffron, Patrick Kerwin, Bruce Kirby, Melissa Lindberg, and Edith Sandler of the Library of Congress; Leslie C. Waffen and Donald Jackanicz of the National Archives; and Kathy Creek with the National Anthropological Archives of the Smithsonian Institution. Other research sources, further afield, include depositories of papers at Fort Sill, located near the city of Lawton, Oklahoma. It is here that Scott spent a seminal part of his early life honing his skills as an advocate protecting the interests of American Indians. Another significant depository is at the U.S. Military Academy at West Point, where he served as superintendent in the first decade of the twentieth century and where many documents beyond the years of his tenure there are catalogued. Cherie Rinehart at Fort Sill provided invaluable assistance, as did Dawn L. Crumpler at West Point. Impressionistic sources beyond letters, reports, and official documents conveyed a more personal understanding of Scott's life. Prior to her passing in 1990, I had the pleasure of interviewing Sarah Houston Merrill ("Houty"), Scott's youngest daughter, who was born in 1900 and who provided invaluable insights regarding her father's personality and the dynamics of her family. And in a different way, a visit to the restored Fort Totten, north of Bismarck, North Dakota, where Scott was stationed early in his military career, gave me a sense of what his daily life was like, complementing the descriptive letters to his family that he wrote from the post. Students of the history of the army's role in the development of the American West may profit too from the publication of Scott's autobiography in 1928 near the end of his life. *Some Memories of a Soldier,* at over six hundred pages, is a mine of detail about daily military life on the Great Plains in the nineteenth century, the dress and culture of specific tribes, and encounters with tribal leaders. It also reveals his interaction with colleagues and officials later in his career in other places where he was stationed and where he resided and traveled in his retirement. Significantly for this study, his autobiography conveys vividly his views and attitudes about culture, race, and the changes in military policy and organization over the span of his career. As such, it provides the reader with a clear understanding of how he wanted to be remembered. A vastly different and unusual source in the life of a late-nineteenth-century frontier officer was the movie he made with synchronized sound in 1930 on the Indian sign language. In the film, Scott introduces some of his tribal friends in Montana who talk about the meaning of the sign language. While the movie sheds little light on Scott's interaction with American Indians that cannot be gleaned from more traditional sources, it is a uniquely fascinating historical record.

On a personal note, several people offered invaluable aid in their review of manuscript drafts, including both professional scholars and individuals initially unfamiliar with the subject matter. These include Allen Cohn, Jason P. Clark, J. Gerrit Gantvoort, James Leiker, William Simons, and James Slaughter. Their literary skills and ongoing patience provided many helpful insights, and I am indebted to them all. In a different way, Molly Murphy contributed to the visual quality of the project with her colorful art work. It is a pleasure to have such talented friends. Perhaps the most valuable assistant that anyone could ask for is a loving understanding partner. I am truly blessed to have a wonderful wife, Carolyn Dupree LaPotin, who not only read and critiqued many of the drafts of the manuscript, formatted the text, served patiently as a sounding board when I verbalized many of my ideas, but equally significant, put up with the presence of numerous archive boxes that seemed to grow well beyond the confines of my study! I owe her a debt that I know I can never repay.

▼ ▼ ▼

INTRODUCTION

Hugh Lenox Scott wanted to be remembered as a soldier of peace.[1] When he died at Walter Reed Hospital in Washington, D.C., on April 30, 1934, newspapers throughout the nation cited his record of military service on the American frontier during the late nineteenth century, overseas following the Spanish-American War, and ultimately, in Washington as chief of staff of the army. His contributions as a peacemaker and peacekeeper among American Indians were particularly noted because of his friendship with them. His study of the use of an Indian sign language, a long-standing means of intertribal communication among Native Americans west of the Mississippi, was also remarked upon. Specifically, journalists at the time of his death documented his long career spent negotiating with tribal leaders as an officer on the Great Plains following the Custer debacle at Little Big Horn in 1876; organizing an Indian regiment of Kiowa, Comanche, and Apache scouts in 1892; and administering to the Chiricahua Apache prisoners of war in 1894 when they were brought to Fort Sill, Oklahoma Territory, from their exile in Alabama. His overseas assignments in the early twentieth century, first as an administrator in Cuba and then in the southern Philippines, were also highlighted. In the latter area, as governor of the Sulu Archipelago, Scott worked with the indigenous Muslim Moro people. While it was his superintendence at West Point and subsequent command of the army's Texas Military Department that ultimately led to his promotion to brigadier general and chief of staff in 1914, journalists noted that Scott continued to play a major role in protecting the interests of tribes, throughout his military career as well as during his formal retirement from military service. Scott continued his work on behalf of tribal groups during the later chapters of his life through his membership on the Board of Indian Commissioners, until its termination on the eve of the Franklin Roosevelt administration.

Scott was unique in several ways as a career officer in the early twentieth century. One was in how he defined his role in military administration. Scott wanted to be known and remembered as a "soldier of peace" because he viewed using overt military force as a last resort, relying on his skills as a negotiator to avoid conflict. Such a position was inconsistent with the goals of a new modern American army that evolved over time to meet the challenges of a nation with overseas possessions to administer and defend.

Scott entered military service in an army too long constrained in size by a nineteenth-century Congress whose members felt threatened by a professional standing military force. This, and a restrictive retirement system that kept senior officers in place long after they were effective commanders, intensified the competition among junior officers of Scott's generation for attaining professional recognition. Compounding the problem for an officer like Scott, who defined his military role more as a negotiator than a warrior, was the United States Army's new objective to help guard the nation's overseas possessions in the first decade of the twentieth century. Elihu Root, the new secretary of war (1899–1904), and arguably one of the greatest military reformers of the twentieth century, noted that "the real objective in having an Army is to prepare for war." Root's reforms, in part to correct the deficiencies of a nineteenth-century military force, resulted in major changes in the training of officers and, ultimately, in the very structure of the military hierarchy itself. Seniority in rank was no longer a viable criterion for professional advancement. What replaced it, the subjective criterion of merit, was interpreted to apply to one's battlefield experience. This hardly served the personal goals of an officer like Scott who considered overt military action as a last resort.

Scott was unique as a military officer in other ways as well. His role as an Indian reformer, one who negotiates with and advocates for the interests of tribal groups, was not seen as a legitimate undertaking for a twentieth-century army. Once tribes were no longer a military threat to the army, it abdicated any responsibility for their welfare. In fact, Scott's efforts to assist them, when doing so directly thwarted the interests of the military, were met with rejection.[2]

Scott began his venture into Native American affairs with little interest in the welfare of tribal groups. As an adolescent, he felt the need to test his endurance and courage in adverse physical environments, in terms of both climate and terrain. His choice of a career in military service was predicated on a desire to continue the adventurous life that he had enjoyed as a youth. Scott was drawn to tribal groups by what he perceived as their ability to live in an environment fraught with danger and uncertainty.

However, in 1876 when he first entered the northern Great Plains as a newly minted second lieutenant in the Seventh Cavalry, tribes west of the Mississippi were already confronting the devastating loss of their reservation holdings and their cultural integrity as independent peoples. Dissident bands engaged in violent raids against western settlers and commercial interests that were increasingly penetrating their tribal holdings. Scott's orders were to subdue the bellicose actions of these tribal groups. Eventually, the Dawes Severalty Act of 1887 allowed the federal government to nullify tribal titles by fiat, and the Supreme Court, in *Lone Wolf v. Hitchcock* (1903), sanctioned the unilateral authority of Congress to abrogate treaties between the United States and Native American tribes. This ruling abolished the treaty system and what guarantees tribal groups had under its provisions. The cumulative effects left tribes confined to designated lands adjacent to agencies where the government distributed provisions and from which it could monitor the movement of potentially dissident groups. Scott embraced the role of negotiator and advocate for tribal groups as a consequence of their poor treatment and condition.[3]

Indian reformers in the late nineteenth and early twentieth centuries were an eclectic group with varied types of education and experiences. Helen Hunt Jackson, author of *A Century of Dishonor* (1881), was one of the first. Her critique of the government's treatment of tribal groups provided the catalyst to inspire many eastern reformers. Critics and reformers addressed what they believed to be the causes of the impoverished state of tribal groups, including the federal government's role in creating the problem, and the solutions that could end tribal destitution. They formed dozens of local and national organizations from 1880 to 1930 to address these issues. Some called for major changes to the Bureau of Indian Affairs (BIA), created in 1824;

others advocated for its dissolution, given the ongoing political corruption of many of its staff. Proposals for solving the "Indian problem" also varied. A few favored a multicultural approach, allowing tribes to maintain and build upon the virtues of their cultural talents and interactions with the broader American society. However, most favored some form of assimilation, whether immediate or gradual. Daniel Smiley, a wealthy prominent eastern Quaker, convened a well-attended annual forum at his Lake Mohonk, New York, estate in the late nineteenth and early twentieth centuries. Here reformers could discuss their views on various aspects of promoting the welfare of "the Indian and other dependent peoples."

Most reformers were white Anglo Protestants, although several, like Carlos Montezuma, an Apache, and Henry Roe Cloud, a Winnebago, were nonreservation Natives. Many of the middle-class professionals were doctors, lawyers, and educators. Not surprisingly, Christian missionaries, both Protestant and Catholic, or those who worked for and with church groups, were well represented, comprising about a third of the Lake Mohonk gathering at its final meeting in 1929.[4]

Religion was a major component in the Indian reform movement. Although not outwardly or overtly spiritual, Scott was raised in a devout Presbyterian environment. Both his father and grandfather were ministers; the latter was head of the Princeton (N.J.) Theological Seminary and a prominent and well-respected theologian beyond ecclesiastical circles. Scott's widowed mother—her husband and Scott's father died when Scott was eight—was another moral force in his life.[5]

There was another element combining both religion and reform. This dynamic was racial marginalization. The defining of people of different races according to a scale of civilization tied to the so-called Anglo race had a long history of accommodation before Scott began his military career. Anglo-Americans used racial marginalization to justify holding blacks in bondage and treating them as inferior human beings, and eventually as second-class citizens. Discrimination also had negative impacts on immigrants lured to the country's shores by the dramatic industrial development in the United States at the end of the nineteenth and beginning of the twentieth century. So, too, racial marginalization was used against American Indians to deny them their tribal holdings.

The proliferation of a polyglot of cultures on America's shores challenged societal norms, the existing social stratification in the United States, and the very definition of what constituted an American. Many scholars, journalists, and literary figures sought some kind of scientific rationale to defend giving privileges to Anglo-Americans who now felt threatened by traumatic cultural change. Anthropologists and sociologists were hard-pressed to come up with a scientific scale that could weigh the numerous characteristics that constituted a *race*, let alone agree what those characteristics were. Nonetheless, their treatises, often called by critics "scientific racism," were used by a number of Caucasian Americans to justify racial marginalization. Popular writers among the intellectual community bolstered the argument for racial marginalization with impressionistic evidence drawn from their study of history.[6]

However, not all subscribers to racial marginalization were prepared to abandon or ignore the status of "inferior" peoples. Some felt morally obligated to assist others on what they perceived to be the path to civilization. Many who embraced missionary work viewed their calling in the field of Indian reform. Others, in professions not tied to the clergy, were equally committed to assisting those viewed as members of an inferior race on the road to salvation.

Hugh Lenox Scott was one of the latter. As both a negotiator attempting to promote peace on the western frontier and an advocate protecting the welfare of tribal groups, Scott saw his role as a mission to promote the civilizing of Native tribes through their assimilation into Anglo society. Scott's racial predilections were evident in his interactions with the Muslim Moros of the southern Philippines as well as with American Indians. He viewed both groups as primitive and childlike, with little ability to reason. His frontier diplomacy, as it were, was predicated on the assumption that both peoples' embrace of violence constituted a critical component of their purportedly primitive cultures. He developed negotiating skills to win their trust by listening patiently to their concerns, promoting their loyalty, and promising them no more than he was capable of delivering. He formed alliances among many of the tribal groups to glean information about possible unanticipated acts of violence—a common occurrence among primitive peoples, or so he believed. However, pacification won them nothing in return. Their compliance with his directives was predicated on the respect that he demonstrated for their culture, but he never believed that their culture was enough to sustain them in an Anglo-dominant world.[7] Moreover, what he, as an advocate, offered them—a plan of assimilation—was predicated on his values, not theirs.

This study will address the complex relationship that Scott had with military service, specifically how he attempted to gain professional recognition culminating in a star ranking while still maintaining his relationships with indigenous peoples and his motivation as a peacemaker. Other aspects of his life warrant investigation, including his role as a reformer, his relationship to other reformers, and his racial proclivities tied to reform. Collectively, they constitute the legacy of his life.

CHAPTER 1

▼ ▼ ▼

THE BEGINNINGS

Starting a Life of Adventure, 1853–1876

> I am the most horribly homesick fellow you ever saw.
> —*Hugh Scott to Tom Ricketts, June 4, 1871*

Hugh Lenox Scott was born in Danville, Kentucky, on September 22, 1853. The child of Mary Hodge and the Reverend William McKendree Scott, he was the second of three sons who survived into adulthood. He was named after his great uncle Hugh Lenox Hodge, a Philadelphia physician. Scott's father died of consumption in 1861 when his son was only eight years old. Growing up with his widowed mother, older brother Charles, and younger sibling William, Len, as he was called, had a near ideal childhood. He later remembered the Princeton, New Jersey, home of his youth as "always a place of mirth and laughter . . . in winter a place of light and warmth; in summer of cool shade . . . where children, friends and relatives and their children loved to congregate; where all found a boundless love and welcome within its spacious walls with peace and plenty."[1] It was a place of intellectual enrichment as well. Scott's maternal grandfather, Charles Hodge (1797–1878), was principal of the Princeton Theological Seminary at the time and was recognized and respected as one of the foremost Presbyterian ministers in the United States in the nineteenth century.

Scott's father had been a ministerial student—some would say a disciple—of Hodge. Following his ordination, William was called to numerous congregations from New York to Ohio and south to Kentucky. In Kentucky, he served as a professor of ancient languages at Centralia College in Danville. Hodge's relationship with William was more than that of a spiritual mentor.

In 1847, William courted and won the hand of Mary, Hodge's only daughter, and regarded by her father as his special child.[2]

Both Len's father—in what little time that he had with his son prior to his death—and grandfather provided him with a foundation for knowledge that would flourish throughout his life. In 1845, William Scott recorded in his diary how he grew from a young boy of modest and humble means, the youngest of seven siblings from an "honest and pious Methodist farmer" in rural Jefferson County, Ohio, to an ordained Presbyterian minister with numerous callings and a posting at the Bible college in the town where Len was born. William Scott partially credited his intellectual epiphany to the discovery of reading from books given to him by an older brother. The brother all but raised him when their father abandoned the farm and his children and moved with his second wife into a neighboring town. Novels such as *Robinson Crusoe* gave him "a joy unknown before." The works of Shakespeare "fixed my destiny. . . . From it I learned history, philosophy, humanity. . . . Henceforth I was a reader. . . . All [books] that I could in any way continue to get my hands on I read on wet days when there was no work to be done out of doors, in the evenings by the blazing coal fire, and, I am ashamed to say, Sunday."[3]

The second cause of the elder Scott's awakening was spiritual and occurred while under the Hodge's tutelage. Hodge's distinguished career in the church included supervising the instruction of more than three thousand ordained ministers, while serving in various educational institutions, culminating in his long tenure at Princeton. His literary accomplishments comprised numerous treatises on theology and church polity, including his magnum opus, *Systematic Theology* (1871–73). He also authored numerous articles in the *Princeton Review* in response to current ecclesiastical issues. Although Hodge advocated strict adherence to the orthodoxy of historical Calvinism, he adopted a more flexible stance in embracing a polity that tolerated different paths to the acceptance of Christ. Among ecclesiastical circles, he was known as the "Pope of Protestantism."[4]

In Len's later relationship with indigenous peoples, he exhibited explicit attitudes his grandfather undoubtedly would have questioned. Nonetheless, both shared fundamental implicit assumptions of Presbyterian theology that defined the relationship between God and man. Hodge and Scott believed that man was created to glorify God and that salvation could only be attained from a path of "good works" or "deeds" that man demonstrated on earth. The tangible process for reaching such a state was to embrace God by learning about the created world and by knowing one's calling—the role that God prescribed for one's life on earth. Recording the path to one's calling through a personal diary like his father had kept or an autobiography such as the younger Scott would later write, was an act not of pretense or vanity, but of humility. Consequently, the path to salvation for both was an *intellectual* exercise and a demonstration of moral faith so one would know the world God created. Education, both formal and informal, was a fundamental process in a Presbyterian's life.

Although his immediate family had to come to grips with his calling to be a soldier on the western frontier, once he decided what it would be, he applied himself diligently in broadening his knowledge of that world, which he perceived as a majestic landscape filled with opportunities to hunt, fish, test his courage, and seek adventure. And here, too, he would find a cause to do good, as a Christian, in helping those human beings his mother and grandfather referred to as savages.

Len recollected his childhood residence in Princeton as "a spacious cultured home," particularly at commencement when "the doors were wide open to the friends who had graduated at College and Seminary and were now returning to renew the ties of friendship—they came from far and wide and looked up to my Grandfather, as did the whole town, with reverence and admiration." However, this "cultured home" would have a more immediate impact on Scott's siblings, older brother Charles and younger brother William, nicknamed "Wick," both of whom graduated from Princeton College. William graduated with honors and went on to Cambridge, earning a doctorate and pursuing a prestigious career at Princeton University as a renowned paleontologist.[5]

Len, possessing a more independent and adventurous streak, selected a seemingly different path, one that his late father may have appreciated or at least understood, while his mother, who came from a family of students that preferred indoor and sedate endeavors, certainly did not. Both father and son shared a love—Scott called it a "passion"—for hunting and fishing. In his father's absence, Scott cultivated the companionship of several peers with whom he shared outdoor adventures during his teen years. He enjoyed spending time in the woods with Robert Dod, one of his many boyhood friends, along with their hunting dogs. Friends and neighbors considered their enthusiasm, stamina, and perseverance remarkable. Mastering classroom grammar and arithmetic was more a chore than a challenge for a boy who longed for the weekends and a respite from study. Indeed, the limited free time that he did have to spend outdoors made those times even more meaningful. Looking back over his early years from the vantage of a military career, he recalled:

> This was the very best school that could have been devised for a soldier, as I found later on the plains; it taught me to find my way about and take care of myself in the woods day and night in all kinds of weather. I could hunt only on Saturdays during the school term and had to take the weather as it came or lose my weekend; so many days in the dead of winter, I would be found starting [sic] a fox at four o'clock in the morning four miles from home with a strong cold wind blowing and a foot of snow on the ground. . . . and night would find us eight or ten miles from home, hungry, wet, cold, exhausted, with clothes torn to rags, and home to find in the darkness.[6]

Implicit in Scott's view was the need to test oneself, to confront the danger of the unknown, with the ultimate gratification, if not euphoria, of mastering one's circumstances in meeting the challenge.

Mary, who had other plans for her middle son, hoped he would strive for a more sedentary profession such as law or medicine as his great uncle and namesake had done, or perhaps even a teaching profession in the sciences, as Len's brother William would pursue. The loss of her husband—Mary never remarried—intensified her interest in and concern for the welfare of her three sons, and although she would accept Len's decision to follow a military career, she considered it "extremely narrow and dangerous." It would cause her no end of anguish and concern.[7]

Perhaps because Len lost his father at a young age, family members took a particular interest in his welfare and encouraged him to form close relationships with contemporary male friends through their common interest in outdoor activities. Specifically, the Scott-Hodge clan provided him with an invaluable network of support at critical periods in his young life. Len's older brother, Charles, and great-"uncle" David Hunter (the brother of Charles Hodge's second wife, Mary Hunter Stockton), whom the Scott boys always referred to as uncle, shepherded him through his teen years and into early adulthood. And his mother as well as Grandfather Hodge were always there to give advice, often unsolicited!

One of the most important decisions in his early life was the choice of a career. The military appealed to Len owing no doubt to his sense of adventure and going to West Point was an option owing to Hunter. He was a brevet major general of volunteers in the cavalry, commander of a regional department during the Civil War, and a friend of Presidents Lincoln and Grant. He offered to secure for his great-nephew a provisional presidential appointment to the United States Military Academy in the class of 1871. Nonetheless, admission was by no means a certainty in 1870 when the offer was made. There was an entrance exam to pass, and the term *provisional* meant that his admission would possibly be contingent on the failure of other applicants to pass the exam or the withdrawal of competing applicants. He could perhaps be admitted to the class of 1872, but that was by no means a certainty either. In one of what would prove to be many examples of support for young Len, the Scotts held a family conference. Mary sought the advice of her oldest son, then employed in Pittsburgh, to counsel Len on his options. Charles was skeptical about the presidential appointment. "Put not your trust in princes or Presidents either," he cautioned, noting that Grant could die or be removed from office in the interim. The fallback plan, which every parent of a college-bound child could appreciate, was to have Len take additional preparatory coursework and then apply to Princeton College. The hope was that he could pass the entrance exam, which he did. Fortunately for Len, the Princeton back-up plan was unnecessary. He was formally admitted to the Academy as a presidential appointee on July 1, 1871.[8]

"I am the most horribly homesick fellow you ever saw,"[9] wrote young Len to a childhood friend shortly after his arrival at West Point as he prepared to take his entrance exam. Homesickness, however, would be just one, and a temporary one at that, of many challenges he would face during his time at West Point. Life there, then as now, presented traumatic changes for a normal teenager going through a period of rebelliousness in search of his identity. West Point, unlike most colleges and universities, imposed a code of strict discipline and regimentation, as well as an adherence to conformity, that was the very antithesis of what young Scott had been accustomed to even under his grandfather's tutelage at Princeton. The carefree joy of hunting and fishing in the woods and streams with friends, oblivious to time or season of the year, was gone when he arrived as a plebe in early June 1871. Given Len's propensity for hands-on experience and learning by doing, coupled with the Academy's academic curriculum and method of instruction, a West Point education seemed a poor fit indeed.

The institution that Scott entered in the immediate postbellum period was steeped in a strict military code of behavior and a system of education that was increasingly anachronistic. The formal education that Scott received placed a heavy emphasis on the mathematical sciences at the expense of history, grammar, English, and geography. Cadets spent almost half of their total instructional time on the mathematical sciences alone. Little attempt was made to introduce practical field experience into the curriculum. To add to the dilemma, the method of instruction, learning by rote or recitation, discouraged creative thinking, something essential to a young officer who would be faced with an elusive and unpredictable adversary on a battlefield. West Point's instructors were part of an entrenched bureaucracy, initially selected among the officer corps' outstanding graduates. They usually had no more than three or four years of field service following their graduation. They enjoyed lifetime tenure. Consequently, it was not unusual for an instructor to serve thirty years or longer prior to retirement. Often the texts they used were adopted when they first began teaching![10]

Moreover, the unyielding tendency to reject change and embrace the status quo was an element of pride among West Point's establishment both within and beyond its hollowed walls. Instructors certainly had a vested interest in defending the institution's methods of instruction, coming as they did from the ranks of recent graduates. And it had produced the officer corps that led the Union so successfully in battle. Reform was deemed not only unnecessary but potentially disruptive, thus providing the rationale used by many to thwart change. Moreover, the country's senior military leaders in the postbellum period—Grant, Sherman, Sheridan—visited almost annually, if not more frequently, reinforcing the Academy's insular view of its own greatness. So, too, its alumni, an eclectic group that came from all walks of life, and who during their careers undertook diverse field encounters, at least enjoyed the commonality of a shared experience there. To many, West Point was their family, and for some, it was the *only* family they knew. The continuity of what they remembered and what was still there, in terms of customs, practices, and traditions, was undoubtedly a source of pride and admiration.[11]

An anachronistic curriculum, a teaching style that stymied creative thought, and an attitude that favored maintaining the way things had always been—none of this augured well for Len's success at West Point. Adding to his dilemma was the fact that its most enduring academic discipline, the mathematical sciences, was his weakest subject to master. Warning his mother and preparing her in advance for an outcome that might lead to his undoing in the fall of his freshman (plebe) year, Scott wrote, "I know that you always wanted me to stand high in my class *but I can never do it*" (emphasis in original). At that point in West Point's grading system, he stood in the sixth section (the lowest) in math. By hard work and diligence, he thought he could achieve at best a fourth- or third-section standing "and stay there though it is the hardest work I ever had [done] before[.] [A]s you know I haven't a mathematical turn of mind." But the way the subject was presented was as much an issue for him as the subject itself. He went on to complain to his mother that the anxiety he experienced "everyday[,] that I am not going to get a good mark for a lesson that would be considered perfect anywhere else is only thought 'so-so' here[,] and they cut down your mark if you don't stand properly or if you take your pointer in the wrong hand[,] and there are so many little things that I don't see how anybody gets any mark at all." Interestingly, his instructor in mathematics, Albert Church, began teaching at West Point in 1828 and would retire in 1878, two years after Scott graduated.[12] Mastering the subject continued to be difficult for him, and his ongoing tendency to procrastinate in completing his assignments certainly did not help.[13]

A more serious and ultimately more ominous challenge that Len faced at West Point was his trouble dealing with the strict regulations governing every aspect and every waking hour of a cadet's life. Cadets generally averaged one hundred demerits a year, from failure to salute the officer of the day to talking during the dinner service. Scott's average was around 20 percent higher. Even during his final year at the Academy, he noted to his mother that "Ive [sic] had so many [demerits]—that I walk a chalk I've marked out."[14]

Scott was blessed with family and friends who offered love, empathy, advice, and encouragement. The support network that he enjoyed when he first arrived at West Point in early June 1871 continued and expanded through his cadet years at the Academy. His mother, Mary, wrote to him on average of at least two to three letters a month. She intermittently challenged him to apply his best efforts, invoking her moral standard of Christian behavior when he faltered or was tempted by drinking and gaming. She frequently reminded him that other family members and friends were counting on him to succeed and willing to do what they could to make it so. Brother Charles, Grandfather Hodge, and even David Hunter expressed similar sentiments, although less frequently. Hunter informed his great-nephew that he rarely wrote letters, and consequently that young Len should feel flattered and special that his benefactor took an ongoing personal interest in his success. Other supportive family members mentioned in Scott's letters include Samuel Stockton, his grandfather's wife's son from a previous marriage, whom Scott also referred to fondly and legitimately as uncle.[15]

Aside from his family, Scott's many friends were an especially important part of his network or more accurately, his safety net. As a teenager he had hunted with most of them. Robert Dod, who corresponded with Scott on a bimonthly basis during his first two years as a cadet, reminisced about the good times they shared and how others admired them for their hunting skills of accuracy and endurance. Dod's visit to the West Point campus in late July of Scott's first year was a testament to their friendship. A few of Scott's older friends were chosen by his mother from among her friends' sons to serve as role models.[16]

Any mother would have probably considered Edward P. Rankin, a friend from Scott's hunting days, and four years his senior, the perfect role model. A minister's son, Rankin wrote letters to Scott that displayed a religious orientation in his attempt to address the importance of developing one's intellect. Inquiring about the library at West Point and whether Scott had time for reading, he noted, "You can not spend too much time in this way. . . . The sooner you make it [the habit of reading] the better for you."[17]

The influence that Scott's network of family and friends had on his development at West Point is difficult to determine with precision. However, indirect evidence indicates that it was significant. His letters home document his determination to justify the confidence that they had placed in his ability to persevere, making it clear that the network was meaningful. One can glean insights into his thoughts from his letters or references to family and friends. For example, his mother reminded her son that family influence had enabled him to get into West Point, and since the choice was his, he had an obligation to be diligent in his studies—advice the young Scott took to heart.[18] Scott's interest in reading and developing a disciplined intellect is another example of how family influence motivated him. Mary was quick to follow up on her son's question of *what* he should be reading. "If you want conversation," she advised

> the best thing is to think about and digest what you read. You can't make conversation on a mere string of isolated facts. Shakespeare and Macaulay's essays are two very good books. I am delighted to see that you have found out your ignorance, for, as Socrates says: "We only go to school to find out how little we know." And I would encourage you in every way to read and improve yourself. . . . Read the newspapers and keep abreast of the times[,] it will give you always something to talk about.[19]

One thing that can be said with certainty is that his family was there to save him when he faced the greatest challenge of his tenure at West Point, and one that threatened his continuing education: hazing. The practice of forcing first-year cadets, or plebes, to perform often impossible tasks of physical endurance and engage in other acts meant to humiliate them was a long-standing tradition at the Academy. Although officially outlawed, with the perpetrator subject to disciplinary action, the practice was condoned by upperclassmen and even the plebes themselves as a test of character and manliness. In an institution that allowed for few diversions, some considered it an amusement. The plebes could anticipate applying the same treatment to a subsequent class of freshmen in their second year as "yearlings." The fear of isolation and ostracism, a common fate of first-year classmen, encouraged plebes to welcome the attention, even if it was negative. The plebes' refusal to reveal the names of those who hazed them, as a point of honor, undergirded the prevalence of hazing.[20]

One's initial introduction as a cadet to West Point's environment often came through the practice of hazing. Plebes spent at least the first three weeks there in "camp," where a selected group of upperclassmen, often induced by peer pressure, would ostensibly teach them the basic fundamentals of soldiering, such as how to march and salute. Over time, this introductory period came to be known as "beast barracks," where plebes were subject to acts that were meant to teach them "unquestioning and instant obedience," and was looked upon as discipline training. "Seps," those entering cadets who arrived during the fall after the summer's "beast barracks" had ended, could be subjected to the same treatment, since they were initially segregated from the other cadets and considered below the rank of plebe (those who had arrived the previous summer).[21]

However, if an incident was reported to senior authorities, they were then duty-bound to act on the complaint. Such action could lead to potentially unfortunate consequences for cadets so accused, possibly leading to their expulsion. Such was the situation that yearling Scott found himself in during the spring 1872 semester when he was formally charged with hazing a fellow cadet. Nonetheless, this was not the first time that Scott had encountered the issue. He engaged in a mild form of hazing in late June 1871. He probably assumed that since he did not find it detrimental when it was done to him shortly after his arrival, it was acceptable to practice it on a fellow cadet. It may also have been a situation where he was dared into doing it by his peers, since reference was made to it as a "class" activity. Whatever the reason, his behavior triggered a sharp rebuke from his mother, particularly because her son knew he could be dismissed from West Point as a consequence. What may have saved her son from disciplinary action the first time was a visit to the Academy by Grandfather Hodge. Hodge's presence on campus may have thwarted any disciplinary action against his grandson. Whatever the cause, the absence of any punishment for the transgression may have encouraged Len to tempt the hand of fate even further![22] In the previous semester, four of his friends or acquaintances were dismissed for hazing and two others received serious reprimands. That should have served as another warning to him, but his response was to note that "neither (of the cadets who were given reprimands) . . . did devil any of (the) 'seps' any more than I did," and hence, from his perspective, did not deserve the punishment. Scott criticized the authorities for censuring the behavior. Again, Mary warned her son not to "hazard your whole career for the short-lived pleasure of hazing."[23] And as before, the family network stepped in to save him. While admonishing his grandson for his behavior yet again, Hodge brought his case to the superintendent as well as to West Point's commandant, Gen. Emory Upton, remarking, "I said all I properly could to make him take a favorable view of the matter but what I have written [to you] is all I could get from him." Len also had the reassurance from his grandfather of knowing that "if the worst should come, you have a home to come to where you will be received as kindly as ever." Mary's reaction was to blame those who reported her son and to pray that "God bless and keep you & help you from your present straight."[24]

Given his disciplinary record on the issue of hazing, Scott probably fared better than he had a right to expect, doubtless owing to the support of his family. He was one of three cadets in his original class held back a year. Looking back on the incident at the end of a long career, he noted how "I and my class were much aggrieved at this severe punishment for what had been a custom ever since the founding of the Academy," but he recognized that "the foundation of all military discipline is obedience to orders, and . . . since hazing has been forbidden by the proper authorities, it cannot be tolerated." Nonetheless, and perhaps as a consequence of his cadet experience, as superintendent of West Point in 1906, Scott declined to reform the practice without the cooperation of the students themselves, whose honor code prevented them from turning in a fellow classmate.[25]

"There is something in [soldiering] I like better than anything else even though I'm only a plebe . . . what must it be if you are a Colonel and command a regiment." So wrote Len to his younger brother, Wick, in his first year at West Point. And despite the setbacks and challenges he confronted, as a senior classman, he never doubted that he had made the right decision in pursuing a military career. On a personal level, his West Point experience taught him respect for order and structure as manifested in a growing sense of self-discipline. The penalties that he incurred there for his behavior doubtless encouraged him to direct his energy in a more constructive direction, although he would continue to demonstrate little patience for what he regarded as the manifestation of senseless authority.[26]

More significantly, West Point gave him a sense of focus in channeling his enthusiasm for outdoor adventure as well as new ways to test his self-reliance. Swimming was one such activity, and perilous enough to challenge his resourcefulness. Prior to the construction of a swimming pool in the Academy's gym, officials allowed cadets to swim discreetly in the Hudson River at twilight in a secluded but dangerous point owing to the river's currents. Scott, perhaps in defiance of regulation and with a determination to test his courage, swam across the river and acquired a reputation as an excellent swimmer.

From his experience at West Point he developed a lifelong desire for adventure through his growing love of horses. He derived utmost pleasure in the challenge of training them and in interacting with their personalities, culminating in the exhilaration of drilling and riding the animals around the trails near West Point. Therefore, a career in a cavalry regiment seemed the ideal occupational path.[27] However, even in the final months of his senior year, that option was far from a certainty. In calculating his chances, Scott had to contend with several factors. Class standing was one consideration since the higher a cadet stood in his graduating class, the more options he had. Unknown to him at the time were incalculable factors such as the influence of well-placed family and friends. Scott pondered his options in his final semester at the Academy. His first choice was a cavalry assignment since officers in these regiments were paid one hundred dollars more a year to offset the cost of maintaining their horses. However, regimental posts in the cavalry were in higher demand than those in the infantry. Nonetheless, there was always the possibility of a posting in one of the army's two black cavalry units, despite their being viewed by many officers as less desirable, although, according to some field officers he had spoken with, these postings were equal in all ways to the white units. Another advantage of such a posting included Scott's belief, whether accurate or not, that the army would not reduce or eliminate these cavalry units since there were only two. Given the fact that they were in Texas, "a Sportsman's paradise," he could enjoy hunting in a hospitable climate year-round. And although he would incur the wrath of his classmates for considering a black regiment, he noted that "negro fever . . . is dying out somewhat nowadays."[28]

Scott's classmates might have believed, erroneously, that "negro fever" was "dying out," but negative racial perceptions of Indians among Scott's generation were quite common. The army life that Scott entered was socially stratified, and standards of behavior, in both prerogatives and limitations, were understood in a descending order of privilege. In that context, most army officers placed Indians on the lowest, "savage" rung of a ladder leading to civilization. Those with little knowledge or interest in Native culture viewed American Indians strictly by their behaviors, such as their gyrations in dances and their invocation of spirits. Scott shared the widely held view that American Indians were racially inferior; however, he believed that if treated with patience and understanding, they could attain a level of civilization equal to that of any Euro-American.

Numerous examples of racial marginalization, the view that the Caucasian race is superior to all others, abound in American history. Some reformers, like Scott, while embracing this view, used it to justify what they perceived as a humanitarian or spiritual necessity to guide "inferior" peoples on the path to salvation. The definition of path would be up to the reformer. For abolitionists, it would begin by advocating for the freedom of enslaved blacks, and once they were freed, educating them for the "responsibilities" of citizenship. The recruitment of black "buffalo" soldiers and Native American scouts into military service, some reformers believed, would inculcate an understanding of, respect for, and an appreciation of the values of a democratic society.[29]

Scott graduated from West Point on June 14, 1876, with a ranking of thirty-sixth in a class of forty-eight, just high enough for a cavalry post with the black Ninth Cavalry originally stationed at Fort Davis in Texas. However, within two weeks of his initial commission, and upon his request, he was transferred to the Seventh Cavalry as a second lieutenant on June 26, 1876, and ordered to report to Fort Abraham Lincoln in the Dakota Territory, five miles south of the frontier and railhead community of Bismarck.[30]

Scott's appointment to the Seventh Cavalry was yet another example of how the family network served to his advantage. To assist him in his desire to obtain a preferred cavalry posting, his mother drafted a letter that Scott sent to Hunter in May 1876, with an additional request to his uncle Samuel Stockton, who, at the time, was a captain in the Fourth Cavalry. Stockton endorsed the letter-writing strategy, noting that Hunter "knew everybody in the War Department." The decimation of the Seventh Cavalry under Custer's command at Little Big Horn in late June altered the equation as well by broadening the number of cavalry postings open to officers. Scott, with the assistance of his relatives, took full advantage of the opportunity.[31]

Scott's West Point years clearly demonstrated the important role that the family network played in furthering his military career and in ensuring he would have one in the first place! Through the Academy, Scott acquired lifelong friendships in roommates Ernest Garlington and Horace Slocum, friends who would share some of his military experiences and enhance his career.[32]

One of the enduring characteristics from his West Point years was his seemingly insatiable desire for adventure. Scott continually tested himself in the face of danger, in an ethical context as well as a physical one. His attitude toward hazing demonstrated a propensity to see how far he could "push the envelope" in the Academy's equivocation over the practice. And his desire to swim the perilous waters of the Hudson River off the shores of West Point revealed a young man determined to test the "hand of fate," as it were. Although finding his place in the military proved to be relatively easy through his initial assignment on the northern Great Plains, searching out a venue for his skill set in a changing military force proved to be more elusive.

Scott addressed the challenge through a consummate ambition that proved to be a driving force throughout his entire military career. For example, and as previously noted, before a posting in the Seventh Cavalry became a reality, Scott was prepared to go with one of the two black cavalry regiments, for "the chances of becoming a Major before I die are twice as great." Although such a move may have incurred the scorn of his more racially biased classmates, Scott dismissed would-be detractors: "I don't care as long as I see it to my advantage."[33] His Academy years demonstrated the usefulness of family and friends as he embarked on his career. He would continue to rely on their influence and that of others in the venues where he was stationed as he sought an elevation in rank.

Before Scott reported to his post at Fort Abraham Lincoln in the Dakota Territory as a second lieutenant, he visited his brother Charles and his new bride in Pittsburgh. In St. Paul, he met with Capt. Frederick Benteen of the Seventh Cavalry, who had recently returned from the Yellowstone River and was hailed as a hero for allegedly saving the remainder of the regiment. Moving west, Scott enjoyed his first of what would prove to be many bird hunting ventures at Fargo on the Great Plains. At night after a day's train ride on the Northern Pacific Railway, he reached Bismarck and the Missouri River, two hundred miles distant. Morning brought a ferry ride down the river whose majestic beauty was described in Frances Parkman's *Conspiracy of Pontiac*, a copy of which Scott carried in his field pack. His autobiography, although written more than fifty years after the event, conveyed his sense of awe and exhilaration upon reaching this vast region so dramatically different from the woods of Princeton or the Hudson river valley. A new world had opened for Scott and a new way of life had begun.[34]

CHAPTER 2

▼ ▼ ▼

THE MAKING OF A FRONTIER DIPLOMAT

I was where I belonged.
—Hugh L. Scott

When Scott began his military career on the northern Great Plains, the region was in a state of conflict and turmoil. The lure of range land and minerals was making the terms of earlier treaties with tribal groups in the region difficult if not impossible to enforce. For example, the Treaty of Fort Laramie (1868), signed by federal officials and bands of the Oglala and Brule Sioux, seemed, on paper at least, to provide these tribes with few constraints on their traditional lifestyles. It designated as tribal landholdings an extensive tract both northeast and to the west of the Missouri River. Military authorities led these tribes to believe that the forts along the Bozeman Trail—a source of concern to them—would be abandoned. The Black Hills, part of these designated lands, were regarded as sacred by the Sioux, where they believed life on earth began. In addition, these tribes, along with the Northern Cheyennes, were permitted to hunt buffalo in the Powder River region to the southwest of the Sioux reservation in an area designated as "unceded Indian Territory." Nonetheless, the discovery of gold in the Black Hills in 1874, near what is now the western boundary of South Dakota, exacerbated relations between indigenous tribal groups, on the one hand, and ambitious prospectors and Anglo settlers, on the other, along with the frontier army charged with protecting and segregating both groups. The army's mission proved difficult to implement. The numerous trails to the Black Hills and the broad dispersion of military forces meant that trespassers lured by the chance of quick wealth could not be thwarted, despite efforts by the military to counter such behavior.

Nor did the Sioux at the time that they signed the Laramie Treaty fully understand that some of its provisions sanctioned incursions on their holdings. To illustrate, the "unceded Indian Territory" lands allocated to the Sioux and Northern Cheyennes were available to them as hunting grounds only "so long as the buffalo may range thereon in such numbers as to justify the chase." Other provisions compromised the integrity of the Sioux reservation itself. For example, Article II allowed for "railroads, wagon-roads, mail-stations, or other works of utility or necessity . . . (to) be constructed on the lands of their reservation." Although the tribe would be compensated, the government would determine the amount. Moreover, a clause in the Fort Laramie Treaty allowed the army to construct a fort on the designated Sioux reservation, which Lt. Col. (Bvt. Gen.) George Armstrong Custer and a large force of men and supplies were attempting to do in 1874. Several bands of Sioux and Northern Cheyennes, who shared their buffalo grazing lands, viewed the construction of a fort as a prelude to additional military posts on their tribal holdings. An offer by the federal government to purchase the Black Hills outright was an acknowledgment that the military could no longer prevent incursions onto these tribal lands by mining interests. These groups were joined by surveying parties planning the construction of a rail line to Bozeman, west of the Sioux holdings. In addition, commercial enterprises sought access to exchange goods with the Crows, the Sioux's archenemies, in the eastern Montana Territory. To make matters even more ominous, Sitting Bull, a prominent Hunkpapa Lakota spiritual leader, served as a catalyst for other dissident Sioux and Northern Cheyenne bands conducting raids against settlers, miners, and traders, both within and beyond the designated Sioux reservation. In the early 1870s, he further consolidated his authority with other bands of Sioux west of the Black Hills near the Yellowstone River. From here, these Sioux and Northern Cheyennes conducted skirmishes against Northern Pacific Railway workers and the soldiers who increasingly tried to protect them. The Bureau of Indian Affairs, which controlled both the Indian agents on reservation lands and the annuities granted to the Sioux under terms of the Laramie Treaty, concurred in the need for an offensive military action if the dissident Natives failed to return to their reservation by the end of January 1876. When they failed to do so, the determination of the army to protect those seeking to extend settlement on the one side, and the ongoing and increasing depredations by the Sioux on the other, reached a tipping point. It appeared that what could not be obtained in peaceful negotiation would be taken by force in war. Custer was prepared to act.[1]

The Great Sioux War (1876–77) that followed manifested not only the use of overt military force but also the strategy that military leaders would use to exploit rivalries among tribal groups. To be sure, Gen. George Crook's victory over Cheyenne dissidents at Big Horn Mountain in November 1877 was a devastating blow in suffering and in the loss of life, but the battle underscored the disunity within tribes, a disunity that Crook, through his use of Sioux and Cheyenne scouts, was all too eager to exploit. So, too, Custer's defeat at Little Big Horn in June 1876 was a rare example of cohesiveness among tribal groups, a unity that quickly disintegrated in the summer when, out of necessity, the tribes moved north to hunt for the buffalo that would sustain them over the winter months. The government's war against the Sioux was the equivalent of a scorched-earth policy, exploiting both the tribe's vulnerable dependence on the buffalo and the animal's diminishing presence over the prairie lands of the Great Plains. By exploiting the rivalries among band leaders and the loss of their ability to sustain their way of life, the government intended to force tribal groups to adopt the white man's definition of civilization through acculturation on the reservation.[2]

In August 1876, less than two months following Custer's defeat, the government initiated discussions with the Sioux bands for the acquisition of the Black Hills. The multiband council, a long-established political structure used by the elders to reconcile differences among the various bands, participated in the process. The chiefs were divided, with Sitting Bull opposed to the loss of the Black Hills. The federal commissioners were determined to get the chiefs to endorse the cession of the Black Hills from the Sioux reservation. They were unwilling to acquiesce to those chiefs like Sitting Bull, who felt that before an agreement could be signed, they needed to consult with the northern bands of Sioux that were not present at the meeting. The commissioners intimidated others by threatening the loss of their annuities if they did not sign off on the cession within the limited time period allotted. Even if a majority of the chiefs present acquiesced to the demand, it was a violation of the Laramie Treaty since

The Great Plains and the Border Lands, 1868–1890. Reproduced from Katharine Bjork, *Prairie Imperialists: The Indian Country Origins of American Empire* (2018), 20. Reprinted with permission of the University of Pennsylvania Press.

the agreement did not represent three-quarters of the Sioux adult population as required under its terms. Nonetheless, the federal government formally took possession of the Black Hills in February 1877. Most of the dissident bands, including some Northern Cheyennes under Little Wolf and Sioux bands led by Red Cloud, Eagle Pipe, Two Kettles, White Eagle, Red Horse, and Spotted Elk, saw no immediate prospect of retaining their traditional lifestyle. They acquiesced to federal authority and agreed to move onto the remaining reservation lands, in subsections according to their band affiliation. At the same time, Sitting Bull fled to Canada, perhaps fearing retribution from the so-called Custer avengers and, at the time, being unable to rally a sufficient number of dissident bands to accompany him. However, despite what appeared to be an unequivocal victory for the army, the potential for trouble remained.[3]

Trouble remained because the cause of anguish among tribal groups was ongoing. Military personnel in the northern Great Plains during this period inherited a legacy of anger and acrimony that many chiefs felt as a consequence of the government's surreptitious tactics in dealing with them. Furthermore, federal policy mandated that these bands remain on the reservation under the control of the BIA. As a result, in lieu of the rapidly diminishing bison herds and symbolic cultural aspects of the hunt itself, the Sioux were now increasingly dependent on the supplies, provisions, and annuities dispensed at specific agencies from staff appointed by the BIA. In 1877, there were four main agencies in "Sioux country": the Red Cloud Agency for the Oglala; the Spotted Tail Agency for the Brules; the Cheyenne River Agency for the Miniconjous, Sans Arcs, and Two Kettles; and the Standing Rock Agency for the Hunkpapas, Sihasapas, and Yanktonais. Further exacerbating the circumstances faced by dissident Sioux was the fact that agencies were often staffed by "spoilers," men who attained their posts through political connections, without regard to their integrity in dealing with tribal peoples. Consequently, the government was often charged for provisions that were not delivered on time, if at all, because unscrupulous agents and their merchant suppliers were taking additional profit. This would prove to be one of the many challenges that Scott would face in trying to maintain peace when the vicissitudes of federal Indian policy created additional tensions among tribal peoples. The process of pacification would not be an easy one.[4]

Although the Great Sioux War formally ended with the Battle of Muddy Creek in May 1877, none of the senior military commanders such as Generals Crook, Alfred Terry, and Philip Sheridan, the commander of the Division of the Missouri, believed that military engagements with the tribes of the northern Great Plains were over. Their pessimism was realistic. One issue was determining exactly who would assume responsibility for the process of acculturation and assimilation. The Custer debacle in June 1876 raised serious questions regarding the army's ability to maintain peace on the frontier. This underscored the ongoing debate between civilian and military leaders over control of federal Indian policy. Historically, the BIA, under the Department of the Interior, had the authority to regulate matters on reservations concerning the implementation of services to Native peoples as designated by treaty. Military personnel could intercede only when so requested by the mostly civilian agents appointed by the BIA. Communication and coordination between the Interior and War Departments at the local level was often poor or nonexistent. Tensions had increased with the pressure of encroachments by Anglo settlers and commercial interests on the lands designated to tribal groups by treaty. The survey and construction of trails and railroad lines through reservation lands, sanctioned in treaties in often obscurely defined articles meant to deceive the tribes, only added to tribal leaders' resentment. And again, exacerbating the situation, as previously noted, was the often corrupt relationship between agency personnel and merchants contracted by the BIA to supply provisions to the Sioux and Northern Cheyennes as stipulated in treaties. They were often in a state of anger and despair following the decimation of wild buffalo herds. Not only did they lose the cultural significance in hunting the buffalo, but their dependency on the herds for physical survival was undercut. Consequently, these tribes, faced with what they regarded as treaties negotiated in bad faith, often took their vengeance out by committing depredations both on and off reservation lands.

Yet another conflict existed because of the imposition of a federal Indian policy. The sophisticated political structure of tribal governance placed decision-making powers in the hands of chiefs. These chiefs led bands of followers within the numerous subcultures of tribal societies, which often thwarted an opportunity for consensus. For example, although the Sioux had a tribal council among diverse chiefs, unanimity was often the exception rather than the rule. Federal commissioners often exploited these differences, playing one band against another, heightening tensions and increasing the likelihood of violence among tribal chiefs and their followers.[5]

What was required of military personnel in order to avoid unnecessary bloodshed was patience, tact, and diplomacy, not only with regard to dissident and diverse tribal chiefs, but also with other government officials, such as agency personnel. Equally significant was the lack of willingness to understand and respect tribal cultures. Needless to say, none of these components were in West Point's curriculum in the 1870s!

The Reverend Charles Hodge was only too aware of his grandson's seemingly carefree and cavalier attitude toward life when he finally graduated from the United States Military Academy in the summer of 1876. Consequently, a Bible seemed an appropriate gift to give Lennie, as he called him. Hodge's bequest came with inscribed admonitions—guidelines, as it were—on how a young Christian gentleman should conduct himself while living in a frontier world his grandfather and mother undoubtedly regarded as savage and heathen:

- NEVER pass a day without reading the BIBLE and calling upon God in prayer.
- Learn to pray always. THE LORD JESUS is ever near you. It does not take long to say, "LORD, Preserve me; LORD help me; LORD keep me from sin." We need to say this a hundred times a day!
- NEVER gamble.
- NEVER drink intoxicating liquor.
- NEVER use profane language.
- Let no corrupt communication proceed out of your mouth.
- NEVER incur debt.
- LIVE PEACEABLE with all men.
- NEVER be afraid to CONFESS CHRIST.
- Let your last words every night be, "I TAKE JESUS CHRIST TO BE MY LORD AND SAVIOR."
- May the blessings of GOD be upon you, ALWAYS and EVERYWHERE.

Your Loving Grandfather, Charles Hodge, September 15th, 1876.

Whether young Scott followed all his grandfather's admonitions is impossible to say. However, we do know that he ultimately took "LIVE PEACEABLE with all men" to heart, though the pacification of tribal groups would not be predicated on a basis of equality for both sides and consequently was perhaps doomed from the start. Scott was asking them to lay down their arms against the onslaught of Anglo incursions on their lands, yet he could not guarantee them what they wanted most: a recognition that those lands were spiritually sacred to them and could not be sold or transferred to another party. Moreover, his journey in reaching the goal of pacification began with an entirely different orientation, a love for adventure. As time went on, however, through different venues and experiences interacting with tribal groups, Scott acquired the skills and the attitude to serve as a "Frontier Diplomat."[6]

Fort Abraham Lincoln, named for the martyred president, was the largest and most important post on the northern Great Plains when it was completed in 1874. Its location, across the Missouri River from and five miles south of Bismarck, in the Dakota Territory, housed 650 infantry and cavalry troops. The infantry was left to guard the post when the Seventh Cavalry departed under Custer's command, once in 1874 and for the last time in May 1876.

The post was being reorganized when Scott arrived among the replacements for the more than 200 cavalry soldiers who perished at Little Big Horn. After General Terry returned from Little Big Horn, the fort was reinforced with 1,200 additional men. Ultimately, there were eight troops of cavalry bivouacked in the upper post and two infantry companies housed in the lower post. The fort's strategic location accounted for its enhancement, and its reinforcement evidenced the army's recognition that the Great Sioux War would not end the resistance of tribal groups. Indian incursions had prevented the construction of the Northern Pacific Railway from traversing tribal lands west of Bismarck. Another potential area for conflict was the Standing Rock Sioux Reservation Agency, just sixty miles to the south, along the Missouri River.[7]

Upon arriving, Scott may have found it initially strange and somewhat disconcerting to billet in field bedding on the floor of Custer's house. Nonetheless, he became well acclimated to his surroundings in a relatively short period of time. To be sure, the brutal Dakota winters, a sampling of which he would face in his first six months at the post, challenged even a young man who had spent long frigid winter evenings rabbit hunting in the fields near Princeton, New Jersey. As he would tell his readers in his autobiography, fifty-two years later:

> Here then before me was this primitive America for which I had sought, and here was I with a spirit attuned to understand it and to rejoice in becoming a part of its life. Many of my contemporaries were children of the East, always looking eastward and longing to get back; but no matter how cold, how wet, how hungry I found myself during all the years of Plains life that followed, I felt that I was where I belonged.

Scott's longing for a "primitive America" extended to his feelings toward its Native peoples as well. Scott saw a relationship between the topography of a region and the character of its indigenous inhabitants. Specifically, he believed that Eastern tribes, because they lived in dense forests, were evil and deceitful. The Indians that Scott negotiated with on the open Great Plains were, in his eyes, devoid of pretense, exceedingly loyal, and trustworthy.[8]

Location had a specific meaning to young Lieutenant Scott. On his first assignment at Fort Lincoln in the fall of 1876, he was ordered to disarm and dismount renegade Sioux at various agencies, who were sending arms and supplies to Crazy Horse and Sitting Bull. Positioned behind the column of troops in a supply train was not where a young adventure-seeking officer should find himself. As early as the end of the antebellum period, troops in the Army of the West were often led by Indian scouts, who were indigenous to the region and consequently familiar with the terrain and the habits of their band or of tribal adversaries. It was at the head of a column that a soldier would first confront the dangers that lay ahead, a position "sought after by the most adventurous lieutenants . . . away from the routine that was irksome." Such a location undoubtedly provided the recipient with "a part in all the excitement," a sense of control, and the opportunity to test one's ability to survive in an initially alien environment.[9] Once again, Scott could draw on the skills he had honed as a youth hunting wild animals. A keen sense of sight or sound could indicate the presence of game. However, here on the western frontier, the sound of leaves rustling, the sudden sight of animals in flight, or the smell of smoke could reveal the presence of a dangerous enemy, placing one in a life-threatening situation. Scouts, often situated on high, well-concealed lookout points and in some cases many miles ahead of a column, were well aware of these signs and were quick to alert troops of impending danger. And, as with hunting game, patience was a critical skill, in both a defensive and an offensive military operation.

Being at the head of a column challenged Scott's intellectual skills as well. He needed to understand what the scouts were communicating to each other about the region they were traversing. His initial option was to learn the Siouan language, and although the post trader at Fort Lincoln had a copy of a Sioux dictionary, he would not sell it to Scott at first. After borrowing it, he scrupulously mastered the dialect, thus affirming his conviction to the book's owner, whereupon Scott was given the volume. Nonetheless, its use would be limited to Sioux scouts. Consequently, Scott quickly learned that a long-standing sign language, presumably developed out of necessity for intertribal trade, was a more practical means of communicating with Indians, not only with the tribes of the northern Great Plains, but those as far south as the Mexican border as well. Each tribe used a specific symbol for most objects of nature, both animate and inanimate. Although Scott first embraced its use as an essential tool in negotiation, he would spend much of his active life in the scholarly pursuit of its origins and the way its symbols were developed and applied. He strongly believed that the seemingly ubiquitous use of sign language among tribes and its endurance over a long period of time could provide meaningful knowledge of "the origin, the life and growth of all language." Nonetheless, that field of inquiry was in his future—for now, it merely provided a pragmatic goal in broadening his horizon for adventure.[10]

The ability to communicate with a broad group of Indians literally opened a new world for Scott, similar to but even more challenging than the physical world he had entered. This ability led to an almost insatiable desire to understand all aspects of American Indian culture, and cultures of indigenous peoples wherever he was posted throughout his military career. He marveled at the way tribal groups adjusted to the forces of nature in their topography and climatic environment and their use of legends and symbols to define their earthly existence. His autobiography is filled with references comparing his seemingly sophisticated Christian society to that of the Indians in the West, whom he chose to see as honest and trustworthy, lacking pretension and any concept of original sin.[11]

What began as a desire for adventure led ultimately to a unique opportunity for a young officer on the late-nineteenth-century American frontier. Over a period of three years, and in venues from Devil's Lake, in the northeastern corner of the Dakota Territory, to the Yellowstone and Missouri Rivers in Montana Territory, Scott honed his skills as a respected negotiator and trusted friend of and advocate for American Indians, earning a reputation that endured well beyond his military career. Perhaps Scott learned more from Chief Joseph of the Nez Percés, Northern Cheyenne Scouts, Red Cloud of the Oglala Sioux, and inhabitants of a Crow encampment than they learned from him. What each took away was at least a feeling of respect if not always admiration.

Scott spent a great deal of time during the first year of his posting on the northern Great Plains in pursuit of Chief Joseph and his Nez Percé followers, who might be four hundred miles from Fort Lincoln. In the early spring of 1877, he was initially stationed out of Fort Benton, at the headwaters of the Missouri River near what would become Helena, Montana. Scott was ordered to lead a mule team to Col. Nelson Miles and his force who were seeking to apprehend Chief Joseph and his Nez Percé followers. Originally located within what became the Idaho Territory, the traditional lands of the Nez Percés were traversed and occupied by miners, traders, missionaries, and settlers who, with the assistance of federal officials, often exploited tribal divisions. A similar scenario would be faced by other tribal groups displaced from their holdings. A treaty signed by the U.S. government and certain "Christianized" Nez Percé leaders in 1863 denied any legal recognition of those Nez Percés who sought to retain their own spiritual faith. Eventually, with the loss of their landholdings, Chief Joseph and his band, "seeing no chance for the peaceful settlement he had hoped for . . . started eastward across the Bitter Root mountains with all his women, children and horses in search of peace in the buffalo country." Regardless of whether the chief's intentions were peaceful or not, military officials feared that his group would join with Sitting Bull, north of the boundary with Canada. Scott's alleged but indirect assistance in the ultimate capture of Joseph, noted below, was only his first encounter with this noble chief who would enhance his understanding of Native peoples. Scott was part of the military escort, under Miles's immediate command, that led

Joseph and the estimated 450 Nez Percé prisoners following their surrender. The march from the Bears Paw Mountains in the north-central region of the Montana Territory to the environs of Fort Lincoln, near Bismarck, occurred in the early winter of 1877. During the journey of more than two weeks, the prisoners stopped at Fort Berthold, in the northwest region of the Dakota Territory, adjacent to the agency of the Arikara, Mandan, and Gros Ventres tribal groups. They came out to see why Joseph was so venerated by his people. It was here that Scott stood in awe, as Joseph, in the presence of 1,500 people conversing in nine languages, addressed them using only sign language to describe the challenges that he had faced. His gestures were understood by the group without a single sound uttered from his lips. Looking back on the event a half-century later, Scott noted that he "never saw a more interesting exhibition of the sign language than was given by Joseph that day."[12]

In the summer of 1877, near the end of the Great Sioux War, Miles ordered Scott to investigate dissident Sioux allied with Sitting Bull's Canadian band near the Musselshell River in the northeastern region of the Montana Territory. Scott selected thirty-five Northern Cheyenne scouts who had previously fought against Custer and had only recently surrendered to Miles. His friends warned him not to go with these scouts, fearing that it would be rather easy for them to kill him and join Sitting Bull north of the border. Scott discounted their fears, noting that "I never felt that way toward them. . . . They were perfectly adapted to their environment, and knew just what to do in every emergency and when to do it. . . . I watched their every movement and learned lessons from them that later saved my life many times on the prairie."[13]

Other venues with different tribal groups proved equally valuable and productive for Scott in honing his skills as a negotiator. One such encounter involved Red Cloud, a prominent Oglala Sioux chief, whose long-standing acrimony against the frontier army was symbolized in an earlier confrontation's being labeled Red Cloud's War (1866–68). Red Cloud also played a significant role in events leading up to the Great Sioux War and beyond. His ongoing defiance of the restraints imposed upon his people on reservation lands posed a special challenge to Scott as well as his commanders, Generals Sherman, Sheridan, and Terry. The assertive and proud Oglala leader was always ready to hold government officials accountable for the promised annuities, and he was not about to allow authorities to mandate where he could reside on reservation land.

In the fall of 1877, a military escort took Red Cloud and his followers ostensibly to settle at the Big Bend of the Missouri River along with other tribal bands, in order to expedite and reduce the cost of delivering food and supplies. Facing an oncoming Dakota winter, Red Cloud refused to proceed, despite threats from both Sherman and Sheridan to withhold provisions allotted to his people. A more contentious situation was avoided when the War Department relented, fearing further unrest and especially the possibility that Sitting Bull might entice Red Cloud's followers to join him in starting yet another major Sioux war. Nonetheless, the BIA insisted that the "Red Cloud" agency, the location for his tribal band, had to be on the shore of the Missouri River. This raised, once again, long-standing antagonisms that previous treaties had never resolved. Among them were who would determine the location of the agencies designated on reservation lands. Red Cloud had been led to believe the issue was settled. As part of a delegation that journeyed east to the nation's capital, they had extracted a promise from President Rutherford B. Hayes to allow the Sioux to select a place of settlement of their own choosing on the "Great Sioux" reservation. The recommendations of yet another commission, authorized by Congress in the summer of 1878, seemed to offer a viable geographic compromise as to where a future Red Cloud agency could be located. Nonetheless, routine bureaucratic procrastination made Red Cloud and his followers "angry & . . . not now to be trifled with."[14]

Such were the circumstances that summer when Scott was initially ordered to join up with the Seventh Cavalry, which was directed to apprehend a group of Northern Cheyennes trying to reach Red Cloud's band of restive Sioux. It was alleged, erroneously, that Red Cloud had killed an agent, although he did steal beef and provisions to feed his hungry people. Scott claimed that the situation was tense when he finally arrived at Red Cloud's camp, with five thousand restive Sioux on one side and eleven troops of the Seventh Cavalry on the other. No interpreters were present. His goal was to avoid unnecessary bloodshed. Scott and Red Cloud began to sign, and Scott learned that Red Cloud had not killed the agent. Presumably, Red Cloud was so impressed with Scott's ability to communicate with him that the Sioux chief took Scott into his lodge, where the two could "talk it out." Scott had the courage and confidence to go into the chief's dwelling alone and, presumably, unarmed. As he noted in his autobiography, and after years of experience in negotiating with indigenous peoples, "Indians are always hospitality itself, and he made me welcome in his lodge. I stayed there three nights, watching. I could not see that anything overt was underway but felt that I had no friends there and that hostilities might be brewing without my knowledge." Courage was not the only trait that was on display in Red Cloud's lodge that summer. Scott also broadened his understanding of the Indian sign language as a consequence of Red Cloud's unique style of signing as the chief "talked" about "everything under the sun."[15]

As previously noted, one aspect of American Indian cultures that attracted Scott to study them was what he saw as their integral relationship to the natural environment. Scott's transition, as it were, from negotiator to advocate began when the natural world in which these tribes lived was transformed by the rapid decimation of the buffalo herds, the ongoing expropriation of their lands from Anglo settlers and commercial interests, and the undermining of their tribal polity—in short, by the loss of their ability to control their own destiny.

Although each of these factors had traumatic effects on Plains tribal groups, the loss of the buffalo and the relative suddenness of their disappearance, was likely the most devastating. The animal provided tribal peoples with a source of food and clothing, as well as being an integral part of their culture. So important were these free-roaming herds that tribal groups hunted them on only certain days and under certain conditions, to enhance the yield of carcasses for feeding and clothing the tribal village. For example, Crow hunters studied the movement of buffalo to segregate sections of the herd, and the braves would then join in the hunt on a given day, slaughtering every animal thus isolated. To hunt on an individual basis would run the risk of scaring away other buffalo, thus endangering the survival of the entire village. The Sioux observed the condition of these wild herds at certain times of the year, such as the density of their mane and the stockiness of their stand, in order to take full advantage of the animal's usefulness as a source of food, clothing, and shelter. The hunt itself took on a unique social and cultural significance for a people that believed in the importance of maintaining a balance with the forces of nature.[16]

The diminishing of herds in the late 1870s was generally caused by nontribal groups' hunting practices. A near global market for tanned hides during this time led to a frenzy of commercial hunting, and consequently, the supply of these animals substantially decreased over a relatively short period of time. Both robes, tanned by Native women on the reservation before they were sent east, and hides, sent east and then tanned, were garnered as trophies, as well as apparel. At the same time, federal officials had a vested interest in encouraging the decimation of buffalo herds. Their loss forced tribal groups onto reservations and to the agencies on which they increasingly depended for their food and clothing.[17]

Scott lamented the indiscriminate slaughter of the buffalo and the waste of the animal's parts, which denied tribal groups what had been their necessities of life. The seeming dramatic and sudden end to the northern buffalo herds by the early 1880s underscored the way the animals were hunted. He observed in 1883:

> There was about three thousand men on the range killing buffalo for their hides. . . . Whenever a dollar can be made on the hide of an animal[,] that animal is doomed. The hunters would sometimes get a stand on a herd of buffalo and kill one hundred or more. The weather was intensely cold, 40 degrees below zero for days and never above 20 degrees below at noon for weeks at a time, and after taking the tongue and skinning one animal, the hides would freeze on the others and would be left untouched by the knife. The waste was terrific.

He felt a sense of shame and anger when "the buffalo never returned, and many Indians starved to death in consequence; starved to death under the American flag, wards of our government, because our government was too weak and too careless to protect their food from wanton destruction by white men."[18]

Through his experience with the Sioux in his early years on the northern Great Plains, Scott gleaned an ability to perceive the challenges tribal groups faced from *their* perspective. For example, while acknowledging that early trappers entering Sioux country might have been mistreated, he noted that "the trappers[,] accountable to nobody[,] often committed intolerable aggressions . . . [and] it got worse when thousands of emigrants went up the Platte on their way to Oregon thru Sioux country." Furthermore, Scott believed that Custer's campaign through the Black Hills in 1874, followed by a rush of gold seekers, was a violation of the Fort Laramie Treaty (1868), which guaranteed the Sioux the possession of their sacred Black Hills. Nor did this treaty mandate that the Sioux had to leave their reservation lands and settle at the agencies. Their failure to do so on the deadline set by government officials was, according to Scott, used as a pretext for Custer to take the Black Hills by force. Scott also questioned the intent of the Sioux and other tribal peoples to confront Custer in June 1876. "Custer went out & fought them—so from this point of view[,] the white man was the aggressor—that is the line I would take if it was my own case," he argued. The white man "was particularly bound to treat the Indian equitably . . . but instead of that he allowed white men to trespass in their country—kill off their food." What would Scott have done had he been able to alleviate a confrontation?

> If there had been an officer high enough in rank & known to them [The Sioux]—bold enough & with enough knowledge of Indians to go off alone into their camp & reason with them he could have led the whole bunch into the Agencies—I have seen some pretty cross Indians but have always found them reasonable and have never failed to get them to see the proper course & if the thing were to do now I would have liked to take an escort of prominent Sioux Indians—taking only enough soldiers to cook, pack & look after the stock & a first class interpreter & go right into Gall's lodge or Crazy Horse's—& patiently sit there for a week or a month allowing no rebuff to change my course—giving reasons at councils. . . . I have never seen an Indian yet who could stand out against me if I was determined to get him to do something[.] He is too wise or able not to see your arguments.

Scott wrote this forty years after his initial posting on the frontier, and after many years' experience in negotiating with tribal groups in a diversity of confrontational situations. Nonetheless, his understanding and appreciation of their culture, and its importance to them, proved him to be a worthy advocate in defending their pride and integrity, while negotiating with them under stressful and life-altering situations. His advocacy broadened as tribes in the American West faced ongoing challenges to their physical existence and their cultural homogeneity.[19]

Scott saw the scenario of white exploitation against tribal groups who hoped to retain their own physical and cultural integrity as a conflict of the strong against the weak. Consequently, he embraced a spiritual aspect of his upbringing that defined his relationship with tribal groups in a paternalistic context. His Christian faith motivated Scott to assist them—"to do good works," as it were—but not, however, as their equal. No matter how pure and devoid of evil a heathen's soul might be, in Scott's view, he must embrace Christian civilization in order to be saved. Scott may have differed from others of his faith in his patience with the process and his more pragmatic definition of "Christian civilization," but his actions in dealing with indigenous peoples reveal a paternalistic relationship.

On a personal level, despite having to endure long, bone-chilling winters and periods of boredom and loneliness, Scott generally enjoyed his various postings in the Dakota and Montana Territories. Aside from his orders involving Indians, Scott was detailed to bury the remains of Custer and the Crow scouts who accompanied him. The remains were identified and hastily buried several days after the so-called massacre in late June 1876, but the graves were hardly deep enough to prevent wind and rain from exposing the bodies. Such was the case the following year, when Scott was detailed to rebury the remains, now partially ravaged by animals. Although no record has been found of his personal feelings, his emotions may well have been mixed. He undoubtedly would have been unable to join the Seventh Cavalry even with a relative's influence, given his relatively low class standing at West Point, if it were not for the opening created by the deaths of his fellow officers. On a more positive note, when weather permitted at Forts Lincoln and Totten and he was not constrained by an off-post assignment, Scott enjoyed hunting wild fowl and prairie chickens to supplement the diet of his fellow soldiers. Learning new skills in a terrain initially unfamiliar to him was another source of pleasure and satisfaction. Navigating a schooner on Devil's Lake near Fort Totten with its windswept terrain, and "fishing" for lake pike with a gun or a spear when they came up to spawn, were challenges that he mastered with delight.[20]

Nonetheless, periods of euphoria were broken by sad news. Dr. Charles Hodge, Scott's grandfather, and a moral pillar in his life, died suddenly. Shortly thereafter, Mary Hunter Stockton, Charles's second wife, succumbed as well. Both, either directly or indirectly, were instrumental in launching their grandson's military career. Recall that Gen. David Hunter, Mary's brother, used his friendship with President Grant to get Scott into West Point in the first place. And Charles used his prestige to keep him there when his grandson's behavior was grounds for dismissal. Frustrating as well was Scott's inability to return to Princeton to be at his mother's side for either funeral. As hard as it was for Scott to deal with the loss, it was more difficult for Mary, his mother. Having lost her husband at an earlier point in her marriage, she now had to deal with the loss of her parents. The concurrent departure of her sons, Charles, Len, and shortly, Wick to careers of their own, was an added source of emotional torment. In a way, Len had been special to her, not because he followed the moral and vocational path that she wanted him to, but because he *did not*! His alleged "transgressions" provided her with the "moral validation" she manifested in chastising his behavior.[21]

Scott's courtship and ultimate marriage to Mary Merrill, the daughter of Gen. Lewis Merrill, in June 1880 began a fifty-four-year relationship with a partner who turned out to be a steadfast advocate in advancing his military career. Scott had known Mary when she was at school in Philadelphia, and when he learned that her father and his family were stationed at Fort Yates at Standing Rock in the Dakota Territory, Scott received a month's leave to court her. He brought his new bride back to Fort Totten, where they spent three years together on an almost daily basis, a prolonged tenure that proved to be rare for them prior to his retirement decades later. Not surprisingly, his mother's feelings about his relationship were mixed. While she could relate to her son's joy, his marriage was yet another reminder of the loneliness she was facing and the feeling of abandonment from the "loss" of her son.[22]

The second phase of Scott's tenure on the northern frontier in the early 1880s was somewhat different from his earlier experiences. The number of "renegade" tribal groups away from their agencies had diminished dramatically. The rapid decline in the buffalo herds led to the forced dependency of the Sioux and Northern Cheyennes in the eastern Great Plains, and of the Crows to the west, on provisions allocated to them at tribal agencies. Equally disheartening, if not more so, was the subversion of much of their cultural heritage as they acclimated to reservation life. Scott's field duties during this time included such relatively mundane but essential tasks as assisting in the survey of a telegraph line and delineating reservation boundaries. One of Scott's few pursuits of dissident tribal groups occurred when a band of Crows under Crazy Head had left their reservation lands. Scott was given command of two officers and seventy-five enlisted men to find them and order them back to their reservation "without delay." He objected to the size of the force in his orders, fearing that "if such a large force were sent out some mistakes would be made that would spoil everything." Nonetheless, his commanding officer, Col. Elwell Otis, was adamant. A compromise was reached. The number of troops would remain as in the original order, but in deference to Scott's concerns, their role as a battle force was significantly reduced. Whether the amendment to the original order would have made a difference is impossible to say. The dissident Crows were compliant in their willingness to return to their reservation agency.[23]

The 1880s marked a major turning point in Scott's professional life as well. The role of a frontier soldier was becoming increasingly anachronist. Tribal groups, with perhaps the exception of the Apaches and the Comanches in the Southwest, were no longer deemed a barrier to Anglo expansion. Consequently, from the army's perspective, they were no longer a military problem or concern. To be sure, some officers ended their military careers as agents on reservations, but they did so reporting to civilian supervisors under the BIA. On a personal level, the Scotts had started a family, with four children born by 1887. Financial challenges, as well, mandated a vocational reassessment.[24]

One option available to military officers in the right venue was the potentially lucrative practice of speculating in western lands. Although the practice existed even prior to the Civil War, the postbellum period, from the 1870s through the 1890s, was an advantageous time for military officers who had an awareness of and access to fertile frontier lands. Knowing where railroad and telegraph lines were to be constructed provided them with a unique opportunity to obtain land and aggrandize their own personal wealth. Scott's commanding officer at Fort Meade in the 1880s, Brig. Gen. Samuel D. Sturgis, was among the more prominent military speculators in the Black Hills region, at least in mining and town settlement. Sturgis praised Scott for his thorough and indispensable knowledge of the topography and resources of the Dakota Territory, suggesting the option of leaving his military career for stock raising. He also offered to find financial backers for Scott. Sturgis was not the only senior officer who offered such assistance. Although he would use his outstanding reputation as a Unionist during and following the Civil War to assist his new son-in-law in attaining professional advantages, Col. Lewis Merrill was also in a uniquely favorable position for investments in land speculation, having been assigned to command the troops guarding the construction workers building the Northern Pacific Railway line through the Dakota Territory. Scott, who had invested in some lands along with his brother Charles, hoped that if their venture were successful, he would invest some of their mother's funds in the land claims as well. The venture was precarious at best, and never led to great wealth for the Scott family. In fact, many of their investments in land over the years turned sour, either because of poor timing in purchasing and selling or because of fraudulent practices perpetrated against them. Although the Scotts would, in retirement, purchase a farm, the cultivation of crops and the grazing of animals proved to be more of a hobby than a reliable and consistent source of income.[25]

Despite the army's success in the military subjugation of tribal groups in the Great Sioux War, not everyone subscribed to its reputation as an institution defending the nation against its enemies and promoting the common good. The stagnant size of the postbellum army, minimally staffed at approximately 28,000 personnel during the period 1875–98, generally reflected the attitudes of a nation fatigued by the recent war and concerned by the unprecedented use of a military force as a posse comitatus in the southern states as well as a strikebreaking force in northeastern cities. Some were critical of a peacetime standing army on constitutional grounds, fearing what they regarded as a growing militarism in American society. Compounding the problem was the relatively large number of Civil War officers who were forced to remain in the service because of a limited and restrictive retirement system. Exacerbating the situation further was a rule (not changed till 1890) limiting promotions to vacancies within an officer's regiment. For example, in 1885, more than one-third of all army officers were forty-one to fifty years old, at least theoretically competing for advancement in their regimental rank before retirement. Of these, many had remained in the same rank for twenty to thirty years. Young

Lieutenant Scott was thirty-two years old in 1885. Consequently, opportunities for advancement in one's military career were few, and competition was often intense. Cultivating familial relationships and those from venues where one served as well as embellishing one's credentials, if possible, were the routine paths to success.[26]

Utilizing the influence of relatives to attain professional advancement was nothing new to Scott or other officers in military service. Members of his family had come to his assistance before. What the Scott-Hodge-Stockton clan may have lacked in affluence, they more than made up for in a reputation for moral integrity and intellectual respectability. As one who wrote a letter of introduction and endorsement on Scott's behalf reminded the recipient: "Lt. Scott has a record as an officer, scholar and gentleman, quite in accordance with the traditions of the stock from which he comes[,] with the blood of a Hodge in his veins, most of us can tie to him without question." The author touted another attribute in favor of Scott's candidacy: "he is the son-in-law of Gen'l Lewis Merrill[,] well known to all students of the War."[27]

Charles Hodge's tenure as one of the early builders of the reputation of Princeton Theological Seminary provides a more significant though circuitous example of how familial relationships opened professional opportunities for young Scott. Alexander Quay was an early-nineteenth-century impoverished Pennsylvania tailor who, in midlife, experienced a spiritual epiphany and felt called to preach the gospel. He entered Princeton Theological Seminary in 1827 and, following his ordination, held several administrative positions in the church. He was also called to several congregations throughout New Jersey and served as an advocate for the manumission of slaves who ultimately would be sent to Liberia. Two of the former positions were with the Presbyterian Board of Education and the Board of Foreign Missions, of which Hodge was an active organizer and exponent. It may well have been through these organizations that Quay and Hodge met.

Quay and his wife had only two of eight children survive into adulthood. The eldest, Matthew, "grew up in a frugal home where the love of God, concern for humanity, and faith in self-reliance were taught." Nonetheless, the younger Quay's ultimate career was in the political rather than the spiritual realm. As a United States senator, Matthew Quay (Pa.; 1887–89, 1901–4) was a prominent and influential political broker on both the state and federal levels. On the national level, Quay served as chairman of the Republican National Committee (1888–91) and assisted in the nominations of Benjamin Harrison for the presidency in 1888 and 1892 and Theodore Roosevelt for the vice presidency in 1900. While the elder Quay's commitment to humanity was in the structured abolition of slavery, his son shared with Scott a longstanding sincere and genuine commitment to the welfare of American Indians. Scott would profit from the access that Matthew Quay could provide through his friends and associates and their friends as well, prior to Quay's passing in 1904.[28]

Lewis Merrill served the interests of his new son-in-law not only through access to opportunities for investment in western lands. Merrill's military posting also provided him with an introduction to individuals who significantly, like Quay and his associates, were civilians, and would later play important roles at crucial periods in his ascent up the chain of command. These included Charles E. Rushmore, an attorney who eventually speculated in mining enterprises in the Black Hills, and John F. McGee, also a lawyer as well as a district judge.[29]

Scott claimed that his reputation as a tribal negotiator owing to his mastery of Indian sign language "soon became known to commanders of every grade, clear up to generals Sheridan and Miles, who befriended me as long as they lived." With perhaps a great deal of bravado, Scott noted that the generals "gave me a freedom and scope I have seen extended to none else in the Indian country." Recognition was critical to a young lieutenant in a highly competitive professional environment. Stopping at the Palmer House in Chicago while on leave, Scott visited Sheridan and his brother to discuss the latest news on tribal activity on the northern Great Plains. Proudly, Scott relayed in his autobiography that "when he called me 'Scott,' placing me on a conversational level with himself, I swelled up with pride so that Chicago could scarcely hold me. Both Sheridan and his brother always asked me to dinner whenever I passed through Chicago, and I never appealed to either of them in vain." Whether a recognition of his work in negotiating with tribal dissidents led directly to his promotion as a first lieutenant is difficult to say, but in June 1878 he was so notified of his elevation in rank.[30]

Sheridan's brief tenure as commanding general of the army (he died in 1888) was not enough to assist young Scott, but another overly ambitious officer, Col. Nelson Appleton Miles, proved to be of invaluable assistance in furthering Scott's career. Scott served under Miles's command when he was ordered to lead a mule train to the colonel's force that was then pursuing the Nez Percés in the Montana Territory, hoping to prevent them from joining Sitting Bull north of the Canadian line. Although Scott had first met Miles a year before at Fort Keogh, their relationship grew when both accompanied Joseph and his followers as prisoners of war from the Bears Paw Mountains to Fort Lincoln near Bismarck, Dakota Territory, in the fall of 1877 on the aforementioned march. Upon reaching Fort Lincoln, Bismarck residents celebrated their arrival by treating all parties to a feast. Joseph and Miles stood together while a band played the National Anthem. Clearly Miles enjoyed the publicity, even suggesting that he and Joseph travel to Washington together, so that Joseph and his followers could learn what Miles wanted to believe were the sincere intentions of the president for their welfare. As previously noted, Philip Sheridan, his commanding officer, had other ideas and a different attitude toward the Nez Percé insurgents. Scott's role in Joseph's capture was minimal. However, as an intertribal sign language interpreter and a soldier who respected Joseph's humanity, Scott could share in the respect if not total adulation extended to Joseph by Anglo and Native alike.[31]

Nelson Miles mentored Scott in many ways, not the least of which was in providing venues that allowed him to expand the kinds of opportunity he could offer tribal peoples. Both men shared a great deal in common: a desire for adventure that the American frontier could provide; a respect for American Indian culture; and a willingness to avoid unnecessary bloodshed when dealing with dissident tribal groups, as Miles demonstrated in his capture of the Nez Percés. Perhaps the most important characteristic that both men shared was a seemingly insatiable desire for professional advancement. Miles placed Scott in positions that he believed would advance Scott's career, where he could meet and work with influential contacts in and beyond the military. Nonetheless, their differences were significant as well. Miles was vain, exceedingly jealous of others to the point that he would denigrate and undermine the reputation of another officer if it would further his own career. Scott was more subdued and diplomatic, priding himself on his ability to get along and often reach consensus with those who initially opposed him. Moreover, Scott garnered a reputation for honesty and integrity, with both his peers and the tribal groups he worked with throughout his life. Obviously, Miles did not see Scott as a threat to his own career, and in his willingness to be mentored, Scott drew on the more positive side of Miles's personality.[32]

Why and how did Scott believe that his military service on the Great Plains warranted the kind of recognition from senior commanders that he claimed? It certainly was not owing to his battlefield accomplishments under Col. Samuel Sturgis's command in the Great Sioux War, which were minimal. Of his three deployments during that conflict, two were in the Dakota Territory, where he was stationed at Fort Abraham Lincoln, shortly after his arrival on the northern Great Plains in the fall of 1876, and both involved preventing dissident Sioux south along the Missouri River from leaving the Standing Rock and Cheyenne River Agencies. His regiment's objective was to round up tribal horses and weapons to prevent the Sioux from leaving the reservation and committing more depredations. These deployments were more like skirmishes than battles. Scott's third wartime encounter was on the Yellowstone River in the Montana Territory in the summer of 1877. In this third deployment for Scott's regiment, he was ordered to participate in scout and escort duty along the Yellowstone and to assist in the exhumation of the bodies of the soldiers killed at Little Big Horn for later burial. Here, too, there was little if any direct confrontation with dissident Indians. It was following this detail that Scott was ordered to the Nez Percé conflict at Canyon Creek and the Bears Paw Mountains.[33]

The answer can be found in how Scott structured his credentials in reference to what he believed to be the army's needs and objectives. The Great Sioux War was a costly venture, culturally devastating to the Sioux and other tribal groups to be sure, but financially expensive to the federal government as well. No military commander believed that dissident tribal groups were humbled by their military defeat as a consequence of the conflict. Crazy Horse's contentious band may have been somewhat neutralized by his death, but Sitting Bull, just north across the Canadian border with 1,200 lodges, was a source of inspiration to other tribal groups and a potential threat to the American army guarding the northern frontier. Those troops, dispersed over a broad area in several territorial regions, could not adequately defend the farmers, ranchers, and commercial interests increasingly pressing westward for frontier land. If the Great Plains were to be settled, tribal groups must be confined, not simply to reservation lands, but to specific designated agencies where the distribution of allotments would constrain their mobility. Such constraints would also minimize the military's role in tribal surveillance, since the BIA would assume primary responsibility for tribal groups who were settled on specific reservation lands. Even if there were a sufficient number of troops to muster an offensive operation—and these opportunities were few and far between—officers were not trained to counter the hit-and-run tactics that tribal insurgents used against them. Winter campaigns, part of a strategy of total warfare, often successfully exploited the vulnerability of tribal groups in their sedentary venues and in the burden of having to travel with their women and children. Nonetheless, the use of such tactics was not unequivocally accepted, even among the military. Many senior officers, including John Schofield, who would become commanding general of the army, believed that such tactics "disregard[ed] the rules of civilized warfare."[34]

Scott had to exercise discretion and tact in how he presented his experience. Senior commanders may have recognized and appreciated his skills from a logistic perspective, because they could help minimize the costs of direct military confrontations with dissident tribes. However, many of them did not share Scott's opinion of what he regarded as the injustices perpetrated against tribal groups through the displacement of their lands and cultural foundations. For example, although Sheridan may have been impressed with "white men who could open up channels of communication with the Indians and deal effectively with them," as his biographer noted in reference to Scott, Sheridan, like Gen. William T. Sherman, his mentor, strongly believed in the efficacy of total warfare. This would include undertaking military campaigns in the winter months with the objective of destroying the food supply of dissident bands to force them onto their reservation agencies. Scott particularly deplored the decimation of the buffalo herds, an integral component of the policy of total war.[35]

As a loyal soldier far down in the military chain of command, however, he discreetly directed his criticism of the treatment of tribal peoples at the BIA and ultimately the Department of the Interior, deflecting the army's role in causing the problem. He believed that these civilian-managed components of the federal bureaucracy were responsible for the dire situation that tribal peoples confronted. Scott's deflection of the military's role in provoking Native

American depredations involved the Northern Cheyennes who, forced by the Department of the Interior to migrate to Indian Territory, were killing "all the white men they could coming across Kansas and Nebraska. . . . with a quarter of the army following them." Scott lamented that "this was part of the harsh policy of the secretary of the interior, to assemble all Indians in the Indian Territory, no matter where their habitat, even if it killed them, as it did very many."[36] Scott discreetly chose his villains when it came to other injustices perpetrated against tribal peoples. Such was the case with Chief Joseph's capture. Miles had promised Joseph in good faith that he and his followers would be permitted to return and settle on their traditional tribal lands in Idaho. Such did not prove to be the case. Sheridan, who still considered the Nez Percés prisoners of war since they had killed soldiers, prevailed upon authorities to send Joseph and his followers to Fort Leavenworth, Kansas, with subsequent banishment to the Indian Territory. Chief Joseph's subsequent life in Kansas and the Indian Territory, where many of his people died, broke his spirit. Significantly, while condemning Joseph's "treatment by the white man," Scott deftly blamed, not the army whose actions led to Joseph's plight, but the "government."[37]

Scott's service guarding a group of Cheyenne prisoners under the command of then Col. Samuel D. Sturgis provides another example of how he sought to embellish his credentials in a way that he believed would work to his advantage. Sturgis was prepared to offer Scott a one-hundred-dollar stipend for his efforts in mollifying the restive Cheyennes as a result of his skill as a "sign-talker." Although doubtless the money would have come in handy, Scott informed his commanding officer that he would rather have a letter in his file affirming his service as an interpreter.[38]

While Scott encountered a diminishing number of field patrols, other opportunities opened up at the posts where he was stationed during this period. One was in the additional time that he could spend with his new wife and growing family. Another was the opportunity to broaden his administrative experience in the numerous staff functions available to officers on their frontier posts. Scott's integrity, reliability, and concern for detail placed him in a favorable position. Consequently, with his new bride joining him, Scott was assigned to Fort Totten (1879–82), where he assumed the role of acting assistant quartermaster and commissary of subsistence. Duties included the ordering of essential provisions for the post, arranging military transportation including the care and upkeep of horses, and providing materials for any additions or modifications to the fort. In the fall of 1882, he was transferred to Fort Meade in the Black Hills, where he rejoined his Troop K. Here he served as post treasurer, and eventually, as the post's judge advocate, arranging cases for courts-martial, adding additional staff assignments to his résumé.[39]

Not all of Scott's efforts to enhance his credentials were successful. To be sure, Scott learned a great deal about Chief Joseph and his cultural pride and skill as a sign-talker when the lieutenant accompanied the chief and his band of Nez Percés to Fort Lincoln and ultimately to Fort Leavenworth as prisoners of war. Nevertheless, it was perhaps his alleged initial encounter with Chief Joseph that Scott hoped would prove helpful in enhancing his résumé. The fear that Joseph's band would join Sitting Bull and other dissident tribes in Canada and launch an attack against military forces and settlements south of the border was only one explanation for military officials' intense urgency to capture Joseph. Another explanation was political and would eventually involve Scott in his ongoing pursuit of professional recognition and elevation in rank. The movement of Joseph's band created a jurisdictional dispute among several rival commanders who themselves were seeking additional professional recognition. Owing to his distinguished service as an Indian campaigner in the Red River War (1874–75) and credited by his superiors with ending the Great Sioux War, Miles, then a colonel in the Fifth Infantry, was given independent command of the District of the Yellowstone in September 1877. The exceedingly ambitious Miles saw the position as an opportunity to prove his worth and obtain promotion to brigadier general. Gen. Oliver O. Howard, commander of the Department of the Columbia, under whose authority the original Nez Percé landholdings were located, claimed that he had General Sherman's authority to pursue Joseph's band beyond his geographic jurisdiction. Consequently, Howard saw Miles as a rival.[40]

Scott's involvement in Joseph's capture began in the early fall of 1877, when he volunteered to be detailed, with Miles's approval, under Lt. Gustavus Doane with Company E of the Seventh Cavalry. Doane was ordered to Judith Gap in the Montana Territory. As previously noted, Miles took credit for the capture of Joseph and his band near the Bears Paw Mountains.

However, Scott claimed that *he* had contributed to Joseph's apprehension when he inadvertently diverted "their advance-guard," which had stolen some horses that Scott was seeking to recover. Scott followed them down the Yellowstone Valley in hot pursuit. These renegade Nez Percés then reported back to Joseph, erroneously, that a large force—Scott had only ten men with him—was blocking their egress in a narrow part of the valley. Consequently, Joseph and his band were forced to move in a northerly direction, through Canyon Creek, where they crossed the Yellowstone River. This placed him within a day's march of Miles's force, which allowed the colonel to overtake them short of the Canadian line, *if* Scott's interpretation is credible.[41]

Scott's claim is disputed, however. An amateur though highly respected anthropologist, Lucullus V. McWhorter, notes that the Nez Percé band had crossed the Yellowstone River and made their way up Pelican Peak before August 26, a week prior to September 2, when Scott claimed that he first encountered the advance Nez Percé scouts. At least several days before Joseph and his band reached the Yellowstone River, they had decided their only avenue of escape was to venture on to meet Sitting Bull's tribal contingent in Canada. Furthermore, Walter Camp, an editor who interviewed hundreds of tribal participants in the postbellum Indian Wars, questioned Scott's claim. Camp had interviewed Yellow Bull, a Nez Percé war chief, who was privy to Joseph's movements prior to his capture. As a consequence of the interview, Camp wrote Scott saying, "I think there was more to this incident than you are probably aware." Other Nez Percés interviewed by Camp who had been present when the Nez Percés surrendered to Miles at the Bears Paw Mountains implied that Joseph may have changed his story, to one different from what "Joseph brought [to Scott] after having visited Miles camp."

Was Scott's "rapid advance" chasing the Nez Percé scouts a valid explanation as to how and why Joseph and his band were ultimately captured? We may never know. Nonetheless, the military confrontation—perhaps "skirmish" is more accurate—gave him an opportunity to document his combat skills.[42]

Scott's field and staff assignments on the Great Plains in the 1880s were balanced by more relaxing and intimate experiences. A four-month leave in the spring of 1884 gave him the chance to visit family and friends in the East. Although Scott could not travel initially with his new bride after their wedding and following the birth of David Hunter Scott at Fort Totten, Scott's mother had the opportunity to see her new daughter-in-law and grandson when Mary went back to Philadelphia to visit the Merrill family the previous year. Scott had the opportunity to meet with his older brother, Charles, in Pittsburgh and his younger brother, William, then at Princeton University as a professor of geology and paleontology. Doubtless, Mary was pleased to see her son as well. Over the years, Len seemed to be closer to Wick than he was to Charles, perhaps owing to personality and the interests that the younger Scott brothers had in common. Both shared an intellectual curiosity about the world around them: Len, in how the cultures of indigenous peoples interacted with their geolandscape, and Wick, in how that landscape was created in the first place.

A more protracted posting in the East was opened to Scott when he was detailed to undertake recruitment for the Seventh Cavalry in Philadelphia from the fall of 1886 to 1888. Scott enjoyed another prolonged stay with his wife, as well as his friends and relatives in both Philadelphia and Princeton. Although unsuccessful in having the eastern posting extended, Scott undoubtedly used what time that he had to explore the contacts he had made and garner additional ones in his campaign for professional advancement. An opportunity arose when it was announced that several openings would become available in the commissary department within a year. If appointed, Scott would be promoted to a captaincy. A plethora of letters soon followed supporting Scott's candidacy for the position, with endorsements from such eclectic and diverse sponsors as a Louisville, Kentucky, attorney and Princeton graduate who was part of the three months' frontier expedition organized by Wick, with a military detachment under his brother's command; the president of Princeton College; senior officers such as Colonel Sturgis; the governor of Pennsylvania; and the president of the Pennsylvania state senate along with twenty-three of his colleagues. U.S. Senators Quay and J. Donald Cameron (Pa.) and Lewis Merrill were behind the scenes soliciting still others.[43]

Ultimately, all was for naught. Given the static growth in the size of the army at the time and the number of officers in rank hoping for promotion, Scott probably did not stand much of a chance. He was granted an additional four months' leave following the end of his recruitment position in Philadelphia. Fortunately, another option opened for him. He would join Troop M of the Seventh Cavalry at Fort Sill, Indian Territory, in February 1889.[44]

Scott's initial thirteen-year tenure on the northern Great Plains underscored a period of maturation in his growing awareness of the opportunities offered in a new frontier environment. As a young officer eagerly seeking adventure, Scott initially brought essential skills that he had honed as a teen in Princeton. His winter nighttime forays hunting rabbits imbued a sense of confidence in his own ability to master a seemingly inhospitable environment, sharpening his visual and audible senses. Scott was challenged by the indigenous peoples who had evolved a diverse culture in such an environment, and his latent intellectual curiosity was aroused to understand their way of life. His knowledge and mastery of the sign language used by tribal groups on the Great Plains provided an invaluable and lifetime conduit to achieve that goal. Awareness of their cultures and of the seemingly unrelenting challenges that sought to destroy them provoked a strong sense of sympathy in him.

Nonetheless, his sympathy had a spiritual connotation derived from his Protestant upbringing. However fascinating he found tribal groups—whether praising the cultural pride shown by Chief Joseph or the hospitality extended to him by Red Cloud—they were still, in the eyes of a Christian, a simplistic people, and one faced with extinction when their lands were taken from them and their food supplies destroyed. The fact that Scott could reach out to them in a language they could converse in was a source of pride and self-adulation. His knowledge of that language enabled him to protect them as a good Christian would or should. His sympathy was predicted on the belief that they were incapable of helping themselves, that they were an inferior race. His role as a peacemaker or peacekeeper initially was to diminish the characteristic that many Anglos found so objectionable in tribal cultures—that is, their veneration of warfare. As a result, and to ease their transition into the Anglos' definition of civilization, Scott embraced mediation and pacification, to avoid overt military confrontations that threatened their very survival. In a broader perspective, Scott's early experience on the northern Great Plains led to an unswerving dedication to assisting indigenous peoples wherever he was posted throughout his military career. Grandfather Hodge would have been proud of him!

Such a role ultimately came at a price. Frontier constabularies were anachronistic in an increasingly professional army that defined as its purpose to train for potential military confrontations, often against more sophisticated forces, and ones that would, increasingly after 1898, involve overseas service. Moreover, competition for promotion was exceedingly keen, owing to a static retirement system and regimental constrictions that straight-jacketed a predominantly young to middle-aged military force in rank for extended periods. Scott was increasingly aware of the challenges he faced given the paucity of his direct battlefield experience. Although he could no longer draw upon his grandfather directly, the elder Hodge's reputation and prestige, and those of the Scott-Hodge-Stockton clan, provided a foundation that broadened to include friends of friends in the civilian and military realms. Consequently, Scott was able to garner political influence to enhance his military career. A mentoring relationship under soon to be General of the Army Miles was one potentially fruitful avenue for professional advancement. In addition, he marketed his credentials to attract a receptive audience, tailoring his duties and skills—not the least of which was his knowledge of the intertribal sign language—to meet what he believed to be the army's needs at the time. He also broadened his documented experience by undertaking staff and administrative postings when active field experiences apprehending dissident tribal groups diminished. Only time would tell whether and how these strategies would be successful in an army in transition.

Scott's Fort Sill assignment, though it held no promise of advancement in rank, would give him additional administrative experience in his role as the post's quartermaster. Managing a budget and advocating for additional funds to address the needs of the post gave him access to influential groups in Washington, both civilian and military. Most significantly, aside from the opportunities available to him as the post's quartermaster, the Fort Sill posting gave Scott additional opportunities to interact with tribal peoples, to mutual benefit.

CHAPTER 3

▼ ▼ ▼

THE FORT SILL YEARS AND BEYOND

Advocacy and Its Limitations

I have the honor to state that these Indians were taken and placed here after great expenditure of blood and money by the War Department to be made self-sustaining at the earliest possible moment. They are now rapidly approaching that condition—the Indians themselves being much encouraged as to their future.
—Hugh Scott to the Adjutant, Fort Sill, August 15, 1897

The Kiowa and Comanche tribes that Scott initially encountered at Fort Sill in the early spring of 1889 were dealing with the same constraints on their tribal holdings and cultural foundations that the Sioux and the Nez Percés had earlier endured. Encroachment on their lands by settlers, facilitated by the construction of railroads, and by other commercial interests such as miners in search of gold created scenarios that were played out with almost every tribe west of the Mississippi by the last third of the nineteenth century. A major difference was the geo-ecological isolation that the Kiowas and Comanches had enjoyed on the southwestern plains for a considerably long period of time, from at least the early eighteenth century. The ancestral origins of these tribal groups can be traced to the headwaters of the Arkansas River where they had first lived among the Shoshones.

The geographic region to which they eventually migrated in their adaptation to a hunter-gatherer culture consisted of a land area of 240,000 square miles, covering parts of what would eventually become the states of Colorado, Oklahoma, Texas, Arizona, and New Mexico. In a region that came to be known as Comancheria, this tribal group, comprising approximately a dozen bands, created what amounted to a military and trading empire based on stolen horses and cattle, and in the taking, trading, or selling of human captives. The key to their success was the acquisition and utilization of the Spanish horse by the mid-eighteenth century. Comanche tribesmen became expert riders in a relatively short period of time, utilizing the advantages of the breed's speed, intelligence, endurance, and ability to live off the grasses of the semiarid Southwest. No southwestern tribe other than the Kiowas, with whom the Comanches formed an alliance in 1790, so successfully engaged in mounted hunting and warfare. With a nomadic range of eight hundred miles, Comanche raiding parties extended as far south as Mexico and as far north as Nebraska, drawing on and enhancing their wealth in horses, skins, and captives. Their territorial control of Comancheria lasted till the early part of the nineteenth century, driving the Jicarilla Apaches from their traditional lands in West Texas and preventing the northern reach of Spanish missionaries. So successful were the Comanches in thwarting settlement until the early nineteenth century that when Mexico declared its independence from Spain in 1820, in an effort to diminish Comanche raids, the Mexican government initially encouraged colonization by settlers from the states of the American South, a decision it would regret within twenty years.[1]

Ultimately, neither military prowess nor commercial hegemony could save the Kiowas and Comanches' way of life from increasing Anglo incursions, both indirect and direct. Tribal populations were decimated by smallpox epidemics in 1816 and 1839, as well as by the ravages of cholera in 1849, the latter disease having been brought by prospectors moving westward to California in the late 1840s in search of gold. The Kiowas lost half their number from cholera, and Comanche bands who interacted commercially with white settlers found their numbers substantially depleted as a consequence of disease. Contentiousness increased in the 1850s with the diminishing of the buffalo herds by commercial hide hunters and the influx of settlers into West Texas. Tribal raiding parties, seeking cattle and captives, were increasingly met by armed Texas Rangers. Settlements in West Texas were threatened by Comanche incursions despite attempts by federal officials to restrict them to a 20,000-acre tract along the Brazos River in north-central Texas south of what would become the Oklahoma Territory in 1890.[2]

The onrush of settlers, ranchers, and other commercial interests into the southern Great Plains following the end of the Civil War and the killing of Capt. William Fetterman and eighty of his troopers at the hands of the Lakota Sioux near Fort Kearny, Nebraska Territory, in 1866 engendered a sense of urgency among federal officials to make a more concerted effort to set aside, and limit by treaty, designated lands where tribal groups could reside. These officials hoped, too, that imposing a more sedentary lifestyle would encourage them to embrace agriculture as a meaningful path on the road to civilization. The Treaty of Medicine Lodge in 1867, which comprised three distinct agreements with different tribal groups, was meant to achieve this objective. Ostensibly, the Kiowas and Comanches were pressured by the so-called Indian peace commissioners to accept a 5,500-square-mile tract in the Leased District of Indian Territory (within present-day Oklahoma) as their reservation. The promise of $25,000 per annum in goods for thirty years was one incentive designed to win their approval. An equally significant enticement was to allow tribal members to journey south of the Arkansas River during the hunting season into northern Texas beyond the confines of their reservation with exclusive rights to hunt in the bison range "so long as the buffalo may range thereon in such numbers as to justify the chase." What the Comanche and Kiowa chiefs regarded as their traditional right, the commissioners interpreted as a privilege.

To the dismay of the commissioners, the Treaty of Medicine Lodge failed to achieve stability and pacification, let alone an avenue of "advancement on the path to civilization." Contrary to its stipulation, considerably less than a majority of tribal males had signed the agreement, and a number of Comanche bands were unrepresented in acquiescing to the treaty's terms. However, the bigger problem in implementing its provisions was the fact that the treaty failed to take into account how tribal groups would likely react to the wanton, willful, and concerted slaughter of the buffalo that they depended on for their very survival and that played an integral role in their culture. Specifically, their exclusive right to hunt the buffalo south of their reservation was undermined by soldiers who even provided protection to commercial tanners and poachers. Consequently, with the diminishing herds of buffalo on the southern plains, Comanche hunters and warriors frequented the region of northern and western Texas to steal and trade horses and cattle, bringing recurrent terror to West Texas settlers. One county in the region saw its population diminish by half in the decade following the treaty's signing.[3]

When Scott arrived at Fort Sill on frontier duty in the early spring of 1889, the Kiowas and Comanches were facing the consequences of nefarious government practices in implementing the treaty. No longer were they the formidable threat against the northwest Texas settlements that they had been for generations. With the buffalo all but extinct on the southern Great Plains, these tribal groups became completely dependent for their very survival on the annual annuities provided by government contractors, many of whom engaged in graft. Such practices as the failure to deliver food and other essential provisions in a timely fashion, as prescribed by treaty obligations, and the diminished quality and quantity of such goods brought starvation and despair to the reservation. Consequently, the Comanche population, estimated to be 1,550 in 1885, had declined by 50 percent since the Treaty of Medicine Lodge was negotiated in 1867.[4]

Graft was not limited to tribal contractors. The Indian Service itself, under the Department of the Interior, was fraught with corruption in its operation as an agency administered through political patronage. Congressional influence was often the primary criteria in the selection of reservation personnel. The result was the appointment of agents who were often totally unqualified to serve. Unfortunately for tribal peoples, these agents, as field staff away from the levers of control, often enjoyed a wide latitude in implementing policies formulated by government officials in Washington. Their base salary of approximately $2,000 per annum was often simply a starting point in aggrandizing additional wealth in the form of bribes from those committing incursions on reservations, as well as from contractors supplying annuities stipulated in treaty agreements. Some agents used their position for political as well as economic advantage, ingratiating themselves to higher public officials at the expense of their alleged commitment to the welfare of Native peoples.

The frequent turnover in agency personnel as a result of successive national Democratic and Republican administrations in the 1880s and early 1890s exacerbated an already irresponsible federal administration of tribes. The Anadarko Agency that served the Kiowa-Comanche people had no fewer than eight agents from 1885 to 1893, intensifying the corrupt practices by agents who knew full well that their time at the "public trough" was limited, and thus that they had to take advantage of every situation as a source of self-aggrandizement. The frequent turnover of agents had other negative consequences as well. Agents came and went, but the cattlemen, reservation traders, and "squaw men"—white males who married Indian women ostensibly for their land titles—remained to continue their often nefarious deeds unabated.

Specific examples of agent malfeasance on the Kiowa-Comanche reservation during this period are all too common. Agent J. Lee Hall, appointed to Anadarko in 1885, committed graft on a grand scale by issuing fraudulent vouchers for goods and services and misappropriating lease money. His addiction to alcohol led to frequent absences from his post and eventual removal from office two years later. His successor, E. E. White, committed nepotism when he illegally placed his brother on the Indian Service payroll, and bribery in profiting from a grazing lease on reservation lands issued to a Texas cattleman. William D. Myers, a Democrat who replaced White, though lacking experience in Indian affairs, nonetheless proved sympathetic to tribal concerns. However, his tenure ended in 1889, when Republican President Benjamin Harrison entered the White House. Charles E. Adams, who replaced Myers, soon became embroiled in scandal involving traders on the post and was forced to resign in the fall of 1891.[5]

Scott had ample opportunity to hone his skills at negotiation and tribal advocacy during his eight-year posting at Fort Sill. The numerous challenges he faced that undermined tribal stability gave him the opportunity to test techniques that he had used on the northern Great Plains among the Sioux, Northern Cheyennes, and Crows and in the Montana Territory with the Nez Percés. Others developed over time and would prove useful in dealing not only with American Indians but also with indigenous peoples in Cuba and the Philippines as well. Specific occurrences at Fort Sill that he encountered early in his administration involved, among others, the amenability of the Kiowas, Comanches, and Kiowa-Apaches to the so-called Ghost Dance religious movement (sometimes called the Messiah Dance). This spiritual movement of renewal captivated diverse tribal groups including those of the northern and southern Great Plains. Other threats to tribal integrity were more ominous and far-reaching. The Dawes Severalty Act of 1887 promulgated the destruction of tribal cultures through land redistribution and mandatory school education. Concurrent with these events was the ever-present criminal activity, from both within and beyond the confines of the reservation. Scott's initial title, acting assistant quartermaster, did not do justice to the actual tasks that he performed at the post. A more apt job description was noted in his *Biographical Register* file as "tours of field duty settling Indian questions."[6]

Perhaps as a reaction to the demoralizing consequences on tribal life at the time, among not only the Kiowa-Comanches but also other plains and prairie tribes as well, there arose a spiritual movement led by a Paiute, Jack Wilson, better known by his American Indian name, Wovoka. Wovoka was credited with inspiring a spiritual following as a result of his first of several divine revelations in the mid-1880s. He never claimed to be a messiah, but he considered himself, and was considered by other eclectic tribal peoples, to be a prophet. His message was one of a spiritual catharsis in which the troubles faced by the tribes, such as the loss of the buffalo and the constraints on their culture life, would dissipate, replaced by a world balanced between nature and the spirits. He believed that it was this world that their ancestors had enjoyed when they were first put on earth. The performance of a special ritual, the Ghost (or Messiah) Dance, was an affirmation of belief. Whether the movement took a contentious tone against white incursions on Native ways of life would be predicated upon tribal interpretation. Whether it would lead to a violent confrontation would depend on how government officials perceived its practice. Nonetheless, although subject to diverse and often conflicting interpretations regarding its bellicose tendencies, Wovoka's message was meant to be an awakening of the soul for a downtrodden and demoralized people. Such was the environment that Scott confronted in the early years of his posting at Fort Sill. Although Scott did not take credit for preventing tribal groups from turning the movement toward violent ends, his comprehensive investigation of its origins and intertribal development enabled him to prevent a tragic misunderstanding like the one that occurred among the Sioux at Wounded Knee in December 1890. His skills as a keen observer, his knowledge of intertribal customs and traditions, and a determination to advocate on behalf of tribal peoples—all would be tested by these and other events.[7]

In November 1890, the War Department ordered Scott to investigate "the feeling and intentions of the Kiowa, Comanche, Apache, Wichita . . . during the excitement over the Messiah Dance." He was directed to determine how and in what way they were influenced by Wovoka's prophecies. Scott spent the next three months in the field visiting different groups, putting to use the skills of observation he had initially developed while watching the Indian scouts leading military patrols on the northern Great Plains. He recorded the movements of each group while they performed the ritual in dance and song, noting important details and indicating the ceremony's significance to its participants.

Although the dancing movements were unique, there was nothing to indicate that the spirited dance was a gesture of defiance—or worse, a prelude to violence—at least among the Kiowas. Many saw it as a spiritual catharsis, an opportunity to purge sins in preparation for a return to the way of life that tribal peoples had enjoyed in the past. Perhaps tied to this was the chance at "meeting" their deceased ancestors in another world. However, most saw the Ghost Dance in a more secular context, as a social gathering and an opportunity to visit with other families. Unlike the Sioux, no Ghost Dance shirts, which that tribe believed to be impervious to bullets, were worn by dancers on the Kiowa-Comanche reservation.

During his three-month field assignment to investigate the Messiah Dance prophecy, Scott had hoped to find Sitting Bull, a Southern Arapaho (not to be confused with the Sioux chief of the same name). Sitting Bull claimed to have seen and spoken directly with the Messiah when he was among the Cheyennes and Arapahos, symbolically disseminating Wovoka's prophecies to other tribal groups by placing a golden eagle's feather in the hands of influential tribal chiefs of many nations so that they may pass the prophet's message on to their people. The Comanches had refused to accept the feather, ostensibly repudiating the relevance of the prophet's message to their tribal group. However, a Kiowa chief had accepted it, passing the message on to a prominent Kiowa, Ah-pia-ton (Wooden Lance). Ah-pia-ton was selected by his tribe as a delegate to find the messiah and confirm his earthly existence. A firm believer in Jesus Christ as a man of peace, he approached Wovoka (who, once again, never claimed to be the messiah, but a prophet). Nevertheless, he became disillusioned and skeptical when he saw that Wovoka's hands were devoid of any scars to indicate he had been crucified. Consequently, he believed that Sitting Bull's enthusiasm led to overexaggeration. Ah-pia-ton conveyed these feelings to his people, thereby earning Scott's respect for his honesty and courage. Although many Kiowas were disappointed in what Ah-pia-ton told them, he ultimately won their respect for his honesty.[8]

Nonetheless, whether some tribal groups viewed the Ghost Dance as simply a peaceful spiritual movement or a prelude to overt violence, neighboring white settlers were suspicious of its practice, more so following news of the Wounded Knee encounter and the fact that it was often performed in secret. Scott had suggested that the dance be conducted in such a way that anyone could see it, to minimize suspicion that it was done with evil or bellicose intent. Moreover, he warned military officials against attempting to disarm Indians on the reservation, given how groups were isolated and widely dispersed. He feared that such a move would be interpreted as an act of provocation. Ultimately, the realization that the messiah had not returned to the secular world led to the dissipation of the movement. Ironically, too, it negated what Scott saw, given his Christian upbringing, as the loss of a unique chance to provide, on a broad scale, an opportunity to bring whites and Indians together around the teachings of Jesus.[9]

Scott's involvement in the "Messiah" movement underscored for him the importance of patience and a keen sense of observation. Nonetheless, Scott would be the last person to claim full credit for preventing a massacre among the Kiowas at Anadarko, Oklahoma, similar to the one that occurred at Wounded Knee. His evolution to a successful peacekeeper included acquiring individual contacts within a tribal community through patience and observation. To the extent that he could, he studied a tribe's history, their interactions with neighboring tribes, their contacts with white settlers and commercial interests, and most significantly, their encounters with military forces. Aside from the knowledge of tribal history, among the prerequisites that he found useful if not essential in selecting such an individual included the person's status within the tribe; his interactions with other tribal members; his willingness to serve as "eyes and ears" for Scott, so that he could anticipate potential discord before it occurred; and how such an ally on his own could dispel anger among tribal members and others beyond the reservation.

Although not entirely qualified on all the criteria, Scott found a loyal ally during the Ghost Dance episode. I-See-O, a Kiowa born around 1851 near Fort Larned, Kansas Territory, left the region following the Custer massacre, ultimately settling with the Comanches who, as noted, had accepted the tribe in the late eighteenth century. When he arrived at Fort Sill in 1889, he was enlisted as a scout by the post's commander. Initially, he served as a courier between Fort Sill and other posts. To Scott, I-See-O's greatest asset was devotion, having recognized early in his life that accepting if not entirely embracing the white man's world was the only option open to his tribe and their Comanche neighbors. As noted by his biographer:

> I-See-O's work was always of the quiet kind. His services have never been measured by heroism in the face of hostile fire, nor by the prowess of his rifle or pistol, but by the struggles that he averted and consequently the lives that he saved. He was usually the intermediary—the man who was Indian at heart, familiar with his vices and virtues, well aware of the power of the American soldier and the futility of struggle when the same ends could be obtained in a peaceful manner. It seems as though his whole life has been dedicated to creating better understanding between the white and the red men. Wherever I-See-O appeared bloodshed and struggle were conspicuously absent.[10]

Scott used and often depended on I-See-O's services throughout his tenure at Fort Sill and beyond. In the Ghost Dance event, Scott credited his ally with preventing violence among the Kiowas and Kiowa-Apaches, noting: "It was largely through I-See-O that I got underneath the surface of affairs. He and I went about together wherever the excitement was greatest, sometimes in the Wichita Mountains, sometimes in the Caddo country, or sometimes 150 miles up the Washita, and between us we pulled the Southern Indians through that troublesome time without firing a shot." Nonetheless, Scott and I-See-O's relationship was not one of equals. I-See-O manifested loyalty to Scott, a quality that Scott depended on and rewarded when he had the opportunity to do so. I-See-O corresponded with Scott, through the Kiowa's nephew, throughout Scott's career and into retirement. Scott successfully advocated for a military pension for I-See-O for his service as an Indian scout. Regardless, Scott described him as "old and mediaeval, his mind is back in the middle ages, and he has simply been stunned by civilization."[11]

Other incidents proved the worth of I-See-O's assistance. One consequence of tribal despair was an increase in criminal activity. Such behavior on the

Kiowa-Comanche reservation was not limited to the illegal incursions by settlers and commercial interests on tribal lands. In January 1891, Scott was ordered to take two troops of cavalry from Fort Sill to Anadarko to investigate the death of several Kiowa children, one of whom had been whipped by the white superintendent of the tribal school they were attending. Evidently, the children ran away after the beating and froze to death in the snow. Subsequently, the superintendent was threatened by a Kiowa at gunpoint, and others sought revenge for the children's tragic deaths. The agent at Anadarko feared for his life and called for a squadron of cavalry. Scott, at night and in the middle of a blizzard thirty miles away at Fort Sill, enlisted I-See-O, who guided the lieutenant with a lantern on a trail familiar to the Kiowas. After calming the agent, Scott subsequently ordered I-See-O to ask the tribal elders to summon a council, thwarting what could turn out to be a major uprising. The last thing Scott wanted to do was to mount a show of force. He knew full well that with tensions already high on and near the reservation, the use of military force would only escalate events further. He hoped as well that consulting with the tribal elders would minimize tensions, which it did. This procedure had two advantages. It enabled him to determine where they stood on the desire of tribesmen to take revenge on the superintendent. It also conveyed a respect for and deference to the tribe's decision-making process. Although not always successful, as time would soon tell, the strategy opened and sustained an avenue of immediate communication, framed in mutual respect and trust. Scott informed both the council and the agent that such action on the superintendent's part was an affront to the tribe's cultural dignity. His action led to the superintendent's removal.[12]

Perhaps the most devastating blow to these tribes' lifestyle and the greatest source of tribal tension during Scott's tenure at Fort Sill involved the passage of the Dawes Severalty Act (1887). This measure negated the very possession of their reservation lands and undermined their cultural existence as a tribal people. The federal law conveyed to the executive branch the authority to terminate reservation lands, while allotting to individual tribal families specific tracts of 160 acres each to be used by them for their own economic development. Surplus tribal holdings would then be sold off to non-Indian settlers, with the proceeds used to provide individual tribal families with the essential resources needed to enable them, eventually and hopefully, to become prosperous American citizens. The measure was premised on several assumptions about the future of American Indian civilization: that tribal peoples could no longer survive in a commercially competitive democratic society and must adjust accordingly; and that the concept of tribal ownership, the holding of lands in common, impeded their survival. The idea was that the custom of tribal holdings did not give them any incentive to cultivate the soil, but that individual land ownership would.

The policy was supported by a divergent and somewhat eclectic group, consisting of eastern reformers and the tribes' predominantly reservation-based clergy as well as would-be western settlers and commercial interests, who coveted the vast tribal holdings. Not surprisingly, these diverse groups had specific plans on how to implement the measure, oriented, to be sure, by their beliefs about the beneficial outcomes that each could obtain. Reformers, the so-called Friends of the Indian, were sympathetic to the plight of American Indians and believed that education was a critical component in preparing them to assume their role as responsible citizens. There were debates among reformers over the specific form—primary, secondary—or curricular objectives such an approach should take. The more pragmatic western land settlers and their commercial cohorts were simply concerned with obtaining fertile soil, as rapidly and as cheaply as they could. The Friends of the Indian, perhaps out of a hope beyond what the actual situation warranted, believed that the tribal family's white neighbors would serve as models, in guiding them on the path to responsible citizenship.

Following passage of the Dawes Act, reformers continued to debate specifics, such as the size, eligibility, usage, and terms under which original Native recipients could sell or transfer their holdings once the lands were allotted to them. Some of these debates produced amendments to the initial measure or led to subsequent congressional legislation. However, one thing was clear: tribal groups would have no voice as to whether their reservation would be subject to allotment. The decision would ultimately rest with the president of the United States in consultation with Congress. Although a tribal council, representing a majority of the adult male members of a tribe, could negotiate the terms of termination, the amount they would receive for their "excess" reservation lands would ultimately be up to federal officials. The Dawes Act's initial implementation called for the creation of a commission, organized in

March 1889 and known as the Cherokee (or Jerome) Commission, named after its director, David H. Jerome, a former governor of Michigan. The commission was charged with the task of negotiating with the tribal council for the price of the "excess" land.

Many of the discussions concerning Indian reform affecting western tribes actually occurred at a location in New York State. Albert Smiley, a prominent Quaker pacifist and wealthy proprietor of a grand hotel in the lower Catskill Mountains known as The Mohonk Mountain House, offered his facilities on an annual basis in the 1880s and 1890s. It was here that eclectic groups shared their experiences and ideas on the plight of American Indians. Significantly, Smiley was a member of the Board of Indian Commissioners, charged with the authority to monitor the annuities and services provided to tribal groups by federal officials under treaty provisions. The board, consisting of prominent citizens who served without pay, was created during the Grant administration as part of the president's "Peace Policy." Periodically, Scott contributed to the conference dialogue, and he subsequently served on the board following his retirement from military service. His input on both bodies will be examined in a subsequent chapter of this study. Other philanthropic organizations, such as the Indian Rights Association and the Women's National Indian Association, as well as numerous religious-oriented groups, shared a concern for the plight of tribal groups during this period.[13]

The commission's time frame paralleled the wave of pressure for the settlement of southwestern lands held by tribal groups. By the late 1880s, the desire for tracts in what was known as the "Unattached Land District" of Indian Territory, northeast of the Kiowa-Comanche reservation, had become intense. The so-called Boomers, potential white farmers and ranchers, literally waited at the border in April 1889 for the specific time allowed for them to stampede across it for a claim to their 160-acre tract, ostensibly provided to them by the Homestead Act of 1862. In 1889 alone, the population of a neighboring county adjacent to the Kiowa-Comanche reservation grew to 5,000 settlers.

Members of the Jerome Commission arrived at Fort Sill (where the initial meeting was held) in September 1892, well versed in how to proceed with tribes to negotiate away their reservation holdings. In the four-year period from its creation in 1889, the commission would negotiate ten agreements with twenty tribes, leading to the loss of 15 million acres of reservation lands transferred to white settlement. As noted, the pressure for tribal holdings in the Oklahoma Territory coveted by Boomers had reached the point where the Comanche reservation would be next. The commissioners used a strategy combining benevolence and intimidation. The benevolence was in the assertion that the government had furnished them with food and clothing, and that funds generated by the land sales from their "excess" holdings would be used "in fixing up their houses" so that they might "live in comfort such as you have never known." The intimidation was in the threat of terminating the annual appropriations that the tribe had depended on for survival for the last twenty-five years, funds ostensibly promised to them in the terms of the Treaty of Medicine Lodge. Furthermore, the commissioners pointed out that the Dawes Act gave the president the authority to allot reservation holdings at "any time."[14]

The tribes hoped at least to forestall the abrogation of their reservation lands. The three groups—Kiowas, Comanches, and Kiowa-Apaches—had anticipated the commission's directive to negotiate with them for the termination of their reservation holdings even prior to 1892 and planned accordingly. Several prominent chiefs—among them Quanah Parker, a Comanche, and Lone Wolf, a Kiowa—initially led the opposition along with other tribal leaders. Parker's mother, a white settler and Comanche captive in her youth, had married Parker's father, a war chief. Parker earned his credentials as a war chief, and the respect of his people, by leading raids against settlements in northern Texas, both prior to and shortly following the signing of the Treaty of Medicine Lodge. A shrewd, consummate pragmatist, familiar with the levers of power in the federal government, Parker could function in the Anglo world as well as in his own. By the time the commissioners arrived on the reservation in 1892, Parker had used his position within the tribe to aggrandize considerable wealth in land and cattle. It is thus difficult for historians to discern whether his negotiating skills were used primarily in the interests of his people or in furthering his own personal wealth. Lone Wolf, the Younger, stood in the tradition of his father, a Kiowa warrior chief of the same name. Unlike Parker, Lone Wolf was initially steadfast and adamant in his opposition to the application of the Dawes Act to the Kiowas, believing that allotments would destroy their way of life. As such, he represented the more conservative faction of his tribe. Parker and others journeyed to

Washington to discuss, among other matters, the commissioners' visit to their reservation.[15]

Not even ten council meetings at Fort Sill and at Anadarko from September to mid-October 1892 could allay the suspicion and mistrust that the tribal delegates harbored regarding the motives of the government's representatives. Most chiefs initially agreed to delay negotiations until the Treaty of Medicine Lodge was due to expire in 1897, on the premise that the treaty protected them from allotment and could not be terminated without the consent of a majority of the tribal males. Of course, the commissioners had a quite different understanding—namely, that Congress and the president could nullify its provisions at will. According to the Jerome Commissioners, tribal possession of the soil was transitory, subject to the discretion of federal officials, and quite different from a status of ownership, such as what a *patent in fee simple* meant. Even when tribal families were eventually granted allotments, the land they held came with constraints on both usage and tenure that no white settler would be subject to in acquiring frontier acreage. Consequently, one of the commissioners warned the chiefs that "it is a dangerous business to go into the waiting business" and lose what little option they had in the termination of their tribal lands. When the treaty's abrogation became a reality, it appeared that both Parker and Lone Wolf were willing to negotiate for the best terms they could get for the sale of their tribal lands. However, Lone Wolf was skeptical that the government would follow through on any terms it negotiated.[16]

Lone Wolf's concerns were justified given the strategy that Jerome and the other commissioners used to attain compliance. One tactic involved colluding with tribal agents who were political appointees and often amenable to bribery. For example, George Day, who was an agent during the commission's negotiations, was promised an allotment for cooperating with the commission against the tribes' interests that he was charged to serve and protect. At times Day either authorized extra provisions for those who would support the commission's recommendations or threatened to withhold same from Natives who were averse to its recommendations. He also prohibited tribal delegates from presenting their position, either directly or through petition, to federal authorities in Washington. A previous agent, J. Lee Hall, even claimed to the commissioners prior to their visit that a majority of tribal members at that time were in favor of allotment. This was far from true. Collusion was not limited to the reservation agents, however. Parker's role in the negotiations during the fall sessions raises suspicion. While advocating publicly for the best terms in the sale of tribal lands, he failed to press for a provision that would have allowed a tribal delegation to go to Washington and negotiate directly with federal officials as to the price of their tribal holdings. Adding to the suspicion regarding his motives is the fact he arranged to meet surreptitiously with the House Committee on Indian Affairs to press his case for immediate ratification of the commission's terms. Other tactics used by the commission included the use of double signing by "squaw men," using both their original and their given Indian name, and misrepresentation of the terms that tribal males were agreeing to.[17]

Whether the tactics used by the commissioners to gain compliance from the three tribal groups were coercive or not, by their final session in October, three-fourths (456 of the 562) of the adult males had signed to accept the severalty of their tribal holdings and receive individual allotments of 160 acres. Critics claimed that tribal members had signed on to the proposal believing that they had an additional four years under the terms of the Treaty of Medicine Lodge (due to expire in 1897) rather than be subject to the immediate loss of their tribal lands. The discrepancy encouraged dissension among rival tribal factions, which delayed ratification. Nonetheless, even when it appeared that the severalty of their reservation lands was inevitable, stalwarts held out to negotiate the best price they could for the sale of their "excess" reservation holdings. The commissioners offered $2 million, with 453,000 acres set aside for tribal family allotments out of a total of almost 3 million acres. The actual purchase price was less than $2.5 million, which was the price the tribal groups were asking. The difference was significant. Calculated another way, the tribes were paid less than $0.80 per acre for their "excess" holdings, far below the per-acre price of $1.25 they would have received had their demands been met. This difference between the commissioners and the three tribes as well as the tribes' claims of fraud, misrepresentation, and bribery held up ratification of the Jerome Agreement for another seven years. Ultimately, these tribes were awarded an additional $500,000 plus more land from what had originally been set aside for white settlement. Nonetheless, the final agreement ratified by Congress did not augur well for the ability of these tribal groups to fulfill the dream of the Friends of the Indian—specifically, to prosper as their white neighbors.[18]

The Dawes Act and its subsequent imposition on the three tribes at Fort Sill led Scott to broaden his relationships with tribal groups, adding the role of advocate to that of negotiator or peacekeeper. The surreptitious negotiating tactics of the commissioners, aimed at fomenting dissension between and among tribal leaders, and the commissioners' willful misrepresentation of the terms that tribal members were approving provoked Scott to take an active role in criticizing both the process of ratification and the final substance of the agreement's terms.[19]

Scott actively attempted to win the support of tribal members who were detached from the more malleable factions led by Parker and Lone Wolf and who appeared willing to capitulate to the commission's terms. Ah-pia-ton, the Kiowa chief who had earned Scott's respect for his honesty and courage, was a prominent member of a delegation sent to Washington that Scott organized in the spring of 1893. The actions of Parker and Lone Wolf, who organized a rival delegation, added to the challenge that Scott's group faced. The Scott party had raised funds through voluntary contributions to send its delegation, only to meet with the refusal of the reservation agent to allow them to go. To compound their dilemma, the agent used the funds that were raised by Scott's group to send the rival delegation of Parker and Lone Wolf, despite a promise to return the funds to their tribal donors! Such were the challenges that Scott faced in his dealings with often corrupt officials in the Indian Service.[20]

Scott's efforts manifest several additional aspects of his role as peacekeeper. The corruptive practices of agency personnel often thwarted his ability to assist tribal groups like the Kiowa-Comanches. The partisan nature of the appointment process had not served the interests of tribal groups, instead subjecting them to the often illicit relationship between and among agents, reservation contractors, traders, nonreservation commercial interests, and the personnel agents appointed to positions that provided tribes with services guaranteed them by treaty provisions. Although George Day, Anadarko's agent during the period when the Jerome group formally met with the tribal council, demonstrated at least some genuine concern for his clients during his tenure, he unequivocally sided with the commission. Others, appointed through the Department of the Interior and subject to the spoils system at the time, incurred Scott's scorn and condemnation. His solution, which met with mixed results, was to seek out military officers to serve as agents on reservation lands.[21]

Scott's reliance on Washington insiders served his interest in protecting Native Americans. Friends in the War Department, such as Miles, had strongly endorsed his sentiment for reform of the Indian Service. Others in Congress proved increasingly useful to Scott. One was senator Matthew Quay (Pa.). Quay's political standing as a recognized Republican Stalwart and political broker and his friendship with Scott assured that the lieutenant would get at least a hearing among the friends of legislative and executive officials, if not the decision makers themselves. One trip to the capital in 1896, leading a delegation of tribal groups who opposed the imposition of the Dawes Act, provided such an opportunity. Scott worked through the War Department and the commissioner of Indian affairs, Daniel Browning, to arrange a meeting with President Grover Cleveland and a group of congressmen. Through the efforts of both Cleveland and Quay, although each represented opposing political parties, Scott managed to call to the attention of Washington officials the tribes' desperate situation, notwithstanding the contentiousness that ultimately permeated the debate for the next seven years. Throughout his military career and into his active retirement, Scott built a network of power brokers that extended beyond partisan politics. Such relationships facilitated not only his work on behalf of tribal groups but his frequent efforts at seeking professional advancement as well.[22]

Other initiatives that Scott undertook on behalf of tribes during this period were more directly attuned to military service. Given Scott's initial experience with Indian scouts on the northern Great Plains in the fall of 1876, it was natural that he would be receptive to an initiative organizing such scouts into regular army units. In January 1891, John M. Schofield, general of the army, had proposed such a plan immediately following the massacre of the Sioux at Wounded Knee. Schofield's rationale was predicated on the idea that if dissident Sioux could be enticed into regular military service, it might neutralize the threat of additional violence and bloodshed stemming from the Indians' embrace of the Ghost Dance religion. Schofield and his military supporters were working on the assumption that tribal groups, owing to what they believed was their veneration of warfare, would be proud to be soldiers in the American army. However, this proved to be far from the case. Field commanders at posts dispersed throughout the West were encouraged to organize and recruit tribal males, many of whom, like those at Fort Sill, served previously as scouts. As an incentive to enlist, allowances were initially made to permit recruits to serve close to their tribal lands and their families.[23]

Scott began his recruiting initiative in February 1892, with mixed success at first. The commitment to a five-year enlistment—which required giving up their freedom for the regimentation of military service—was a hindering factor. The Comanches, perhaps more constrained by the trappings of civilization than their Kiowa allies, were particularly difficult to recruit, especially when Quanah Parker adamantly disapproved of the plan. Scott, true to his role as a peacekeeper cultivating alliances with influential tribal leaders, enlisted the support of his now trusted friend and Kiowa leader I-See-O. Thanks to I-See-O's influence, within ten months of the initial order to organize the Indian troop, its strength stood at fifty-four, mostly Kiowa men, with some Comanches and Kiowa-Apaches.[24]

Challenges to the project persisted, at least in the first few years. One challenge was encampment. Cognizant of the desire of enlistees to live with or near their families, Scott tried to quarter them on ten-acre parcels each with provision for the building of cabins. However, no funds were available to procure materials for the construction of housing the recruits with their families. Consequently, they lived in canvas-covered tepees just north of the trading post. Instructional training was another problem. The army was revising its training manuals in drill regulation at the time, necessitating a delay until officers could master the new procedures. A measles epidemic that started in the Kiowa school at Anadarko presented a potentially more ominous threat to the entire reservation. Knowledge of appropriate medical practices among tribal families was nonexistent; consequently, at the height of the epidemic in the summer, two hundred Kiowas died in one month alone. By the time the epidemic subsided, the Kiowas had lost one-fifth of their entire population. The Indian soldiers and their families were luckier than most, having access to army medical procedures. As a result, only seven fatalities occurred among the troop.

On a more positive note, Scott had the support of the officers, both above and below his command. Nelson Miles, since 1890 a general in the regular army, commanded the Military Division of the Missouri. He and his immediate post commander at Fort Sill, Lt. Col. C. A. Carlton, were encouraging and accommodating. Equally important, Sgt. Ernest Stecker and 2nd Lt. Andrew Greg Curtin Quay both shared Scott's view of the challenges that tribal people were facing at the time and what advantage they believed recruitment into regular military service could provide. Both were also exceedingly loyal to Scott, as was Curtin Quay's father, the senior senator from Pennsylvania. All shared an affinity for tribal groups within the regular military structure but held a position to advantage their cause. Troop postings appeared to go well at first. On one campaign, the new, all-Indian Troop L joined other soldiers in maintaining an orderly process in the opening of the Cheyenne-Arapaho reservation to white settlement. Posted on the southeast corner of the tract and situated over a ten-mile line, 5,000 would-be settlers were held in check until a signal was given to advance into the territory. Moreover, Scott's efforts in training the Native soldiers received high praise from the numerous military inspection teams that observed their performance on the field. Endorsing Scott's work, Stecker could report, when his immediate commander was in Chicago on business, that the troop was "doing well and that we have had no trouble of any kind."[25]

However, the Troop L's status soon became more challenging and complex with the arrival of a group of Chiricahua Apaches, some of whom had fought with Geronimo against southwestern settlers a decade earlier and were all now labeled as "prisoners of war." Initially sent east to Florida and Alabama following the final apprehension of Geronimo in 1886, the approximately five hundred men, women, and children were decimated by disease in Mount Vernon, Alabama, owing to conditions unfavorable to the natural environment that they had enjoyed in the Southwest. Settlers in the New Mexico and Arizona Territories were assured that Geronimo and his band would never be allowed to come west of the Mississippi River again. However, their squalid conditions in the East and their apparent willingness to embrace a more sedentary lifestyle encouraged Nelson Miles to recommend that they be transported to Fort Sill, Oklahoma Territory, in what was purported to be their permanent home. Scott was charged with the responsibility for the care and settlement of the approximate 260 surviving Chiricahua Apaches at Fort Sill, with a strong recommendation from Capt. Marion Maus, First Infantry. It was Maus who had commanded a body of Indian scouts against Geronimo in the Southwest and befriended Scott when both were stationed on the northern Great Plains during the Nez Percé expedition in 1877. Given Miles's ongoing support for Scott's interest in tribes, the general doubtless needed little convincing. Nonetheless, Maus praised his friend to Miles for "his wide knowledge of the Indian character and great experience (which) eminently fit him for such duty."[26]

The Chiricahuas arrived in October 1894, with little more than the clothes on their backs, to face what proved to be one of the coldest winters in the Oklahoma Territory. Scott's goal for their assimilation was to turn the Apache families into economically self-supporting ranchers, living on farms in modest wooden homes on forty-acre allotments, and with enough land in common to raise cattle herds. Upon their arrival, it was understood by the federal authorities that had approved their relocation—the War Department, the Department of the Interior, Congress, and the Grover Cleveland administration—that Fort Sill would be their permanent residence. It can also be assumed that all parties saw the Fort Sill Apache settlement, given the tribe's bellicose history, as a test case for acculturation on the road to what was defined for them as civilization.

Evidence of Scott's commitment to the success of their resettlement abounds. In their first year at Fort Sill, Scott declined to leave the Chiricahuas under his care for more than half a day's journey from the post. He kept detailed records on the state of their health to document that the move to Oklahoma had led to a diminishing death rate from the diseases that many had succumbed to in Florida and Alabama. More pointed examples included the acquisition of additional land on the Kiowa-Comanche reservation to make the resettlement plan economically feasible; a rigorous campaign to obtain funds for supplies and provisions as well as for services he deemed essential to the project's success, including construction materials for homes, cultivating tools, seeds, and cattle; a determination to hold sutlers and post suppliers of provisions accountable for their delivery of goods at reasonable prices and of good quality; initiatives in what he believed to be a way of enhancing their dignity such as by recognizing the importance of their tribal family structure and by recruiting them for military service; and an ongoing and enduring advocacy for their interests.

Scott recognized that his efforts to resettle the Chiricahua Apaches would not be successful unless sufficient land was available for raising cattle. The Kiowa-Comanche Tribal Council was rightfully suspicious of their former archenemies. Nevertheless, based on the trust that Scott had engendered with them since 1890, they were willing to allow the Chiricahuas to reside on the military tract that was part of their reservation; the council held title to this parcel by congressional authority, and it was eventually to be returned to the Kiowa and Comanche tribes "when no longer required for the exclusive use for military purposes." This phrase was, at the time, essential to assure the sufficiency of additional land for these Apache settlers; and for Scott, the assurance meant that the lands would not later be opened to individual allotment by white settlers. Also, the assumption was that if the military wanted the tract, it would have to purchase it from the tribes. Moreover, the land was a loan to the Chiricahuas and not a sale. In 1897, the tribal council approved an arrangement providing the Chiricahuas' 160-acre allotments for a total of approximately 50,000 acres, including enough pasture to graze their cattle. Of course, all of this was prior to the final ratification of the Jerome Agreement by Congress in 1900, which Scott and tribal members came to regard as fraudulent. Subsequently, the phrase "use for military purposes" would take on another meaning once, as prescribed in the Jerome Agreement, Kiowa-Comanche tribal lands were placed in severalty.[27]

The Chiricahuas' time of arrival and the paucity of provisions for their very survival necessitated immediate action on Scott's part. The absence of more secure shelter obligated the use of canvas, borrowed from the troops at the post, for the construction of wickiups. Provision was made to guard them as prisoners of war, but little restraint proved necessary, as they cut and hauled the timber that would eventually provide them with a more secure shelter. Although a special fund of $15,000 was set aside by Congress for their use, appropriations were initially restricted, pending approval from the quartermaster general's office. It seems, contrary to Scott and Congress's understanding, that the army was defining the word "settlement" in a narrow and constraining way. Scott immediately pressed the issue, and the fund's use was broadened to include, among other provisions, the purchase of livestock.

While the families were in Alabama, two teachers from the Northeast served the fifty-six children of school age. When the families arrived in Oklahoma, the teachers' services were no longer available. With the approval of the reservation agent, Scott arranged to have the children transferred to the Kiowa-Comanche school.

In contrast to his more optimistic view of agricultural practices among the Kiowa-Comanche tribal groups, Scott seemed to understand that, for the Chiricahua Apaches, utilizing the land solely for farming would be insufficient to sustain them economically. In his view, part of the problem was also cultural, as they "have little idea of taking care of themselves and unless prevented[,] would dispose of their crops for anything they can get no matter how small the sum and use up the results of a year's work in less than a week." He believed that a cattle herd of 3,500 would be necessary to sustain them economically, which would require 36,000 acres for pasturage and grazing.

Although the climate—frigidly cold winters and drought-stricken summers—was a major challenge in the Chiricahua settlement's first two years, Scott took advantage of conditions as they existed, utilizing every measure to make the settlement a success. He researched the applicability of planting kafir corn, a sorghum varietal particularly resilient in drought conditions. Fences needed first to be built enclosing the Chiricahuas' range land before cattle were purchased to ensure that their livestock would not graze over the Kiowa-Comanche reservation holdings. Nonetheless, when Congress appropriated annual funds for the purchase of cattle, Scott immediately bought some, not wanting to risk the loss of the funds in case they were not spent during that year; nor was he certain that funds would be available in the future.

Scott was fortunate to have several civilians at the post who were not only involved in the commercial activities at Fort Sill, but were willing to assist him directly and indirectly with his Chiricahua settlers. George Wrattan, a post trader, served as an Apache interpreter following their capture and was with them at Fort Sill. Married to an Apache woman, Wrattan served an indispensable role, since the Chiricahuas had no understanding of the sign language that Scott had used with great success on the northern Great Plains. Wrattan taught them how to herd cattle, assisted Scott in the selection of Chiricahua headmen, and employed some of the tribal youths in his store. Although not directly involved in Chiricahua resettlement, William Quinette proved to be a supporter of Scott's efforts to assist them as well as the soldiers on the post. Quinette arrived at the trading post at Fort Sill in 1878, as an employee of a firm that he would eventually co-own. By the time Scott arrived, Quinette's generosity to all was well known and appreciated. For many years, he sponsored an annual field day, welcoming and recognizing the tribal people on the reservation. Over the years, Quinette extended credit to them for the purchase of necessary goods, with payment made from the annual "grass" money that the Indians received. Quinette's sense of fairness was, it must be said, more the exception than the rule when it came to dealing with tribal clientele.

Scott dealt with merchants who were often quite different from Quinette, and he determined to hold them to account. At least one merchant was chastised by Scott for "delayed shipments of lumber & paper" that "have put me to untold inconvenience. You have shipped a worthless quality of paper and charged a first-class price for it and the lumber has been of an inferior quality."[28]

Scott's understanding of Apache culture and his sympathy for their dignity as a distinct people guided him in planning the structure of settlement for the Chiricahua families. Twelve villages would be constructed, each with a designated leader or headman whom Scott would appoint, and who had earned the respect of the family in their evolution from the confinement in Florida and Alabama to their settlement in Oklahoma. These headmen, former scouts, were expected to keep order in their communities and supervise the cultivation of the fields. In structuring patterns of settlement, Scott recognized that the Chiricahuas were matrilocal; therefore, a newly married husband was expected to live with his wife's relatives. So, too, Scott recognized that interfamily animosities did exist, so he designated allotments in such a way that families would reside near their friends and away from those they disliked.

A more telling example of Scott's commitment to enhance the dignity of the Chiricahuas was in his desire to recruit them into his all-Indian Troop L. To accomplish this objective, he turned to tribal leaders and scouts among the Chiricahuas to supplement the ranks of the mostly Kiowa Natives in his initial Troop L. Forty-three were ultimately recruited. Perhaps as a way of orienting his original troop to the new arrivals, Scott ordered several members to an area of his choosing to arrange for the grazing of cattle for the Chiricahuas. The headmen and respected leaders among their people had been made part of Company I of the Twelfth Infantry in Alabama while still being POWs, an arrangement Scott found strange and which he determined initially not to maintain. Although he understood that his relationship with the Chiricahua soldiers was different from that with the Kiowas and Comanches, he admired the former for how they excelled in military drill, in keeping illegal white traders off the reservation, and in branding tribal livestock. He found them honest and trustworthy, so much so that he was prepared to defend them against acts of what he believed to be military discrimination after they joined his original troop.

For example, Scott organized a spirited campaign in the summer and early fall of 1895 when his recently enlisted Chiricahua recruits were denied membership in and profits from the post exchange. The source of Scott's perplexity—the anomaly of Indian soldiers serving in a regiment in the regular army while being concurrently considered prisoners of war—was one reason they were being denied membership in the exchange. Another was their alleged distance from the location of the exchange and their limited use of it given the fact they had been banned from the bar room, a main source of revenue for the exchange, when they were stationed in Alabama as part of the Twelfth Infantry. Scott rallied support to overturn what he believed to be a gross injustice and discriminatory act against the soldiers in his troop by the Post Exchange council, the body that administered policy on each military post. Over a two-month period, in no fewer than sixteen endorsements, Scott answered in detail each of the arguments that the council presented in support of denying the Apaches Post Exchange privileges. Initially, he enlisted the testimony of Lt. Allyn K. Capron, who had brought the infantry from Alabama to Fort Sill and who claimed that the Apache soldiers in Alabama were never barred from membership in the exchange. Scott's adamancy was such that he ultimately appealed to Col. Edgar R. Kellogg, adjutant general of the Division of the Missouri, in hopes of reversing the council's decision. Unfortunately for Scott, his appeal was denied. Kellogg conceded that while

> Captain Scott is probably correct in making this claim, these Apache soldiers were, and are, in law, organized the same as white soldiers-troops

and are entitled to the same "rights and privileges." . . . [Nonetheless] their status as soldiers is not the same as other troops. . . . While nominally and legally soldiers, these men are not employed as such—only in the most restricted manner. They are actually laborers under surveillance receiving the pay, clothing and allowance of soldiers.

Consequently, the incongruity that initially puzzled Scott, that as soldiers they were still considered as prisoners of war, was used as the basis for denying the Chiricahuas equity with their fellow soldiers.[29]

Two years after the Chiricahuas' arrival at Fort Sill, Scott could report favorably on their resettlement, as he fulfilled his charge to make them self-supporting. He noted that more than $15,000 dollars of the three-year appropriation of $32,500 had been used in the purchase of cattle, both bulls and two-year-old heifers. Additional expenses included building materials, plows, farm wagons, mowers, and rakes. All this, and the account still had a balance of over $7,000 from the total credit appropriations on deposit with the assistant treasurer at St. Louis. As a result of their labor and with the assistance of key personnel, the Chiricahuas had constructed sixty-nine houses and a storehouse. Five hundred acres of prairie sod had been broken and fenced, and enough hay had been cultivated to bring the cattle through the winter. In addition, and despite a summer of excessive heat and drought, three hundred acres had been cultivated, enough to provide melons, kafir corn, and sweet potatoes. All told, more than $10,000 profit in cattle and fruit had been generated through the labor of the Chiricahua resettlers. The Chiricahuas were well on their way to economic independence and self-sufficiency, or so it appeared.[30]

Although Scott was doing all he could to retain his Troop L Chiricahuas as well as Kiowas and Comanches, and despite all the accolades he received for his work in turning "blanket" Indians into a disciplined troop, senior officers well above his command were having second thoughts. Perhaps part of their decision to terminate the project was predicated on the view that Indian affairs were no longer a concern of the War Department and should be transferred to Interior. Part of the decision involved the Indians themselves. Many had difficulty dealing with long-term enlistments, duties assigned in regions away from their families, excessive manual labor, having to reside often in framed dwellings, and perhaps of equal significance, having to wear short haircuts. An additional dynamic was said to be their difficulty in transferring loyalty from one officer to another, a necessity in any mobile military force. By the time that the Chiricahuas joined Troop L, the number of Kiowas and Comanches was down to twenty-three. However, Scott saw the termination of these soldiers as a strictly racial matter. Compounding the issue was the assumption that their presence was displacing an equivalent number of Anglo soldiers who could have been recruited for service, given the stagnant size of the army at the time. Troop L, the last Indian troop in the army, was terminated at the end of May 1897, when it conducted its final drill and returned all equipment to the post authorities. Even prior to the troop's termination, Scott had made efforts, partially successful, to transition his soldiers back to military scouts, with the rationale that no appropriations had been made to enlarge the reservation's police force and, consequently, they were needed in that capacity. Ultimately, twelve of the forty-nine Chiricahua soldiers were reassigned as scouts and served on the reservation. The rest, along with their families, were left on the reservation, where there were few jobs available. Although the Chiricahuas who joined the troop were initially promised that their POW status would be lifted once their enlistments ended, the pledge was not honored.[31]

Throughout his early career on the northern Great Plains and at Fort Sill, Scott had always believed that the War Department, rather than the Interior Department, provided the most prudent and balanced administration of tribal affairs. As earlier noted, many of the reservation agents appointed by the Bureau of Indian Affairs owed their position to partisan politics rather than to documented ability in their line of work. Such was the case when Scott arrived at Fort Sill in 1889. Though enacted in 1883, the Pendleton Civil Service Act provided for only a gradual process of reform in the creation of a comprehensive civil service devoid of partisan politics. In addition, Scott's hands-on approach to administration in the field made it difficult for him to deal with the BIA and the Interior Department, with their proclivity to control field personnel, perhaps a necessity given the graft and corruption that then existed in tribal administration. Compounding the situation, the relationship between the War and Interior Departments in the 1890s was often tenuous and contentious. While the army had the responsibility for keeping the peace on tribal lands and the authority to pursue tribal groups who left their reservations, agents appointed by the Department of the Interior were charged with determining when and where troops needed to be called onto reservations to maintain peace. Although he was amenable to the BIA's appointment of agents and other officials on the reservation who appeared to be eminently qualified as administrators and sympathetic to the needs of tribal groups, Scott made an effort to select or encourage the selection of military officers to positions of tribal administration. As a peacemaker and peacekeeper, Scott was reluctant to call in a military force when he believed that contentiousness could be dissipated through direct negotiation with the parties involved. He applied that strategy several times successfully during the Ghost Dance episode and on other occasions, when agents at Fort Sill believed that a show of force was the only necessary course of action following criminal activity on the reservation.

Upon his departure in August 1897, Scott favored the appointment of military officers as reservation agents. However, he feared that their posting solely based on seniority would not necessarily lead to the best candidates, precluding cultural sensitivities. Nonetheless, his determination to defend military officers in the Indian Service who shared his commitments to tribal groups did not always work out as intended. One example was Capt. Frank Baldwin, on detached leave and assigned to the Indian Service as an agent in the fall of 1894. Scott had met Baldwin during the Nez Percé campaign. Having made a name for himself as an Indian fighter, Baldwin then honed his skills as a negotiator with the Sioux and experienced an epiphany, as it were, following the Wounded Knee tragedy. Consequently, he greeted his appointment at Fort Sill as a unique opportunity to demonstrate his sympathy for tribal groups in a positive and meaningful way. Admittedly, Baldwin had entered a reservation that was in "administrative chaos." The Jerome Commission exacerbated, if it did not initiate, the factions within the groups of Comanches, Kiowas, and Kiowa-Apaches. So-called Sooners, Anglo settlers who illegally entered Oklahoma prior to its designation as a territory, were infringing on tribal lands, indiscriminately mining, cutting trees, and grazing their cattle. Squaw men were pressing their claims to receive tribal allotments. Illicit traders were cheating Indians with exorbitant credit arrangements and selling them alcohol contrary to law. Baldwin made his first mistake by openly siding with a faction that supported Quanah Parker, in opposition to a more traditional faction that had been headed by Isatai, a Comanche warrior and medicine man. Baldwin was a strong proponent of Indian education, defined perhaps in the framework of what many Friends of the Indian saw as a tribal path to civilization. He successfully persuaded the tribal council to concur in the appropriation of $25,000 in "grass" money for the construction of a reservation boarding school. His efforts to strengthen the tribes' commitment to education—by holding what he hoped would be annual meetings of teachers, students, and their parents—was not well received among more traditional groups. Perhaps Baldwin's greatest mistake was to go after the Sooners and reservation traders, who had powerful allies in the Oklahoma legislature. Specifically, Dudley Brown, a trader, filed a claim against Baldwin accusing him of excessive drinking. Although Scott had defended Baldwin's work, the controversy had become increasingly contentious, and undermined the agent's effectiveness. Baldwin was eased out of the agency in 1896, when Miles, who was then commander of the army, temporarily placed him on his staff in Washington.[32]

Other officers with whom Scott worked directly had a more stable career in Indian service. One was the aforementioned 1st Sgt. Ernest Stecker, who served as the immediate commander of Troop L and as a quartermaster at the post. Stecker would later serve as a captain in the Philippine scouts, returning, near the end of his career, as superintendent of the Indian school and as agent at Anadarko for the Comanche and Kiowa tribes in 1907. Stecker endured a number of challenges in the administration of four thousand tribal people, not unlike those he and Scott confronted when they first worked together at Fort Sill. Dealing with "leases and unknown numbers of selfish interests," the latter including post contractors, occupied much of his time. Scott's strong recommendation of Stecker's work in the Indian Service, to Indian commissioners Francis Leupp and Robert G. Valentine, affirmed the captain's view that when military officers manifested a commitment to the welfare of tribal groups, they were in a strong position to deal with the graft and corruption that permeated the service at the time. Several others were equally worthy of Scott's praise. Lt. Allyn Capron, originally of the Fifth Infantry, had been with the Chiricahuas when they were in Alabama and was determined to work with them as an officer of Troop L, where Scott facilitated his transfer. Also high on Scott's list was Lt. Francis Beach, whom he had recommended to succeed him when he left Fort Sill for Washington. Following Scott's departure and the withdrawal of most of the garrison, Beach was challenged by a rumor, followed by a panic among neighboring white settlers, that Geronimo was prepared to take the warpath again and return to where the Apaches originally resided in Arizona. Beach weathered the crisis from the unsubstantiated rumor. On a more positive note, Beach encouraged the Chiricahuas' cattle production, perhaps realizing that cultivation-centered agriculture itself would not lead them to economic self-sufficiency. Equally important in a spiritual context, Beach encouraged the building of a church and a school, on the Chiricahuas' lands at their request. Before he left the Apache settlers in 1899, Beach was as optimistic as Scott had been two years earlier regarding their path to economic self-sufficiency.[33]

What neither could foresee at the time was the subtle shift in the War Department's administration of tribal groups that ultimately negated all the efforts of Scott and his military allies in assisting the Chiricahua settlers on their path to economic success. Whether the army's initial rationale—that military personnel were in short supply owing to an impending war with Spain and therefore could not be utilized in tribal administration—was valid or not, the reality was that the department saw the need for military personnel only when tribal groups were perceived as bellicose and, consequently, called for military suppression. One manifestation of the policy change was the diminishing influence of officers in their attempts to safeguard the interest of tribal groups while serving as reservation agents.

Capt. Farrand Sayre ultimately succeeded Beach as the Chiricahuas' officer-in-charge in the summer of 1900. Sayre, who shared the concerns of his immediate military predecessors for the Apaches' welfare, faced several major challenges, not the least being the need for appropriations to repair or replace essential items. The financial problem was partially solved by using revenue generated by the sale of additional cattle. Nonetheless, other revenue sources were needed to sustain the settlement. In the fall of 1901, Sayre requested a $5,000 appropriation from the War Department, which continued to have jurisdiction over the Chiricahuas in their status as prisoners of war. The request was denied. Brig. Gen. John C. Bates suggested that, since their status as prisoners was nominal, their affairs should be transferred to the Interior

Department, which was then currently undertaking the administration of all tribal peoples. Although Sayre's appropriation request was ultimately approved by Congress, the War Department continued its rule over the Chiricahua settlement, albeit with increasing reluctance to lead them on a path to economic independence. One manifestation of the War Department's indifference to their welfare on the post level was the appointment of a new Fort Sill commander, Maj. Henry Ripley, who had little understanding of or sympathy for the increasingly precarious position of the Chiricahuas and viewed the status of the Indian agent as under *his* ultimate military command and control.[34]

Despite earlier assurances from all sides that the Chiricahua resettlement in Oklahoma was to be their permanent home, both the War and Interior Departments ultimately had a different agenda. At issue, or rather what the military advocate general believed to be the issue, was the status of the tract temporarily and conditionally ceded to the Chiricahuas in 1897 that supplied them with sufficient grazing land and the potential for 160-acre individual family allotments when the land was developed for what they believed would be their permanent settlement. Nonetheless, when Congress finally ratified the Jerome Agreement in June 1900, opening the Kiowa-Comanche reservation to potential white settlement, Fort Sill, where the Chiricahuas had settled on land they had improved, was now the property of the War Department in fee simple. The immediate response of the Fort Sill Chiricahuas was one of anger, frustration, and uncertainty when they realized that the land that had once been promised to them as their permanent home, together with all the improvements they had made on it, could now be taken away by fiat. These Apache settlers lingered in a state of anguish for more than a decade while the War and Interior Departments were seemingly deciding their fate. The War Department was more than willing to rescind their POW status, placing the responsibility for their resettlement and administration on the BIA, paving the way for the army's exclusive use of Fort Sill. Interior officials believed that the Chiricahua settlers should remain where they were, perhaps not wanting to incur either the expense of resettlement or the political repercussions of having to deal with Geronimo's reputation among white settlers and even that of other Apache tribal groups. It soon became evident that the Chiricahuas' fate had been sealed.

One consequence of the new modern army with its overseas mandate was a recognition of the need for professional training in warfare among its branches. Consequently, a confidential report of the new War College Board in May 1903 recommended that the Fort Sill military reserve be used as a school of instruction in field artillery, all but assuring the mandatory displacement of most if not all the Chiricahua families that had settled on the post. In justifying the army's prerogative to reclaim the post for its exclusive use, Gen. George W. Davis, judge advocate general, in 1910, broadly interpreted (or misinterpreted) the phrase "for exclusive use for military purposes," construing the word "use" to mean "possession."[35]

Within two years of the Chiricahuas' arrival at Fort Sill, and despite assurances to the contrary, Scott became concerned about the commitment made to them that the Oklahoma Territory would be their permanent home. The land deal that he negotiated with the Kiowa and Comanche tribes in 1897, for the use of additional acreage to make the Apache settlement economically viable, was not his first attempt at ensuring the permanency of the Apache settlement. While hoping that the Jerome Agreement, which he regarded as fraudulently obtained, would be renegotiated to allow the Kiowas and Comanches to retain their reservation lands, he believed at the time that they had title to the additional acreage in the military reserve, and the authority to sell it. Ideally, he hoped that the buyer would be the War Department. Given the pressure on the settlement of Oklahoma lands, such a sale, if executed, could prevent white farmers and ranchers from infringing on what he hoped would be permanent lands for the Chiricahua Apaches. He also believed, quite correctly, that the Kiowa-Comanche tribal groups would rather have the Chiricahuas as their neighbors than more aggressive and potentially threatening white settlers. He feared that, given the potential change with a Republican (McKinley) administration, if the title issue was not then settled, "it will end in a few years in the Apaches being dispossessed and thrown on the world without a protector." Nonetheless, a second attempt by Scott to execute such an agreement directly with the Kiowa-Comanche Tribal Council met with failure.[36]

Consequently, despite Scott's efforts to thwart the War Department's plan to turn most of the lands that the Apache settlers had inhabited and improved into a post for field artillery instruction, he could do little to help them. One explanation for his lack of success is that the controversy occurred at a critical period in Scott's career, when family matters and pressing vocational decisions were more paramount in his thoughts. A more telling explanation is that there was little that he could do to alter the outcome because the new secretary of war, Elihu Root (1899–1904), was dramatically changing the mission and administrative structure of the American army! Fighting for Chiricahua settlement at Fort Sill could no longer be Scott's primary consideration, even if he were willing to sacrifice his military career for what, clearly, would never result in a favorable outcome for them. To be sure, he was not prepared to abandon his interest in their welfare, as noted by his correspondence with Stecker when Scott was serving as the superintendent at West Point. His role changed, however, from one of advocate on the Chiricahuas' behalf to one of negotiator trying to obtain the best option regarding their cultural and economic future.

Meanwhile, the morale of the Chiricahua settlers had declined dramatically following the military's decision to claim the land that they believed had been promised to them. Additional improvements on the acreage would be futile, and the cattle that they had raised would now be sold at a potential loss. Compounding the U.S. government's problem of where to settle them was the erroneous belief that these were Geronimo's Apaches, even though most had had nothing to do with his exploits on the southwestern frontier thirty years earlier, and many had been born well after the Apache campaigns. The war chief's passing in 1909 mitigated that aspect of the dilemma, but it appeared that neither the War nor the Interior Department wanted to take the responsibility for resettling them.

Scott officially reentered the debate over the resettlement issue in 1911, following a request from the War Department, undoubtedly made because of his familiarity with the situation and his now long-established reputation as a tribal negotiator. He immediately called in Robert G. Valentine, the BIA commissioner, to get his view of the situation. Valentine believed that the Chiricahuas, where possible, should be settled at Fort Sill, but held out the prospect—albeit a voluntary one—that they be permitted to join their cultural relatives on the Mescalero reservation in northern New Mexico. Whether his view gave Scott an out, a possible solution to an increasingly uncomfortable situation, is open to debate. In any event, the War Department saw it that way, and Geronimo's passing made it more likely that the Mescalero would accept their cultural brethren. Scott's initial conference with the Chiricahuas in September 1911 began to take on a pattern that he had used before, and would use again, both with American Indians and indigenous people in the Philippines. Letting the Apache settlers talk over their grievances would by itself hopefully mitigate much of their anger and frustration over their precarious position. This time, however, it did not work out that way. Many of the angry Chiricahua headmen felt betrayed by Scott, undermining what trust they had had in his past assurances. Despite what he had claimed previously on many occasions, he took the War Department's position: that Fort Sill had never been promised to them as a permanent settlement to possess—only to use and occupy. In one of several meetings that were held with the Chiricahua elders, Scott offered them the option of joining the Mescaleros, with the lure of the War Department's rescinding of their prisoner of war status. Conversely, those who remained at Fort Sill—and Scott would have the option of deciding who they would be—would still be considered POWs.[37]

Shortly thereafter, Scott organized a delegation of Chiricahuas to visit the Mescalero chiefs and discuss with them a possible migration of interested Chiricahuas who wished to settle on their lands. The Apache chiefs who they met at Warm Springs in northern New Mexico Territory were pleased to accept them, but the lands offered to them, approximately twenty miles north of where most Mescalero then resided, was of such an altitude and mountainous terrain that farming and ranching would be difficult.

The locus of anger against Scott's plan came from Vincent Natalish, a Chiricahua educated at Col. Richard Pratt's Carlisle Indian School and a resident of New York. Natalish had engaged in a spirited advocacy campaign throughout the first decade of the twentieth century when it appeared that his people would be removed from their Fort Sill settlement. Contrary to Scott's claim that the Mescalero lands offered "good hunting (and a place) where they could live their Indian life," Natalish pointed out that the reservation's "rocky terrain would not offer adequate sustenance." It was obvious that the Mescalero option would not mitigate the frustration that the Chiricahuas now felt, and in no small part because it was proposed by the soldier they had believed would always look out for their welfare.[38]

While recommending legislation in November 1911 to facilitate the resettlement of those Fort Sill inhabitants who were willing to move to the Mescalero reservation and hence would no longer be considered prisoners of war, Scott addressed the guidelines and conditions for those who remained at the fort, creating two separate groups. One group, who would retain their prisoner of war status, would continue to hold their share of cattle and implements. A second group, up to ten in number, who "have trades, are sober, industrious and . . . able to make their way among white men" would have the option of obtaining allotments from deceased Kiowa-Comanche families on their reservation or in such areas "where they will not interfere in the military use of the reservation." This select group would be turned over to the Interior Department and released from POW status. Scott did what he could to discourage the first group from remaining at Fort Sill, noting that if they "were hoping for allotment there (and) were to be treated in the same way (as the other Fort Sill) group, they would in all likelihood pawn or sell their property in the near future for drink and continue in the neighborhood of the past[,] a reproach to the war department as long as they live."

Based on Scott's recommendation, and with political maneuvering among officials in the Departments of War and the Interior, the Senate, and the Indian Rights Association, Scott Ferris, an Oklahoma congressman, introduced a bill that ultimately resolved what was referred to as the "Chiricahua problem." It took Scott and his supporters two years to press for the inclusion of some items, such as a $200,000 payment to the Mescalero Chiricahuas for the loss of their cattle herds, which they were forced to abandon in Oklahoma, and financial support for their new environment in New Mexico. Of the remaining group of 261 Chiricahuas who were descendants of the original 516, 183 chose to relocate to the Mescalero reservation.[39]

However, despite these encouraging legislative efforts, Scott undermined his credibility with these Apaches who had been originally brought to Oklahoma Territory in 1894 under his charge. Initially, he denied that the lands provided for them by the Kiowa-Comanche Tribal Council were meant to be their permanent home, despite his assurance and that of military officials to the contrary at the time. Then he antagonized some of the Chiricahua headmen when he placed himself in the position of selecting the few whom he deemed of such a character as to be worthy to both remain at Fort Sill and lose the sigma of their status as prisoners of war. Although he fought for just compensation for the losses of those who resettled in New Mexico, they never fully attained what Scott had led them to believe would be a self-sustaining existence. As one historian described it, "Scott emerged from the Fort Sill predicament tragically compromised."

To his credit, near the end of his military career in 1918, and as a member of the Board of Indian Commissioners, Scott visited the Mescalero reservation and met with the Chiricahua Apaches. Their tract, in a remote region known as the Whitetail District, was far from the reservation agency and even farther from any off-reservation towns. Moreover, the narrow fertile valley near them, though rich in timber, was at such an altitude that winters were cold and growing seasons short. Their homes at Whitetail, of shoddy material and construction, provided hardly any protection from the bitter winter winds. On a more positive note, the Apaches had the support of several denominational churches and a government school administered by Dutch Reformed missionaries. Tuberculosis, one of the major diseases that ravaged reservations during this period, was declining. Viewing their conditions, Scott apologized to them for what he had done in imposing their migration and offered them lands in Oklahoma. Few accepted his offer, perhaps as a tribute to their growing sense of independence in their new home.[40]

Scott acquired a growing sense of purpose in his relationship with tribal groups from his superintendence of the Fort Sill Apaches and the remorseful encounter with the displaced Chiricahuas. Over the years he seemed to have developed an awareness of the importance of federal wardship, viewing his advocacy on their behalf as a responsibility of the federal government to protect them and safeguard their welfare on the diminishing reservation lands that they still held following the passage of the Dawes Act. Scott interpreted such a commitment in a way that revealed much about how he viewed his own culture in relation to those of indigenous peoples.

Scott's posting at Fort Sill gave him the opportunity to hone his skills in peacemaking and peacekeeping. His knowledge of Kiowa, Comanche, and Apache culture was useful in understanding the dynamics of intertribal differences when it came to education on the reservation and military training in the creation and organization of Troop L. His deference to the views of tribal councils, when it came to incidents such as crimes on the reservation and the challenge posed by the Jerome Commission, enhanced his credibility and respect among tribal groups. His determination to limit the use of military force and only employ it as a last resort may have saved the reservation from the overt violence that occurred among the Sioux, when they embraced the more pernicious aspects of the Ghost Dance religion. His desire to befriend specific leaders among tribal groups such as I-See-O, the Kiowa scout, gave him, among other advantages, insight into their culture and knowledge of the terrain where the tribe resided. Equally significant, the contacts he made among powerbrokers in Washington helped to provide his Indian constituents with meaningful ways to respond to the challenges that tribes confronted in preserving their cultural integrity.

Such techniques enhanced Scott's ability to advocate on their behalf, whether Comanches, Kiowas, Kiowa-Apaches, or Chiricahua Apaches. He was also successful in recognizing and in many cases alleviating the corruptive influence of certain agency personnel and subcontractors at the post through transfer or termination. He undertook efforts to expand the use of Indian scouts in preventing crime, perpetrated both within the reservation and by external groups infringing on reservation boundaries. Although not the first to do so, he was quick to embrace the War Department's initiative in recruiting Indian soldiers into the regular army, and he tried to save what he could of the plan when it was no longer supported by senior officers in command. When it came to the question of needed improvements on the Kiowa-Comanche reservation and appropriations for the Chiricahuas' original settlement at Fort Sill, he solicited financial assistance from Washington. Generally speaking, when Scott saw or learned of substandard treatment of tribal groups, he was prepared to raise concerns with higher-level officials in the Departments of War and the Interior.

Nonetheless, there were limits to what Scott was willing to do or thought he could do on their behalf. He was not prepared to fight for the right of the Chiricahuas to retain their improved settlements at Fort Sill, and even denied the fact that he previously had told them otherwise. Ideally, he wanted them all to move to the Mescalero reservation. In addition, there were the constraints imposed by those prospective western settlers and their legislative allies determined to abolish reservations and claim tribal landholdings. Scott also was constrained in terms of his prerogatives in the face of impending military reform, and by the personal and professional challenges that hindered him from doing more for indigenous people.

Once Congress passed the Dawes Act and implemented it with the creation of the Jerome Commission, there was little that Scott could do to nullify the process, other than denounce the surreptitious way commissioners sought to win the tribes' approval. Scott faced formidable opposition even from the Friends of the Indian who had rationalized the severalty of reservation lands as beneficial to tribes themselves. Nor could he do much to alter the decision of senior commanders to abolish the enlistment of Indians in the regular army, no matter how much he verbally opposed the decision. The army's reassessment of its use for Fort Sill in the first decade of the twentieth century, part of a broader plan for the training of officers in military service, could not have been altered by Scott, no matter what he attempted to do or say when the Chiricahuas first arrived at Fort Sill in 1894.

Perhaps another limitation to his role as advocate was more personal than professional. On a personal level, Scott's earlier work on the frontier had come at great sacrifice to his family. His wife's ongoing frail health, owing to tuberculosis, frequently prevented her from joining him at both Forts Totten and Sill, a source of continual anguish and loneliness to him. Indeed, Mary's health was so precarious that Scott at times had two of his children with him in Oklahoma when on military assignment, while she recuperated in Philadelphia or Princeton. Finances were another growing concern. With a family of four children and ostensibly two residences to maintain, it became increasingly difficult to make ends meet, even with his promotion to a captaincy in 1895. A new posting, ideally in the East, with an enhanced salary that an additional elevation in rank could bring him, would provide another incentive to move on.[41]

Hugh Lenox Scott and Mary Merrill Scott at their residence, Washington, D.C., 1914.
Prints and Photographs Division, Library of Congress.

Maj. Gen. Nelson A. Miles, official portrait, 1898.
Prints and Photographs Division, Library of Congress.

Matthew Quay, U.S. senator from Pennsylvania, 1903.
Prints and Photographs Division, Library of Congress.

Sergeant I-See-O, army scout for fifty years, saluting John W. Weeks, secretary of war, 1925.
Prints and Photographs Division, Library of Congress.

Maj. Gen. Leonard Wood, n.d.
Prints and Photographs Division, Library of Congress.

Major Scott, military governor of the Sulu Archipelago, Philippines, with Sultan Jamal ul Kiram II and local government officials, 1905.
Prints and Photographs Division, Library of Congress.

Brigadier General Scott as acting secretary of war, 1914. Not suited to a desk job.
Prints and Photographs Division, Library of Congress.

Brigadier General Scott *(right front)* and Pancho Villa *(center)* at a racetrack in Ciudad Juárez, 1914.
Prints and Photographs Division, Library of Congress.

Newton D. Baker, secretary of war, 1916.
Prints and Photographs Division, Library of Congress.

Albert B. Fall, U.S. senator from New Mexico, ca. 1922.
Prints and Photographs Division, Library of Congress.

Major General Scott, as army chief of staff *(left)*, with his successor, Maj. Gen. Tasker Bliss, at the War Department, 1917.
Prints and Photographs Division, Library of Congress.

Major General Scott (ret.) at Camp Dix, New Jersey, 1918.
Prints and Photographs Division, Library of Congress.

Prominent members of the Board of Indian Commissioners at their annual meeting in Washington, D.C., 1925. *From the left*: Samuel Eliot, Scott, Edward Ayer, Flora W. Seymour, Malcolm McDowell, and Daniel Smiley.
Prints and Photographs Division, Library of Congress.

Maj. Gen. Hugh L. Scott (ret.) *(second from left)* and Maj. Gen. John J. Pershing, *(on left)* at the dedication of the Camp Merritt Memorial Monument, Cresskill, New Jersey, 1924.
Prints and Photographs Division, Library of Congress.

John Collier, 1930.
Prints and Photographs Division, Library of Congress.

CHAPTER 4

▼ ▼ ▼

A PEACEKEEPER'S DILEMMA

The Challenge of Military Advancement

Indian Service, even if creditably done, was of little or no advantage to an officer.
—Capt. Ferrand Sayre, Indian agent, Fort Sill, Oklahoma Territory, 1904

"Moving on" in the spring of 1897 meant once again addressing the challenges to professional advancement that Scott had long endured in his former postings. Those challenges had been intensifying and at times seemed insurmountable in this period of rapid change and uncertainty when the army was redefining its objectives as the United States entered the world stage as an imperial power. One recurring problem was Scott's stance in his role as a negotiator, peacemaker, and advocate, among and for dissident tribal groups, premised, as it was, on the belief that military confrontation should be used only as a last resort. Such a view appeared to be the very antithesis of the bellicose role that one needed for professional recognition and elevation in rank. During the nine-year period of his overseas postings, and particularly in the southern Philippines, Scott equivocated in the application of military force, believing perhaps that just one more effort at diplomacy could avoid loss of life. Often, he felt the need to convince Mary and, perhaps more significantly, himself that its use was justified in a particular situation.

Compounding his dilemma was the need to address the distinct and seemingly alien cultural characteristics of the Islamic peoples that he interacted with in Sulu Province, where he was stationed. The learning curve in understanding the Moros' definition of provocation and their interpretation of diplomacy was a sharp one fraught with potential misunderstandings. Nonetheless, Scott's efforts at diplomacy may have been as considerable in his dealings with his new mentor, Leonard Wood, as with the Moros themselves. Wood had no such qualms in indiscriminately exercising overt force and, in doing so, often undermined Scott's efforts to avoid what he believed to be unnecessary bloodshed. Nonetheless, Scott's frustration was tempered by what Wood was doing for him, both in assisting him with his personal affairs and in campaigning for his advancement in rank. Wood demanded unswerving loyalty from those in his inner circle under his immediate command, and Scott complied, perhaps even to the point of compromising his sense of integrity.

All these dynamics played out in an environment of major change in military administration and ultimate uncertainty as the War Department, reactively more than proactively, confronted a war with Spain and the consequent administration of overseas possessions. As previously noted, advancement in rank in the late-nineteenth-century army was stagnant, forcing postbellum officers of Scott's generation to wait a considerable amount of time for professional recognition in their military careers. Moreover, a regressive retirement system compelled older officers in the higher ranks of the military to remain, often well beyond their years of effective command. And with a rigid seniority rule governing promotion prior to the early twentieth century, opportunities for professional advancement were scant and highly competitive.[1]

Nonetheless, change was about to take place in military administration as the War Department wrestled with the new reality of an American army charged with the task of protecting and administering the nation's new overseas possessions. As with most any major challenge, however, the military hierarchy embraced change slowly, perhaps too slowly for some. Personnel accustomed to traditional ways of performing tasks felt threatened or saw no reason to abandon what seemed to have worked in the past. Competing agendas coupled with the fear of losing one's authority often thwarted change. One thing was certain: the experience of preparing an army for war with Spain in 1898 and the often poor quality of battlefield commanders in leading their troops into combat underscored the detriments of a system of promotion based entirely on seniority.

Although so called military reformers might have initially differed on specifics regarding the knowledge that officers needed to acquire and how they needed to acquire it, they all recognized a need for additional professional training. This would consist of both classroom and field instruction, learning the tactics and logistics of warfare. Mandated examinations to document proficiencies in the exercise regimes required of officers both to retain and advance in rank became the norm. Significantly, too, the army increasingly embraced the criteria of merit over seniority in determining whether an applicant was qualified for promotion.

The new criteria of merit, however, had its own challenges. In the evaluation of professional competency, determinations as to who was best qualified for promotion in rank inevitably introduced the factors of bias and subjectivity. The task of eliminating seniority in an army in the process of reevaluating its objectives for overseas service allowed for broad discretion in determining who had the best skill sets to meet the military's needs.[2]

The measures undertaken by the McKinley administration leading up to war with Spain had broad ramifications for officers like Scott seeking to advance their professional careers. One factor was the president's equivocation in seeking to avoid such a war. While somewhat sympathetic to the Cuban insurrectionists opposing Spain's authoritarian rule in 1897, the president was cognizant that a move of military support would destabilize trade and antagonize economic interests in his own party. However, the sinking of the *Maine* in Havana Harbor in February 1898 turned public opinion in favor of military retaliation. Military planners in the War Department believed that it would be the navy and not the army that would take the primary role in defeating Spain, as evidenced by Como. George Dewey's utter devastation of the Spanish fleet at Manila Bay in the Philippines on May 1, 1898. Consequently, aside from shore defenses, the army's predominant role initially was to establish training camps in preparation for land invasions of Spain's former colonies if and when such force was needed.

McKinley's decision to incorporate the politically powerful National Guard and state militia units, albeit now under the nominal control of officers in the regular army, into a training regimen for the war with Spain was another factor that influenced career planning in the officer corps. Rather than limit the number of such volunteers, McKinley adopted a course that was politically expedient, if not militarily sound, allowing for the recruitment of approximately 125,000 men. Moreover, in the spring of 1898, following the formal declaration of war, no one could predict how long military conflict would last, and what resources would be needed to combat Spain. The initial limited duration of the direct conflict with Spanish forces created a situation where, at times, more troops were available than were needed in combat.[3]

These several unforeseen factors influenced career planning among postbellum officers in the regular army. Although calculating time in rank was an issue for officers like Scott, given that promotions were, until 1890, limited to one's regiment, the kind of experience in one's military service—defined subjectively as merit—was now a more important factor than how long one had remained in rank. Experience in the Indian Service such as Scott's, especially as it was predicated on negotiation and pacification, was of dubious advantage in an army whose objective was now to prepare for war. Consequently, Scott had to edit his credentials in terms of what he had already accomplished in order to enhance his chances for advancement. And in his career going forward, it was critical for him to find the right venues where he could demonstrate skills congruent with the army's new mission. To accomplish both, he had to seek out the right people, who could document his accomplishments and who had influence with those in command of the decision-making process.[4]

Scott's battlefield experience, at least up to the eve of the Spanish-American War, was scant. In his first assignment, as a newly minted second lieutenant at Fort Abraham Lincoln in the fall of 1876, he was ordered to apprehend renegade Sioux and Northern Cheyennes who were sending arms and supplies to Crazy Horse and Sitting Bull, then taking refuge in Canada. In addition, Scott claimed, perhaps with more bravado than veracity, that he played a major role in a military maneuver that ultimately led to the capture of Chief Joseph and his band of Nez Percés. Nonetheless, his accomplishments, prior to the articulation of the army's new overseas role in 1898, were largely in *avoiding* military confrontation.[5]

Another possible avenue for advancement, and one that Scott hoped to exploit as well in the future, was through the army's delineation between line and staff positions. Unlike line officers, those who held staff positions were not subject to the regimental restrictions in determining seniority prior to the abolition of the rule in 1890. Preceding the Military Reorganization Act of 1901, staff officers enjoyed what amounted to permanent tenure in the administrative bureaus where they served. Generally, too, those who held staff positions prior to the passage of the act, were grandfathered in. As a bonus, staff officers with longevity and influence enjoyed the perquisites of a venue in Washington, where the politically influential military bureaus were centrally located. However, line officers in field postings often performed administrative tasks as part of their duties, functioning as assistant quartermasters in supply or assistant advocates general, filing paperwork for essential record-keeping on their posts. Though technically not classified as staff bureau personnel, they often embellished their credentials in such venues to win support for a staff line. Scott had enhanced his résumé in such a fashion, citing his service as acting assistant quartermaster and commissary of subsistence at Forts Totten (1879–82) and Meade (1882–84), where he served as post treasurer and eventually as the post's judge advocate. While it did not get him a staff appointment, it may have enhanced his credentials sufficiently to warrant his promotion to the rank of captain in January 1895. At the time, it remained to be seen whether such a posting would help him in the future.[6]

McKinley's call-up of 125,000 volunteers, both state militia and National Guard, concurrent with the declaration of war against Spain in the spring of 1898, presented officers like Scott with both opportunities and challenges. The recruitment of volunteers during the Civil War had established a precedent whereby many officers in volunteer service had earned their commission in and transitioned to regular army units in military careers during the postbellum period. McKinley's federalization of the National Guard and state militia units for the conflict with Spain provided officers like Scott the opportunity to advance in rank as volunteers (vols.), well beyond their standing in the regular army, and, with a consummate increase in compensation. The downside was that a volunteer rank could be canceled at any time if and when the president and Congress decided that an enlarged military force supplemented by volunteer enlistments was no longer needed. Nor can the long-standing acrimony between professional soldiers in the regular army and citizen soldiers in the National Guard and state militias be ignored. The former disparaged volunteers as poorly trained, with an officer corps selected by state officials based on their political influence and social relationships, and not on their battlefield experience or knowledge of military tactics. Moreover, regular army officers complained that volunteer soldiers practiced with archaic weapons and conducted tactics that were no longer relevant to a modern army. Acrimony existed on the other side as well. Many National Guard personnel considered the existence of professional soldiers an affront to a democratic society and prone, as a class, to urge battle solely out of the veneration of warfare, evoking a long-held fear of what the nonprofessionals regarded as the pernicious nature of permanent standing armies. A more immediate concern to officers like Scott was that if precedent allowed the professional soldiers to advance in rank, it might also allow officers in volunteer regiments to displace those in the regular army, where advantageous venues were critical to permanent advancement.[7]

Once again, as he had in the past, Scott enlisted the contacts he had made at both the state and federal levels and in civilian and military venues to influence those he believed could help him to advance professionally. Mary, too, continued to play a pivotal role in pressing his interests when her husband was away from the capital and the War Department.[8]

The uncertainty resulting from McKinley's equivocation in planning for war with Spain, the army's role in such a conflict, and the tenure of the conflict itself were all variables that would influence how Scott would proceed on his path to professional advancement. The criteria of merit in the promotion of a middle-aged officer with a scant record of battlefield experience, the viability of gaining a lucrative staff venue, and the challenges posed by the influx of volunteer enlistments that doubled even the enlarged size of the regular army were additional considerations that Scott had to weigh in determining his strategy for promotion.

Nonetheless, in the spring of 1897, the immediate need was to alleviate the loneliness that he faced at Fort Sill, often owing to the absence of Mary and of their children who remained with her. A posting in the Northeast seemed ideal, near Philadelphia and Princeton perhaps, where they could all live among relatives and friends. Advantageous to Scott, at least in the interim, was an offer from James Mooney, director of the Smithsonian Institution in Washington, to work on Scott's research on the Indian sign language. However, while tribal research at the Smithsonian was an enticing option, it would not place him in a position to broaden his opportunity for professional recognition and added financial remuneration.[9]

A venue of both appropriate command and proper location could enhance Scott's chances for promotion beyond an immediate elevation in rank. An anticipated opening of a staff position in the Adjutant General's Office as assistant to the adjutant general at the War Department in February 1898, with the rank of major tied to the posting, initially held out some promise. Once again, whatever forces of influence Scott could marshal would be essential, but would they be enough to overcome the efforts of rivals using a similar strategy? Initially, Scott seemed confident that they would. He garnered the support of officers in the army's bureaus to write letters citing specific incidents in Scott's prior field service and documenting his character and inserting them in his official military file. In May 1897, Scott was exceedingly optimistic. He met privately with President McKinley, who assured him that he would give Scott's credentials his "personal attention." Determined and confident, he wrote Mary with the good news and the strategy he would follow. "I have now the Executive branch solid I think and can go to the Senate Com[mittee]—confident that if then they call on the EX[ecutive branch] for a report that I will be backed up—and I will commence on them tomorrow—with a lot of letters that I have from different sources."[10]

Despite all the efforts of his advocates, Scott's appointment in the Adjutant General's Office in February 1898 did not materialize. Several reasons—none mutually exclusive—may explain his failure. One might be that the candidate who was awarded the appointment had greater influence with the decision makers than did Scott. So, too, that individual may well have had more experience in performing staff assignments, or simply more influence with the president and the War Department than Scott possessed. Once again, the ongoing paucity of promotions among army officers in general and those seeking staff positions in particular would indicate that his chances were slim at best. And perhaps equally detrimental, his work in the Indian Service, however meritorious in the past, would no longer be an important consideration for professional advancement.

Historical speculation suggests another reason: General Nelson A. Miles's growing alienation from the executive branch in his role as commanding general of the army. Miles's efforts, both personal and professional, in aiding Scott were long-standing and ongoing. Nonetheless, the general's loyalty and assistance, while abundant, were limited to officers he did not see as posing a threat to his own professional career and increasingly inflated ego—a shrinking list. As Miles rose in rank based on seniority through 1895, he resisted reforms. He also rejected the idea that the secretary of war, with the approval of the president, should appoint the army's commanding general rather than allow seniority to be the sole basis for promotion to such a rank. Miles's obstructionism vis-à-vis several secretaries of war led to his virtual isolation as a source of advisement in military strategy for the executive branch. Consequently, a recommendation from Nelson Miles in 1897 would not help a candidate's cause.[11]

Scott's discouragement continued when it did not initially appear that the impending war with Spain in the spring of 1898 would hold opportunities for him. However, it opened options that Scott was determined to explore. The administration's mobilization strategy was to call up all National Guard and state militia forces and federalize them by placing them nominally under the command of regular army officers. They would be trained in recently constructed southern camps from which they could eventually be sent overseas through the port of Tampa, Florida, as they were needed. Consequently, in May Scott accepted a position as major (vols.) with an assignment as assistant adjutant general of volunteers at the headquarters of the Second and Third Division of the First Army Corps at Camp Thomas, Georgia, under Gen. James H. Wilson.[12]

Once again, a downside was that federalizing the National Guard and state militias provided unwelcome competition from those in volunteer ranks whose professional elevation was often predicated on nothing more than political influence. This was another consequence, albeit a negative one, of the postbellum precedent established when volunteers filled their states' Civil War regiments, eventually to embark on military careers as officers in the regular army.[13]

With little chance of making his way to the front in Cuba, Puerto Rico, or the Philippines from the late spring of 1898 and on into the following year, there would be no opportunity to enhance his credentials with battlefield experience. Part of the problem was that, like Miles, he now had fewer major sources of influence. If this situation was not bad enough, Mary, who had suffered from lifelong respiratory trouble, found the humid air in

Washington, D.C., intolerable. Consequently, Scott, who had relied on her as an indispensable conduit of information in advancing his professional career, was in a state of deep despair over his future, with seemingly no chance for overseas service.[14]

No clear path to professional advancement appeared over the summer and fall of 1898, but Scott's physical environment improved greatly. By late August, Russell Alger, as secretary of war (1897–99), directed the inspector general, Joseph Breckenridge, to relocate Scott's Third Division, First Army Corps, to Camp Hamilton, in the healthier and more hospitable climate of central Kentucky, near Lexington. The cooler and more temperate climate coupled with an abundant supply of fresh clean water were not the only virtues of the new location. Danville, about thirty miles southwest of Lexington, was Scott's birthplace, and where his father, William, had taught at Centralia College. A colleague of William's at the college, who knew the Scotts prior to his father's death, shared his familial recollections with the son. This experience and the general hospitality of the residents in the region were welcome distractions from the ongoing administrative workload that Scott faced, as well as from the besetting uncertainty of where his next posting would be.[15]

While Scott was in a state of near despair, anguishing over his career and inability to obtain any field assignment, his mentor-to-be, Leonard Wood, was enjoying notoriety in what was nothing less than a meteoric rise through the military hierarchy. Although Wood could claim no Academy credentials—he was an army contract surgeon when assigned by Miles to Fort Huachuca in the Arizona Territory in 1885—his successful though controversial capture of Geronimo, the elusive Apache chief, earned him accolades. Miles ultimately campaigned successfully to have Wood honored with the Congressional Medal of Honor, bringing him to national attention and bestowing upon him the recognition that Wood himself believed he justly deserved.

Wood enjoyed an additional source of favorable publicity and ultimate influence from his initial acquaintance in 1897 with then Assistant Secretary of the Navy Theodore Roosevelt. Both men shared a common interest in adventure and in a desire to test their prowess through physical activity. While "Colonel Roosevelt" recruited his "cowboy volunteers" for the initial invasion of Cuba, leading to his notoriety in the Battle of San Juan Hill (1898), Wood, as commander of the regiment, provided at least an aura of military legitimacy to the engagement. As long as Roosevelt advanced through the executive branch, Wood's ascendance in the military hierarchy was assured, and ultimately by a commander in chief who believed professional advancement should be based on merit and not seniority.[16]

For Scott, the beginning of 1899 initially brought both personal sorrow and cautious optimism. On January 5, he received a telegram from his brother William informing him of their mother's passing the previous evening. Mary had been a moral compass in Scott's life, and although opposed to her son's vocational choice, she had stood by him during his maturation. Adding to Scott's sorrow was the suddenness of her passing, as he had not realized she was ill. Scott could not even attend her funeral. As the only regular army officer present in Tampa, he was mandated to assist his Second Division, First Army Corps, with the deployment of troops to Cuba. His wife, Mary, served as his surrogate.[17]

Scott was cautiously optimistic when Maj. Gen. (vols.) William Ludlow was appointed commander of the city of Havana. Ludlow, whom Scott served under as an assistant adjutant general in the Second Division of the First Army Corps in Columbus, Georgia, had requested that Scott's Second Division accompany him to Cuba, and ultimately the request was approved. The downside, once again, was Mary's departure from Washington, which left Scott feeling that, whether true or not, there was no one there to advocate for his interests.[18]

Ludlow was exceedingly loyal to his staff and, most importantly, willing to help them in furthering their professional careers. Such was the case with Scott. In March 1899, Congress approved a provision under the authority of the secretary of war to open up vacancies in the Adjutant General's Office to any "captains of the line [which Scott was then] who have evinced marked aptitude in the command of troops." Such officers were to be recommended by their regimental commanders to compete by examination, and if successful, they would be awarded a rank of major (regular army) in the Adjutant General's Office. Both Ludlow and Gen. James H. Wilson, Scott's former corps commander in the reorganized volunteer army, endorsed Scott's credentials. As time went on, Ludlow offered to take Scott to Washington in December while on leave. Scott's letters to Mary were increasingly encouraging, even though his workload grew as a result of the furlough of several staff officers.

The only drawback to this posting was that he and Mary could not be together. However, that opportunity would come, at long last, when Scott was granted a month's leave to go to Washington in October.[19]

His work in Havana continued to bring him immediate, if relatively modest, professional recognition. In the late summer, he learned belatedly that the War Department had promoted him to lieutenant colonel (vols.) the previous March. While the promotion gave him a modest increase in pay, his personal expenses had increased as well. Mary was now pregnant with their fifth child, and both the costs of schooling for the older children as well as the expenses incurred by her frequent moves added to his financial concerns. Professional recognition came in other ways as well. Scott was well respected by and on familiar terms with the officers on the island and, most importantly, General Ludlow. A testament to Ludlow's confidence in Scott is seen in his willingness to leave his junior officer in charge of the department while he went back temporarily to Washington.[20]

Nonetheless, it was not Ludlow whom Scott ultimately owed for his recognition but Leonard Wood. Scott first met Wood at the new governor's welcoming reception in early January 1900, when a longtime friend of Wood's approached Scott to ascertain whether he had any interest in joining Wood's staff in Havana. Wood claimed that he had Scott in mind for his staff and meant to "weed out his officers" at Tampa and offer Scott a major's (vols.) rank, but their "hurried departure" to Cuba prevented him from doing so. As Scott would soon learn, many of the personality features ascribed to Miles could also be attributed to Wood![21]

Scott was somewhat ambivalent in working under Wood in the early months of the year. He noted to Mary that "Wood is very pleasant in every way but '*Timeo Damaos et dona ferentes*' [Fear the Greeks even when they bear gifts]." Nonetheless, Wood's offer seemed to be his most viable option at the time. With four growing children and another on the way, perhaps the most important consideration for Scott was financial. An overseas posting would allow him to hold his elevated rank as a lieutenant colonel (vols.) rather than having to revert to his regular army rank as a captain if he were posted stateside. The additional pay commensurate with the volunteer standing would remain if he continued in Cuba. Moreover, Wood was prepared to offer Scott the position as his chief of staff. The provinces of Havana and Pinar del

Rio as well as the city of Havana (Ludlow's former command) would also be placed under Scott's jurisdiction. By early March, Wood seemed prepared to sweeten the deal by holding out the *possibility* of an adjutant general's posting following the departure of an officer who was ill. For Scott, the position of adjutant general of the division in Cuba was "a place that I would never have any right to expect . . . [and] the most important position in Cuba after Wood's." It was increasingly apparent that Wood very much wanted Scott to remain in Cuba as an important member of his staff. Given that Wood already had confidence in him from observing his work under Ludlow in Havana, and would be working closely with him, the position opened additional opportunities for Scott to win Wood's endorsement, as well as those of his influential friends, for his professional future.[22]

Yet, the downside of accepting Wood's offer also had to be considered. Although his financial remuneration would increase, alleviating a concern for his growing family, it would come at the cost of a prolonged absence from his wife, at a critical time in her pregnancy. Adding to Scott's burden was the need to provide for the education of Hunter, his oldest son and the pride of his father, who sought an Academy appointment. Moreover, the work as an adjutant general was arduous and exceedingly time-consuming, limiting what personal contact he could have with his family, as well as the time he would need to study for the mandatory examinations now required for promotion. Also, although not fully understood or appreciated by Scott at the time of Wood's offer, his future mentor was a demanding commander, and most significantly, given their future relationship, one with an insatiable desire to seek for himself a battlefield venue wherever and whenever he could. Perhaps Wood's intent was to prove himself worthy of command to his Academy-educated fellow officers and to defend his Congressional Medal of Honor award against his detractors.[23]

Wood applied stringent standards in selecting his senior military staff. He scrutinized their work prior to appointing them in order to determine whether and how their talents would meld with his own in implementing his vision of the army's new role as an overseas occupying force. Frank McCoy, a young lieutenant, proved to have the talents that Wood was looking for and was appointed his aide de camp. Tasker Bliss, a cerebral officer in the military commissary and a classmate of Scott's, was appointed by Wood as

Cuba's collector of customs for his administrative skills, attention to detail, and integrity. Wood's selection of Scott as adjutant general and eventually as his chief of staff in Cuba was made using these selective criteria, partially predicated on Scott's administrative skill and patience in undertaking and accomplishing often exhausting logistic assignments. So, too, Scott's ability to settle disputes among diverse groups of people in both military and civilian venues was undoubtedly a major asset to the commander of an army of occupation in a foreign environment.[24]

The most important characteristic that Wood demanded was unwavering loyalty. He could not deal with anyone who overtly opposed either his policies or the way that he reached his decisions. Part of Wood's genius as an administrator was in selecting junior officers who possessed the talents that he needed, one of which was a willingness to maintain order. Another lay in demanding that his subordinates follow the rigorous work schedule that he set for himself. Eighteen-hour days were more the norm than the exception, with Sundays and holidays often part of the grueling work regimen. Scott's rigorous schedule was such that he could not even obtain leave for the birth of his youngest child in June 1900, when Wood claimed that he needed his entire staff to supervise Cuba's first democratic election.

Along with loyalty, Wood demanded trust from his staff, and he amply rewarded it when it was tendered. In the twenty-nine months that Wood and Scott worked together in Cuba, they developed an enhanced respect for each other based on a strong sense of trust.[25]

Over time, Scott was amply rewarded for his loyalty to Wood, both personally and professionally. The Scotts' finances were an ongoing concern, exacerbated by Mary's frequent moves, necessitated by her health; the cost of living when she was in Washington; and the demands of a growing family of now five children. Family friends offered financial assistance in the form of gifts and loans, and Scott was forced to sell some of his Native American artifacts in order to meet current living expenses. Wood was aware of Scott's financial situation. Scott noted to Mary that "Gen. Wood is doing everything he can to keep me here in my present position with increased pay from civil duty from the Island funds and . . . sending the Chief Clerk to Washington to negotiate it[.] [He] wrote two strong letters yesterday without anybody suggesting it to him to clinch it if possible."[26]

A related personal matter of growing concern to the Scott family was the situation involving David Hunter, their oldest child. Known simply as Hunter, he was born at Fort Totten, Dakota Territory, in the fall of 1881 after the Scotts were married in June of the previous year. Today, one might call the adolescent a "late bloomer"; he caused Mary and her husband no end of frustration. Hunter showed little self-discipline or interest in pursuing a vocation. The father's hope, if not the son's desire, was to have him admitted to the United States Military Academy, but the effort proved difficult if not impossible, given Hunter's unwillingness to study. Hunter's situation became so difficult for the parents—particularly given Mary's precarious health—that Scott took his eldest son under his wing, bringing Hunter to Cuba in the spring of 1901, in hopes of inculcating a sense of motivation and discipline in the youth. At the time, the move did little to change the boy's attitude about studying, but surely tested the limits of his tolerant father's patience![27]

Here, too, Wood offered his assistance in what Scott sought for Hunter. He wrote letters to friends and influential associates seeking help for Hunter. Given his age and lack of preparation, however, his road to maturity, emotionally and intellectually, would prove to be a long and a twisted one.[28]

Professionally, Wood's insistence on keeping Scott with him in Cuba had other advantages for his junior officer, even if it would not directly lead to a promotion. His Cuban posting gave Scott the opportunity to utilize and even enhance his skills as a negotiator and provided him with the opportunity to apply them in a different cultural environment. "The Latin-American is very punctilious in his courtesy," Scott observed, "and expects you to be the same. Our American brusqueness turns his fur the wrong way. He would rather have you refuse his request with courtesy than grant it without. I was most careful in my courtesy." Scott's deference to cultural sensitivities was coupled with a keen understanding of human nature, as he noted in 1928, looking back on a long career:

> It requires patience to listen all day in the tropical heat to a succession of empty speeches. Each one however, was entitled to his day in court, and I saw that he got it. . . . They use up their power in talk; when they *say* something they feel like they have actually *done* something and their

desire for action is satisfied. When negotiating with armed and angry Indians[,] I am never anxious over the voluminous talker, but I watch the silent one in the corner. His desire for action is not dissipated in talk, and he may act. When they talk out all their opposition, there is no power of resistance left, and they must fall like ripe fruit into your hands. I have seen this happen times without number, not only in Cuba, but in Mexico, in the Philippines, on the Plains of the West. One only needs an unfailing and sympathetic courtesy and an unconquerable patience. If you have not these qualities try some other business, for diplomacy is not for you.

He applied his diplomatic skills successfully in settling both a labor dispute and a contentious situation among importers and exporters in the port of Cienfuegos. He also generated a spirit of harmony and accord among the eclectic group of officers who were cycled into and out of their Cuban postings during the period of American occupation.[29]

Scott weighed his options when he returned to Washington from his Cuban assignment in May 1902. His strategy was twofold: to find a venue that would give him the best opportunity to demonstrate his worthiness for a promotion of command, and, at the same time, to determine what influence he could exert and where it would prove most beneficial in achieving his professional objective.

While his administrative work in Cuba met with praise, there is little indication that it would bring him the kind of recognition that he sought and needed. Moreover, Scott was acting under a time constraint, both in an immediate sense and within a broader framework. The precarious status of a volunteer rank was his immediate concern. Rumors were circulating that Congress intended to muster out the volunteers, which would leave Scott with only a captain's rank in the regular army to fall back on. Aside from a major loss in pay, such a situation would, in effect, denigrate his service in the training of troops during and immediately following the war with Spain, as well as his meritorious service in Cuba. Within a broader chronological context, given Scott's age—he would be forty-nine in September 1902—and with a mandatory retirement age of sixty-four, his chances of earning a position of command in the regular army were rapidly diminishing. In addition, the stress had taken a toll on him physically. Perhaps he reasoned he had little to lose in pressing for a star ranking.[30]

Scott believed that a battle posting would give him the best opportunity for the professional recognition that he felt he needed. However, by 1902, U.S. forces were no longer needed in China following the end of the Boxer Rebellion, and the insurrection in the northern Philippines had already ended. It appeared that his best opportunity for promotion rested in his association with Wood, who was to be posted in the southern Philippines. It was there that a military conflict with the indigenous Muslim peoples known as Moros was ongoing. This venue represented an opportunity to demonstrate his worthiness to senior military staff, or so he reasoned—assuming, of course, that Wood was willing to recommend Scott to serve under his command. As events turned out, Wood was more than willing to assist Scott, who had served him so loyally in Cuba and with whom he had built up a relationship of trust and confidence. Scott's strategy continued both prior to and following his posting in the southern Philippines in March 1903, illustrating the logic that he believed would best obtain his goal. For example, Scott used the impending promotion of his friend and colleague Tasker Bliss to the rank of brigadier general in the regular army (from a similar rank in the volunteers) as a justification for his own elevation to a star, noting that it "would throw discredit upon me if I got nothing[,] being very mortifying to a man who had occupied the 2nd place in the island [Cuba] & had not been called in question as to any of his acts by the Dept responsible not only for Bliss' Dept but for every other also. It would look as if the Dept had not valued my services."[31]

In another example, playing up his peacemaking skills and using Mary as a sounding board for the talking points that Wood could use in advocating for his elevation to a star rank (BG, or brigadier general), Scott argued:

> That my going with him as a Brig. Gen. & succeeding him to the command of Mindanao is essential to the success of his policy & he should go to the President & tell him so at once and explain . . . that the Dept of Mindanao is the sore spot now for the administration. He [Wood] is being sent there to get rid of polygamy & slavery before the next political campaign comes in lest the Administration be attacked on those

grounds.... They [the Moros] are very powerful & will make a great deal of resistance in case of war. The administration doesn't want any war either on the eve of an election & it is going to take *some exceedingly fine work* [emphasis mine]—which Genl Wood will not have time to carry out himself to this end as he cannot rush those peoples and must go to command the Div. at Manila before long. Bliss and Carter are going out there but they have had no experience in dealing with Savage peoples & besides[,] he needs a man there he knows will be faithful to him & knows nothing but fidelity and will watch his interests... & should tell the President that he wants to take me out as a BG.... that it is essential to his policy that the BG be given to me.[32]

Notwithstanding Scott's high optimism in anticipation of a star rank, and his belief that Wood's close relationship with the new president would play to his advantage, all was not as positive as he assumed. While Scott was strategizing on the future of his military career, Roosevelt, by elevating Wood to the highest levels of the military hierarchy in the regular army, was paying a high price for his unwavering loyalty. Theodore Roosevelt's ascendancy to the presidency, following the assassination of McKinley in September 1901, and his noted desire to run for the office in his own right generated fear and animosity among his critics, who resented his ongoing support for Wood as a candidate they deemed unworthy and unqualified for the army's highest command.[33]

The first thing that Roosevelt did in March 1903 after approving Wood's posting in Mindanao, with Scott under his command and in consort with Root, was to send Wood, Scott, and McCoy out of the country to their post in the southern Philippines. Roosevelt recognized that Wood's obstreperous manner would not help his cause. Given Roosevelt's anticipation of what he would go through politically as a result of Wood's promotion, Scott had no chance of attaining a star rank in the regular army at that time. To grant his request would mean that he would jump over eight hundred officers on the seniority list, and Scott's combat experience was even less than Wood's.[34] What Roosevelt was willing to do was to offer Scott a major's rank in the regular army, if the president could be assured in advance that the Senate would confirm his nomination. Both a West Point posting, recommended as a possibility by Roosevelt, and the consideration of a star rank would be taken up following his stint in the southern Philippines. Scott quickly marshaled his allies in the Senate who had been sympathetic to his situation in the past, and his promotion was approved by Roosevelt shortly thereafter.[35]

Scott may not have received the rank he believed he deserved, but under the circumstances, he fared rather well. His attainment of a senior ranking in the regular army provided more security for him than did the precarious nature of his previous volunteer commission. Moreover, his command in the southern Philippines eventually included a military commission as well as a civil one. Scott was the only governor of the five districts under Wood's command to enjoy both, a testimony to Wood's confidence in his ability and his loyalty. It would give Scott the potential for battlefield experience, and consequently, a stepping-stone to further advancement, given that the Sulu District where the Moros resided was considered to be the most volatile area of all. Consequently, Scott was treated quite well by both Roosevelt and Wood as a major in the Fourteenth Cavalry, as governor of the Sulu Archipelago, and eventually, after some administrative challenges, with a military command. Not to be overlooked was the fact that the posting held out the possibility of substantial added compensation that could bring his monthly income to $590, or more than $7,000 a year![36]

However, even if his monetary hopes came to pass, he endeavored to earn every dime of it. Scott's skill as a diplomat would be tested not only by the indigenous peoples that he would encounter in the islands, but by the commander that he served under as well. Wood's initial behavior in the southern Philippines was overly aggressive, timed to his confirmation hearing in the Senate thousands of miles away. He was attempting to prove his qualifications for command, but in so doing, he complicated Scott's efforts to promote peace and stability.[37]

The broader challenge to Wood and Scott underscored an ongoing dilemma faced first by Spain and now by the United States in their attempts to control the southern province of Mindanao and the Sulu Archipelago. When Spain conquered the Philippines in the sixteenth century, spreading the Catholic faith to much of these islands, they met formidable resistance from a group of people in the southern islands of the Sulu Archipelago and in the province of Mindanao to the east, who were called by the Spaniards Los Moros. The

Moros were a Muslim sect. Their cultural, geographic, and economic isolation from their northern neighbors bred a spirit of independence, making them a formidable challenge for any imperial power to colonize.[38]

At the heart of Moro resistance was an adherence to a religious faith equally as strong and unforgiving of dissent as that of the Catholic Filipinos to the north. The Moros' interpretation of the Koran's teachings mandated the implementation of the orthodox legal code of sharia, which affirmed the practice of slavery and polygamy, as well as *juramentado*, literally meaning "those who take an oath." More precisely, in Tausug, the Moros' native tongue, these oath takers were known as "suicide warriors" who adherents believed had a duty and responsibility to slay *kāfirs*, or infidels, defined as anyone who did not adhere to what the Moros regarded as the teachings of the Koran. The exercise of juramentado was especially destructive because of its suddenness, subduing an opponent completely by surprise, and was defined by American administrators as "running amok." When used against a large group of soldiers, its consequences could be devastating. The perpetrator would swing a machete-like bolo knife in trying to kill as many infidels as he could, knowing full well that he would die for what he believed would be a better world in the hereafter.[39]

The sultanate's authority in the southern Philippines was contingent on the sultan's wealth in cattle and slaves, as well as the degree to which he could persuade others to follow him. Ultimately his authority depended on alliances with thedatos, or tribal chiefs, who often had far greater influence than the sultan. A dato had the supreme authority to execute the provisions of sharia law among his followers, who resided in communities known as *cottas*. If a dato did not maintain a level of prosperity and stability within the cotta or failed to protect the safety of his followers from other rival datos, he could be abandoned as a leader. Military alliances among datos were quite common and deemed necessary for trade and, perhaps increasingly, for common defense. Over time, too, the Sulu Archipelago became a region of active trading within Southeast Asia, and consequently, of growing contentiousness among and between Moro cottas.[40]

When the treaty ending the war with Spain was signed in 1898, the United States assumed the challenge of establishing political stability among a native population restive under colonial rule. In June 1903, the Moro province was officially organized by the American army as the Department of Mindanao and divided into five military districts under Wood's command. Four of these were in the province of Mindanao proper. The fifth, the Sulu District, was a separate entity comprising islands to the southwest that were divided from the mainland by the Sulu Sea. Its capital and military fortification were at Jolo, on one of the larger islands. This Sulu Archipelago was inhabited by those Moros deemed to be the most "restive," given their history of piracy and slave trading.[41]

Prior to that time, in August 1899, Brig. Gen. John C. Bates, commander in the region, signed an agreement with Jamal ul Kiram II, the sultan of Sulu. Under its terms, each would recognize the sovereignty of the other, with an annual payment by U.S. officials to the sultan and his entourage. Given the scant size of the American force in the southern Philippines—the bulk of the army of occupation was in the north engaged in a major insurrection—regional peace and stability was crucial.[42]

The content of the so-called Bates Agreement allowed both sides to walk away believing that each had protected its interests and recognized those of the other. The young sultan's primary interest in the agreement was not in the alleged safeguards that it extended to the Muslim culture. Rather, it was the tribute that American officials would pay him to maintain his stature. Bates believed that the sultan commanded the authority of all the datos, but this was not the case even in the archipelago. On the surface, the agreement appeared to be a "live and let live" arrangement, and to the extent that U.S. forces could not do otherwise at the time, it was just that.

Consequently, under their understanding of the Bates Agreement, the Moros, particularly those living in the Sulu region under the sultan, had every reason to believe that the American occupiers respected their cultural practices. Moreover, the Moros claimed precedent from a prior treaty they had signed with Spain in 1878, allegedly acknowledging their sovereignty, and the acquiescence of Spanish authorities to refrain from collecting the cedula, or head tax, on individual Moro families. Whether that treaty was still valid at the time that the United States acquired all the Philippines was an open question. The Moros *wanted* to believe that it established a precedent sanctioning their financial hegemony while limiting that of the governing power.[43]

However, both in process and in implementation, the Bates Agreement may have lulled each side into a false sense of security, which did not augur well for its future success as a means of accommodation between two disparate peoples. The sultan's weakness in the Moro political structure placed warring datos in a position where they could easily reject the terms of the agreement by claiming that the sultan did not represent them when he signed it. Moreover, to a Moro, the imposition of the cedula tax was a concession of tribute. Further complicating the implementation of the agreement was the word "sovereignty," particularly as it was later used as a wedge by American colonial officials to justify the repudiation of the entire agreement. One historian notes that the word was left out of the Moro version of the agreement altogether![44]

Compared to previous venues where he served, Scott's posting in the southern Philippines was unique, both militarily and culturally. The military resistance to the American occupation of Cuba was minimal and effectively neutralized by Wood, through what succor he could provide to unemployed *insurrectos*. Such was not the case in the southern Philippines. There was no civil administrative structure in the Moro-populated islands, and no such tradition of one for a Muslim people who viewed their faith as all-embracing in their daily lives. Moreover, Scott would now be dealing with a race whose morals were largely repugnant to Christian civilization, perhaps even testing his ability to pacify a people deemed by many to be beyond salvation.

Wood had no intention of embracing a policy of military restraint toward the Moros. However, he concealed his real intentions when writing to the president. For example, he neglected to tell Roosevelt that he organized a large show of force in August, shortly after his arrival, and summoned all Moro chiefs in various regions of the Sulu islands to let them know that American sovereignty meant, among other changes, the abolition of slavery. In so doing, he not only rescinded the Bates Agreement by fiat but also ignored the more moderate guidelines formulated by the Philippine Commission, a body created by an act of Congress (1902) to provide for the orderly transition from military authority to civilian control in the Philippine Islands. Among other directives, it prescribed a gradual end to slavery through financial compensation to dato slaveholders or by allowing slaves to buy their freedom. Wood also failed to tell the president about the actions of the legislative council he was mandated to create by the directive of the Philippine Commission. Although three of the civilian members were appointed by then governor-general William Howard Taft (1901–3), the two army officers appointed by Wood gave their commander veto power over the actions of the commission's appointees, since Wood, as provincial governor, enjoyed two votes. The civilian members were thus subject to the four-to-three majority of Wood and his appointees. The council, which met weekly and in secret, exercised its legislative prerogatives to pass eighteen acts during September 1903 alone, thereby creating a civil government for Moro Province. By implication or outright design, the measures repudiated virtually all aspects of the Moros' existence, since secular matters were subsumed by their spiritual customs and traditions under sharia. A particularly noxious measure allowed for the imposition of the cedula, a tax of one peso per each Moro family. As was the case in Cuba, Congress proved unwilling to fund the cost of colonial government, and while the tax was imposed on the northern Philippine islands as a matter of precedent even under Spanish rule, Spain had intentionally refrained from imposing it in the Muslim-populated islands to the south. Hence its unprecedented use there was interpreted by the Moro people as an unwarranted infringement on their sovereign rights; ominously, it precipitated much violence between and among the tribal chiefs and U.S. forces. The secretive nature of their passage, coupled with Wood's unwillingness to allow "savages" representation, added to the provocative character of these laws.[45]

What General Wood did convey to Roosevelt was his determination to conduct what amounted to an offensive military campaign around Lake Lanao in the fall as a show of force, ostensibly to demonstrate his prowess in battle. While praising the success of the Lake Lanao campaign that the young Capt. John J. Pershing had undertaken the previous year, Wood used the pretext of Pershing's failure to abolish slavery and polygamy among the Moros as an additional rationale to revisit the region with a large force.[46]

While Wood's imperative was to destroy the Moros' Islamic culture, Scott was prepared to work within the hierarchy of Moro relationships, manifesting respect for Moro customs and traditions, however repulsive other Christians may have considered them, as he had done with tribal groups on the northern Great Plains and in the Oklahoma Territory. Consistent with his view of Native Americans, Scott regarded "the colony of Mohammedans"

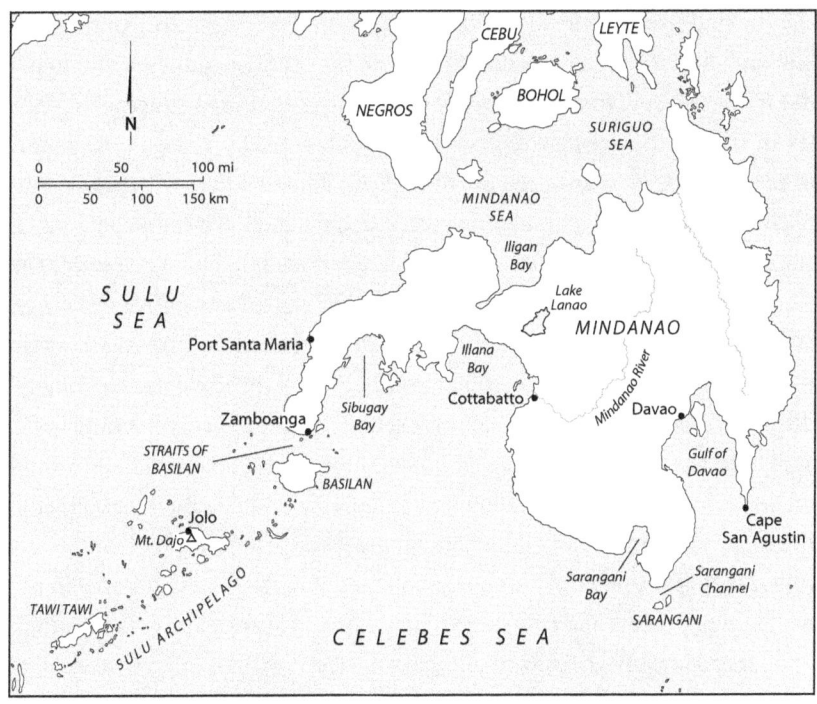

Moro Province in the Southern Philippines. Reproduced from Jack C. Lane, *Armed Progressive: General Leonard Wood* (1978).
Reprinted with permission of the University of Nebraska Press. Copyright 1978 by Jack C. Lane.

as an inferior race, who displayed primitive and childlike characteristics that hindered their ability to become easily or quickly civilized. He believed that they were guided by their emotions and, collectively, had little ability to reason or to think critically. What made their actions potentially ominous was their dismissive attitude toward the quality of human life, coupled with their veneration of violence to settle disputes. Scott embraced a policy of patience and firmness, much as a parent would use in raising a child: patience in listening to their disputes in his role as military governor of the province; firmness in promising no more than he could deliver and keeping his word when he agreed on a course of action. The latter proved difficult when Wood was prepared to undertake swift and overt military action without informing Scott of his intentions.

Consequently, Scott's negotiating skills were put to the test. In his interactions with Moro leaders, he did not have the benefit of the sign language that he had used so effectively in his years on the American frontier, and although his interpreter was skilled and had the confidence and trust of many datos, there was always the chance of misinterpretation. A graver challenge ley in the Moros' propensity to commit *juramentado*. These random acts of mass murder were unpredictable and put those soldiers who believed in pacification and cultural understanding at a decided disadvantage when it came to anticipating a Moro's intentions. Scott also had to overcome of the fact that in Moro culture, negotiation itself was viewed as a sign of weakness. While many Moros might see Scott's respect for their culture in a positive way, he needed to earn their trust initially. Also significant was the Moros' disgust with the concept of surrender even in the face of overwhelming force. Scott had to confront a people who saw no glory in subjugation and would rather die what they perceived as an honorable and spiritually rewarding death, leaving no one left to negotiate! Another potential problem was his initial inability to identify and assess the reputation of specific datos in the negotiating process and to discern their relative influence vis-à-vis the sultan and other Moros in their cottas. Perhaps mitigating this weakness somewhat were Scott's keen observation skills, which undoubtedly had saved his life when he was negotiating with tribal leaders on the Great Plains. Most of these challenges required time as well as patience in building understanding, respect, and trust. His commander's agenda, which encouraged provocative acts to justify the use of force, did not always allow for such considerations.[47]

Wood's initial attempt in 1903 at intimidating Moro leaders on the Sulu islands by summoning them to meet with him in August, and with a show of force, did not stand well with all of them. The acting sultan of Sulu, Raja Muda, failed to appear as ordered, claiming that a boil on an intimate part of his body had prevented him from travel. Wood ordered Scott to find Muda and verify his situation, thereby denigrating the dignity of a spiritual leader by humiliating him in front of his followers, and ultimately making it more difficult for Scott to build trust among the Sulu Moros. Unfortunately for Scott, that would not be the only time that Wood placed him in a situation where he was forced to act against his better judgment. Within a month of his arrival, Scott was confronted with an incident involving a Moro named Biroa, who was still at large after murdering another Moro and kidnapping a girl. Technically, according to the Bates Agreement, Scott had no authority to intervene, since the crime involved only Moros. Nonetheless, Wood ordered him to demand that the sultan bring Biroa in within five days. Fully aware that such an order violated the agreement, yet respecting his mentor's authority, Scott sought what he believed to be a compromise solution. As he noted in his autobiography twenty-five years after the event, "I could see but one way out, and that one very dubious; to keep on worrying the very life of the sultan until he either effected Biroa's capture or acknowledged that he had not the power and asked me to make the arrest as his agent for trial by Moros, according to the [Bates] agreement."[48]

As a result of his skill with the sultan, apparently through flattery, Scott persuaded him to send a powerful dato, Panglima Indinan, to apprehend Biroa. Indinan located Biroa and succeeded in gaining the release of the girl. He then retired to his own cotta without Biroa's capture. Scott visited Indinan and convinced him to bring the girl to Jolo. In addition, he again pressured the sultan, who now ostensibly enlisted the support of Panglima Hassan, a well-known powerful dato in the Sulu Archipelago, along with Scott, to arrest Biroa. Patience and courage were foremost. Scott negotiated first with Biroa's father since Biroa had fled to his father's well-fortified cotta and had initially refused to come out and talk to Scott. When the son finally agreed to parley, in what turned out to be an all-day affair, Scott addressed both father and son. Initially Biroa's father said that he did not want to meet. Scott, who was unarmed and accompanied only by his interpreter, responded with controlled and calculated intimidation, "I had been misinformed about the Moros, for I had been told that they were a brave people but this showed [that] they were afraid of even being scratched. . . . It must be that Biroa's father is a Filipino, hiding like a rat between the rocks; he can't be a Moro!" Scott defused the standoff to the extent that Biroa agreed to go to Jolo under Scott's protection, to be tried in a Moro court. Ultimately, it was Scott's skillful negotiation with Biroa that led him to return peacefully to Jolo.[49]

Although it ended with the successful apprehension of Biroa, the incident had ominous long-range consequences for Scott. Hassan felt both insulted and resentful: insulted in that the crime Biroa committed was *only* the killing of a slave; resentful that both Scott and the sultan believed they had the authority even to request Hassan to arrest Biroa, which implied, to Hassan, that they had sovereignty over the Moro Province. In Biroa's case, while the process of pacification succeeded, the circumstances under which it was applied placed Scott in a precarious position. Scott's problem was twofold. The first was that he had little understanding initially of how to assess a dato's intentions based on his Islamic culture. Specifically, he did not realize that Hassan would feel indignant when asked to apprehend a Moro over the killing of a slave. The second problem was Scott's initial ignorance of the relationships among datos, and between them and the sultan. For example, Scott did not realize at first that the sultan of Sulu, Raja Muda, although a spiritual ruler, had little authority over datos in the region and none relative to the most powerful dato in the Sulu Archipelago. Hassan was not about to take orders from the sultan, and certainly not through Scott's directive as the secular American governor of the region. Consequently, his introduction to Hassan did not augur well for a harmonious relationship. Attempts to negotiate with Hassan proved futile. And the relationship went downhill from there, leading to a confrontation that nearly ended Scott's military career—if not his life! Under the circumstances, when his troops were attacked, Scott believed that he had no alternative other than to use overt force. Nonetheless, the decision, when it came, was not an easy one and was accompanied by much soul-searching. Upon his arrival in Manila in July, Scott had sought to belay Mary's concerns saying: "You may rest assured that I will always try peaceful means to the limit altho I know well that drastic measures are better for me personally." However, his convictions would soon be put to the test, along with the need to rationalize and justify the use of overt force not only to his wife but, perhaps more importantly, to himself as well.[50]

Nonetheless, there were other essential conditions for a successful negotiation that Scott needed to learn and develop. Whether a manifestation of cultural respect would necessarily lead to a dato's willingness to negotiate with Scott was another matter. Scott's premise was that a Moro would rather save his own life if he knew that it would not be taken by an enemy, but his pacification strategy assumed, sometimes erroneously, that a Moro would *not* want to seek a glorious death taking one or more infidels with him. Put another way, the question might be: would a Moro slay an infidel if the individual were at least sympathetic to the Moros' faith? Of course, if a Moro believed in a strict interpretation of sharia law, *any* effort at pacification was likely to prove useless.

Fortunately for Scott, he could readily adjust and accommodate himself to a relationship with many other Sulu Moro leaders, thereby allowing him to win their loyalty, cooperation, and respect without the use of overt force. Scott encouraged them to meet with him in his Jolo headquarters or at their request, in their cottas, and on a casual basis. It was in such an environment that each had an opportunity to interact with the other, in the absence of pretension and formality. Unlike Wood, who sought to abolish the dato structure of leadership, Scott used it to build loyalty through a recognition of the importance of the datos' role, even though they may have been his adversaries in the past. Pershing used similar practices with Moro headmen and cotta members in the Lake Lanao region on the main island of Mindanao.[51]

Winning the Sulu Moros over to his side involved advocating on their behalf, both collectively and individually, against measures that Wood and the Philippine Commission were pressing on them. One such measure was the unpopular cedula tax. From the perspective of senior colonial administrators, the tax, along with maritime tariffs that were imposed on the people of Sulu, were sources of revenue essential to maintaining the colonial administration in lieu of any congressional funding. Scott, for his part, was sympathetic to the consequences that its implementation would have on the Moros' culture, traditions, and practices. Noting that they regarded its imposition as "an attack upon Islam," he believed that it was "most ill-advised at this stage of progress." Nonetheless, as an officer, he was duty-bound to enforce the law even though he may not agree with it, "for anarchy is invited when we attempt to choose which laws we will obey and which we will not," as Scott wrote at the time. His solution was to persuade the datos to collect it, giving the Moro chiefs the deferential authority to enforce it. Scott also scrutinized other measures initiated by either Wood or officials on the Philippine Commission.[52]

While Wood was seeking to disarm the Moros by force, recognizing that arms and munitions were more often sold to the most disaffected cottas, Scott proposed an "arms buyout plan," whereby datos loyal to him would secretly buy arms from other cottas and ultimately receive just compensation from American authorities who would then purchase the guns. When his plan was rejected by Wood and the Philippine Commission, he noted that its disapproval "cost far more in both money and blood to effect the same result in the end." Other legislative measures, promulgated from Manila, were equally damaging to the Moros' economy and spiritual traditions. One attempt on the part of the Philippine government involved confiscating, without compensation, the lucrative pearl beds that had provided a livelihood for Moro families from one generation to the next. Others, directed at specific individuals within the Moro community, were equally onerous to Scott. A measure to reduce the sultan's income and that of his advisers, despite prior guarantees to the contrary, met with scorn. Yet another struck at the very core of the Moro political and social structure: the hereditary rights of the datos. Scott pleaded the Moros' case on these and other measures before the Philippine Commission with mixed success. His defense of the dato system, with its vestige of hereditary title, might seem surprising for someone raised in a Christian and democratic society, but it attests to the value Scott placed on the importance of cultural deference in winning Moro leaders over to his side, and on rewarding loyalty. As he noted:

> Some of the rights appear to us as illegitimate, but they were vested rights nevertheless among the Moros and had come down through their families for hundreds of years.... I felt outraged at the injustice myself; those high-born men had been accustomed to be carried on the backs of slaves all their lives; and now, with their income gone, and their slaves freed without compensation, they were totally unable to make a living unless they should take to robbery and murder.[53]

Some aspects of his advocacy on the Moros' behalf resembled that of an American legislator assisting a constituent. When a Moro's boat was unintentionally sunk in the Sulu Sea by a vessel of the quartermaster's department and his claim for reimbursement was ignored, Scott enlisted the support of an old Senate friend and advocate, who successfully obtained compensation in Washington. Undoubtedly, as Scott noted, that simple act of assistance could build a sense of trust in the American system of justice.[54]

Winning datos over to his side through advocacy of their interests was not the only way to promote peace. An ongoing problem was the potential for American soldiers to act out their prejudices in such a way as to provoke a violent military confrontation. Compounding the problem was the turnover in military personnel, and the time and effort it took to retrain new recruits. Scott could do little about the turnover. But he initiated a training program on methods for interacting with Moros, short of the use of overt force, for new units that were cycled in under his command. He may not have succeeded in eliminating the biases of American soldiers stationed in the southern Philippines, but at least he presented them with the potential consequences if and when they acted on them.[55]

Working through the Moro leadership structure—specifically, winning the loyalty and trust of Moro headmen—provided Scott with four advantages. One was the ability eventually to establish a foundation for a local constabulary that could supplant some of the tasks of the occupying forces, and ideally minimize the hostility that the presence of troops incurred, as it had done in the northern Philippines. Another advantage was in the willingness of datos friendly to the American authorities to recruit others, once they saw that the occupiers understood and respected their Islamic culture and traditions, and would protect them to the degree that they could. Personally reaching out to individual datos may also have minimized Scott's need for negotiation with Moros who committed crimes that a dato could now adjudicate under the sanction of U.S. authorities. A fourth advantage, and perhaps the most important one in the early years of the American occupation of the southern Philippines, was the opportunity that it gave to authorities for intelligence gathering, to know exactly what was going on in the cottas of a particular region and consequently defuse potentially hostile situations. Although not always successful, Scott replicated many of the practices he had honed in dealing with American Indians on the northern Great Plains and at Fort Sill prior to his overseas assignments.[56]

Scott was exuberant in what he believed was his ability to win over possibly adversarial Moros, as he explained to Mary in October 1903: "I feel that I am getting to understand these people already—and can work on them as I used to on the Kiowa & Comanche—the same way seems to be successful with the Moros." However, his optimism did not last long. Shortly thereafter, friendly Sulu datos informed Scott that a party of Moros, perhaps as many as a thousand, were convening within six miles of the Jolo fortification with the probable intent to overrun it. Hassan and members of his cotta were thought to be among the group, presumably to take revenge for what Hassan regarded as an affront to his stature as well as his dignity, during the Biroa affair. Scott believed that he had enough forces in Jolo to counter Hassan's threat, and did not need any military assistance from Wood. Although the rationale for Scott's decision to act unilaterally is uncertain, one possible explanation may have been what he saw as an opportunity to demonstrate a show of overt force, giving him the battlefield experience he so desperately needed for an elevation to a star ranking. A second possible explanation, and one that does not preclude the first, is that Scott, ironically, was trying to protect his mentor. As he noted to Mary at the time: "I am trying my best to keep things quiet until the Gens nomination is thro the Senate lest his enemies attack him . . . but do not know how long I can hold out on that line [refraining from the use of troops]." While Wood may have viewed the timing of events in Washington as a fortuitous circumstance to demonstrate his military prowess once again, Scott saw the hearings as a formidable reason for his commander to exercise restraint.[57]

Scott's biggest problem was not a lack of sufficient forces to engage in an offensive operation, but the morale of his troops, many of whom were intimidated by the Moros' bellicose behavior so close to the Jolo settlement.[58] Scott took a troop of cavalry and made a "reconnaissance of force" to a region where Hassan was reported to be hiding. As Scott approached, Hassan and fourteen Moros were armed with guns, barongs, and spears while guarding their encampment. They were promptly disarmed by Scott's forces. Scott then ordered Hassan to surrender and informed him that he was taking him to Wood. He also warned him that "any treachery would result in his being killed first." Hassan's armed guards began firing in Scott's direction as Scott reached for his gun, and several bullets pierced his hands. The injury resulted in the partial or full loss of several fingers as well as major trauma to joints in his hands. Though not immediately life-threatening—he was brought to an army surgeon in relatively short order—the extent of the injury required additional surgery, skin grafting, and extensive application of sulfa drugs to ward off infection. As Scott noted to Mary, his left hand "looks now more like a pile of cat's meat intended for a disreputable cat." Perhaps of greater discomfort to Scott was the psychological impact of the injury. Scott had to maintain a degree of immobility and physical restraint to allow the injury to heal sufficiently to preserve maximum use of his hands and fingers. He often disregarded the surgeon's advice to remain sedentary or at least semi-sedentary. Within a month of the injury in mid-October, Scott was seen touring the island of Jolo in a gunboat and working at his desk. One of the people who saw him was his surgeon, who promptly marched him back to the hospital! By the end of December, the pain in his hands had diminished, sufficiently that he could move the fingers of his right hand and perform some normal tasks with it. Ultimately, Scott was left with a right hand missing the tip of a forefinger and most of a third finger. The third finger on his left hand was weakened owing to the loss of a half inch from the length of his metacarpal bone.[59]

His injury did not stop Scott from pursuing Hassan and other dissident datos in the first part of the new year. He rode with both hands in casts on a mounted pony or donkey to alleviate the stress from a normal mount, and with a doctor and hospital corpsman accompanying him to dress his hands frequently in the field. Scott was as stable as his condition allowed. Apprehending Hassan was the primary objective in the first months of the year, but he was not the only Moro that Scott was pursuing. Others were accused of murder, stealing horses and pearls, kidnapping, and general violence in rivalries among and between datos. Often relying on navy patrol boats to move his troops, Scott traveled to some of the more remote islands in the Sulu Archipelago in search of his adversaries. If Scott's commander and mentor were leading troops to catch these fugitives, Wood would certainly have used the Moros' crimes as a pretext to justify the use of massive overt force. However, if these transgressors and their allies did not fire on Scott's forces and were willing to lay down their arms when confronted, as Scott always preferred, then the use of force could be avoided. Nonetheless, the risk of an ambush was always present, and the dense jungles and steep mountain grades challenged the stamina of any soldier, let alone one whose mobility was impaired. The inhospitable terrain was not the only challenge the injured major faced. Compounding his problems was the ever-present threat that a Moro adversary would commit juramentado. All in all, Scott confronted his Moro enemies with a great deal of courage, fortitude, and patience. Many of these encounters ended by negotiation without the use of overt force, though the threat was always present.[60]

The campaign for Hassan's capture on the Sulu islands of Jolo and Luuk warranted the inclusion of heavily armed personnel as Scott and his forces pursued Hassan and those datos allied with him. Friendly datos, allied to Scott through a relationship predicated on trust, provided him with information on Hassan's whereabouts. Intensive fighting included assaulting and penetrating well-fortified cottas, where Hassan and other dissidents were believed to be hiding, warding off juramentado charges, and defending against Moros who attempted to surround them in dense jungles. Part of his strategy to capture Hassan and his followers was to turn them into pariahs among other Moros, who would see them as "a swarm of bees that nobody cared to have rest on him." The challenge was daunting. Hassan was "well-armed . . . and is desperate; he knows every foot of these jungles and can hide within 50 feet of you without you knowing it, and has many friends." Another problem that Scott encountered was trusting his troops' judgment. However brave and courageous they were, they did not know Hassan by sight, and with a number of loyal Moros after Hassan, there was always the chance that Scott's forces could harm Moro allies with friendly fire.

Such concerns turned out to be justified when it came to the fate of Hassan. In early March, Moros loyal to Scott learned that Hassan was hiding in a grass hut in the volcanic crater of a mountain known as Bud Bagsak, thought by the Moros to be impenetrable to attack. Scott, with a great deal of assistance given his injured hands, determinedly climbed the mountain on near-perilous paths with his men, surrounded the edge of the crater, and waited till dawn to undertake an assault. Hassan and several of his followers, gathered within the lighted hut, began to sing a Moro death song, emerging armed from the hut at daylight. The American soldiers opened fire, killing two men and wounding a third. The wounded Moro was Hassan, who rolled into a small ravine, firing his Krag-Jørgensen from a position that was inaccessible to return fire. One of Scott's officers worked his way down the ravine and killed Hassan. Scott's courage and stamina were well demonstrated. Being literally led into battle through a dense jungle with both hands in a sling, unable to mount or dismount without assistance, and carried up the side of the mountain to the rim of the volcano—Scott's presence with his troops was a testament to his fortitude as well as his determination to put an end to the Moro insurgency in the Sulu Archipelago. Once again, however, Scott felt it necessary to justify his use of overt force in his search for Hassan by describing the numerous challenges that his troops had to endure in penetrating the walls of heavily fortified cottas as well as in facing the intense firepower of the Moro insurgents. Here, too, Scott presented his usual rationalization, justifying the use of force only as a last resort, and only when his adversaries refused to lay down their arms when confronted. Scott's ambivalence over its use was such that even when Wood embellished a recommendation emphasizing Scott's battlefield experience, which Wood undoubtedly saw as a way of assisting his junior officer's advancement, Scott took umbrage. Criticizing Wood to Mary, he noted that the endorsement "gives one no credit . . . for bringing these people in . . . with many chances to shed blood that were only avoided by the most patient diplomacy, and in fact gives me no credit for what I am most proud—the diplomatic results." That he felt compelled continually to justify the use of force to Mary and to Capt. Oscar Charles, an old, devoted friend in the Tenth Infantry, who now served under him as secretary of Sulu Province, by demonstrating his belief that he had no other option, is a testament to a man who prided himself on his ability to negotiate with his adversaries, and who was frustrated when he could not.[61]

From the perspective of his military career, the question was whether his documented battlefield experience, with a wound under fire, and his determination to lead his troops into combat against his Moro adversaries in spite of his injury gave him sufficient credentials for a star ranking? Only time would tell, but if Wood had his way, Scott would indeed be rewarded with such a rank for his efforts. It is plausible to assume, given Charles's near veneration of Scott, that the five multipage letters (that read like reports) he sent to Mary from the late summer to the early spring were written not only to inform her of her husband's undertakings, but to serve as detailed documentation of Scott's battlefield experience. Lieutenant McCoy was even more candid and forthright with Mary. In a letter to her, written prior to Hassan's fatal encounter, and in a section marked "Personal and Confidential," he reminded her that now was the time to push for a star ranking for her husband. "Don't fail to let it be known that he is in the field, doing things with his wound of November still open[,] being led around by a pony with his hands swathed in bandages, and not letting his wounds interfere with his duties." He also informed her that Wood had strongly recommended to Roosevelt that Scott be promoted. Meanwhile, Scott was determined to hold out for a West Point posting that Roosevelt had allegedly promised him before his venture in the Philippines.[62]

However, both when and even if the Academy posting would occur remained open questions. Tied to that issue and of even greater concern to Scott was his prospects for elevation to a star ranking. His strategy remained the same: pressing Wood and supportive members of Congress to influence the decision makers, Roosevelt and now Taft, as secretary of war (1904–8), while speculating on his competition and calculating who might soon be retiring with a brigadier's rank. Although Scott's initial fear, that he would be passed over for another candidate, caused him much anguish, there were other developments that occupied his time, and that would extend his Philippine tenure beyond his anticipated transfer stateside. One was illness, Wood's as well as his own. His commander suffered from a chronic brain tumor that caused periodic paralysis on the left side of his body as well as partial blindness. Several surgeries brought temporary relief, but the tumor was never completely removed, owing to the limits of medicine in the early twentieth century. Eventually the condition proved fatal. In late 1904, Wood suffered from another bout of seizures and experienced numbness in parts of his body, necessitating a return to the States for surgery the following May. The procedure was a temporary success, in that Wood regained his strength during a period of recuperation, enabling his return to the Philippines in late October. Meanwhile, Adj. Gen. Henry C. Corbin served as department commander, a posting that Wood had originally thought would be his on his path to be a major general. However, Corbin took ill after a year's service (1904–5), necessitating his surrender of the post. Consequently, upon his return, Wood was at first temporarily reinstated in command and given a permanent assignment as commander in Manila on February 1, 1906. During the transitional period following Wood's return to Manila, his aide de camp, Capt. George Langhorne, was placed in the position of secretary as well as acting governor of Mindanao Province, presumably because Scott, with Wood's full endorsement, was seeking the West Point superintendency.[63]

Scott suffered from recurrent headaches that sapped his energy, possibly caused by the trauma to his body from his hand wounds as well as the stress he endured over the uncertainty of promotion and the West Point posting. Adding to this, and preventing an immediate leave of absence stateside, was a request from Taft that he extend his Sulu posting an additional year because of Wood's medical leave. As a loyal officer, Scott agreed to the request. However, he concluded that he could now be of little additional benefit t to the Moros. Mary's equivocal plans to visit him in the Philippines were another source of frustration. Her letters to him had become irregular and infrequent, adding to his loneliness. Ultimately, though, Mary's health improved such that she could make the trip, along with their youngest child, Houston, now four years old. The much anticipated visit occurred from mid-December 1904 to early April of the following year. Meanwhile, Hunter's willingness finally to "buckle down" was now a source of relief to his parents. Although no longer eligible for a West Point placement, he was determined to pursue a military career, following his father as a commissioned officer in the army, through attendance at one of the service schools, which would enable him to attain proficiency in the needed subfields of military science.[64]

At this point, near the end of Scott's tenure in the Philippines, an event occurred that would reverberate in Congress and in the American press and that tested the perimeters of Scott's pacification initiatives. As previously noted, the Bates Agreement never resolved whether U.S. authorities held the prerogative to impose the cedula on Moro residents of the southern Philippines. Once again, American authorities maintained that the tax, along with duties imposed on maritime traffic in and around the Sulu Sea, was essential to provide necessary services to colonial inhabitants on the road to civilization. This followed the precedent of the imposition of such a tax in Cuba under American occupation as well as in the northern Philippines at the end of the insurrection. Wood was emphatic in its implementation, an initiative endorsed by the legislative council that he convened in September 1903 shortly after his arrival. Perhaps of greater importance, both Wood and Moro leaders viewed imposition of the tax as an act of sovereignty. The latter held that the failure of Spanish authorities to impose it on the Moros in the treaty of 1878 between Spain and the sultanate established a precedent, implying that the treaty was still in effect. To the Moros, then, the tax, no matter how small, signified that their rights and privileges were subservient to U.S. authority. Moreover, given that the Moros did not differentiate between the secular and the spiritual realm, the tax was perceived as an affront to the very foundation of Muslim faith, which was exactly what Wood had in mind in enforcing it. Ominously, the Moros' opposition to it gave him yet another reason to invoke overt force against them when he saw an opportunity to do so.

Scott, as noted, had a different perception of the tax. While acknowledging the right of American officials to impose a revenue-generating measure, he criticized the method of taxation. Consistent with his view of the Moros' spiritual orientation, and contrary to that of his mentor, he worked through the dato structure to collect the tax from Moro leaders within their cottas. The premise was that they were willing to collect it based on their faith in Scott's integrity. However, the procedure had its shortcomings. Dissension soon erupted between cottas whose datos collected the tax and those datos who refused to do so. Pala, a dissident Moro who seemed to thrive on instigating violence, took up the anticedula cause, along with other datos, thereby stirring up the passions of those Moros who opposed its collection against both the loyal datos who had agreed to collect it and U.S. officials who demanded its immediate implementation. Consequently, a disheartened Scott lamented that "the cedula has about ruined my hard work of nearly two years."[65]

Scott's despair was well founded. The contentiousness between those datos loyal to Scott and willing to collect the cedula and those opposed to its implementation under any circumstance only increased, as between the anticedula Moros and American authorities. Some of these dissident datos, in their effort to evade American authority in the late spring of 1905, migrated to an inactive volcano on a mountain known as Bud Dago, only six miles from Jolo and at an elevation of at least two thousand feet. Its steep trails made it a nearly impenetrable redoubt. Although not all of the Moros at Bud Dago were seeking refuge from the imposition of the cedula—allegedly some were robbers, kidnappers, and murderers escaping from the law—many saw the migration as a permanent habitation and were prepared to stay there at the cost of their lives. Consequently, they brought their families along. With an abundant supply of water at the base of the volcano, they were prepared to cultivate crops that would sustain them in the event of a protracted siege.[66]

In June 1905, in what he hoped would be his final year in the Philippines, Scott attempted, through intermediaries, to negotiate with these Bud Dago dissidents, confident that he could convince them to come down from the mountain without loss of life on either side. His decision to adopt a wait-and-see posture was predicated in part on logistic considerations. Scott believed that the 2,000-foot elevation and the muddy soil exacerbated by heavy and recurrent rain on near-inaccessible steep-graded trails would result in the loss of half his command if an assault were attempted. So, too, he saw no need for overt military action if the Moros remained peaceful and did not directly challenge American authority. He also believed that if negotiations failed to lead to their surrender, he could starve them out.[67]

Nonetheless, the situation became increasingly precarious in the summer and early fall. Scott's policy of pacification was premised on both the inability of the dissidents to sustain themselves over time and the fact that their mere presence on the mountain would not be construed as a provocation or threat to American authority. Arguing against the success of any pacification initiative was the fact that these Moros could not be starved out. Even without their abundant supply of foodstuffs from the crops they had harvested in the volcano, the seemingly endless supply of fresh water and the trails, familiar to them but obscure to others, leading to the base of the mountain would have enabled them to cultivate a food supply and bring in needed provisions for a long siege. Nor had it been determined with any accuracy how many insurgents committed crimes other than refusal to pay the cedula. It was alleged that criminal activities, such as theft and kidnapping, were occurring through their access to those obscure trails. In addition, although some insurgent leaders allegedly promised Scott that they would comedown off the mountain after they harvested their crops in the fall, they had failed to do so. One could argue that simply by occupying the mountain in defiance of any law promulgated by colonial administrators, the Moro dissidents were committing a provocation, a direct challenge to American authorities. Other Moros, seeing restraint as weakness, would be encouraged to defy colonial authority altogether.

By December, immediately prior to his leave, Scott's situation became increasingly dire. Anticipating the worst, he informed Wood of the weakness of his force, in both offensive and defensive capacity. He reiterated to Wood the challenges that his forces confronted in terms of staging an attack on the mountain, noting that it would be "the most difficult situation I have ever seen." As to defense, his fear was that should dissension spread beyond the volcano—a clear possibility given the dissidents' knowledge of the terrain and the proximity to Jolo city proper of the mountain, his forces would be unable to handle it. He also notified Capt. George T. Langhorne, his replacement, that the unrest among the Bud Dago Moros "may turn serious. . . . [I] am doing the most we can do and pull through and get our ends without proceeding to extremities." His only recourse was to place his faith in the ability of a long-trusted Moro to negotiate a peaceful resolution, as he had attempted to do for months. This ally now feared for his life when he entered one of the cottas in the volcano. Such was the situation in Jolo when Scott left for his much delayed and anticipated leave at the end of December 1905.[68]

The success of Scott's pacification plan, refraining from the use of overt force, was contingent on the willingness of his adversaries to surrender when confronted with armed force. This plan, in his absence, would require the willingness of American forces to give these Moros the opportunity to surrender. However, preparation for a possible use of overt force against the Bud Dago dissidents began soon after Scott left in January and rapidly proceeded.[69]

While Wood was increasing the number of people who could be held responsible for what bellicose action military forces on Jolo might take, Capt. James Reeves, sent by Wood, was justifying the use of a preemptive campaign to dislodge the dissident Moros. In a letter to Langhorne on March 1, he outlined in detail what he saw as Scott's earnest yet ultimately failed attempts to get the dissident Moros to come down peacefully from the Bud Dago volcano. He also noted that, simply by their continued presence on the mountain, they were defying American authority and posing a threat to American sovereignty:

> They are protecting violators of the law, they are allowing and encouraging other people to come up and join them, they are making a daily boast that they have established a strong point, in fact, an impregnable position, and that they are in open defiance of American authority, and that we cannot take their position, that we cannot force them off the hill and cannot force them to obey the laws. . . . They claim to be a set of patriots and semi-liberators of the Moro people.

Nor did Reeves believe that future negotiation was even possible, for neutral datos, whom Scott tried to enlist before his leave, "had frequently told . . . [him] that these people were beyond them and from under their control."

What transpired in the first two weeks of March was devastating. At the sound of a bugle, the soldiers opened fire. The soldiers faced minimal return fire, and within ten minutes, four hundred Moros lay dead, with bodies piled four deep in places. A subsequent assault the following day on another part of the rim brought the total death toll from all engagements to approximately eight hundred Moros, two-thirds of whom were women and children. There were only twenty-one American casualties. The disparate ratio of fatalities points to the way the battle—aptly described as the Bud Dago massacre—was fought.[70]

The ramifications of the battle were broad and far-reaching. The American press had a veritable field day with front-page coverage, including the headline in the *New York Times* on Sunday, March 11: WOMEN AND CHILDREN KILLED IN MORO BATTLE.

Once the story of what appeared to be a massacre broke, Wood was immediately on the defensive, fearing that his career would come to an ignominious end. He fervently defended his behavior and that of his troops against charges that the battle was a massacre.[71]

Scott, now stateside in the East, was caught in an awkward position. Reporters were looking to him to ascertain the veracity of what had occurred as well as the events that led up to the confrontation. To escape from the press, he went into hiding for ten days, north of New York City, until Secretary Taft ordered him to Washington to address why he believed that overt force against the Bud Dago Moros had been necessary. Given the adverse publicity for the administration, and out of a desire to contain the fallout, the secretary of war took advantage of the fact that the Republicans were in control of the Senate. Taft immediately appended Scott's "Memorandum for the Secretary of War" in its entirety into the Congressional Record, pursuant to the investigation being conducted by the Senate Committee on Military Affairs.

In his report "The Moros of Jolo Island," Scott claimed that the Moros on Bud Dago were "being kept down" by a highly respected dato. Conceding that "while the elements of trouble were still there (the elements of trouble are always somewhere in Jolo) . . . it was thought that I could leave them as well as at any other time." However, as previously noted in letters to Wood and Langhorne, Scott was far from confident that the matter could be settled peacefully. On the contrary, he left Jolo with a great deal of foreboding, fearing that his force there would not be able to defend the post, let alone undertake an offensive operation. He also claimed ignorance of what was going on in Jolo immediately prior to the confrontation in March, noting that, in his last contact with authorities there, on January 29, "the Dajo question not being mentioned, it was supposed the Moros remained quiet at least until that date." His further characterization of Wood's view of any Moro resistance was, however, inconsistent with both his mentor's behavior and what he had previously felt about Wood's actions in a battlefield venue. For example, his official report in the *Congressional Record* on March 20 noted:

> The policy of General Wood in that archipelago has always been to bring about peace and order as gently and with as little loss of life as possible. In every case, when it has been necessary to arrest Moros charged with crime and they have gone into their strongholds and called their friends and relatives about them to resist arrest, every possible effort, extending in some cases over weeks and months, has been made to bring about the arrest without bloodshed.[72]

In addressing the option of surrender before applying the use of overt force, Scott made it sound as if Wood had followed that practice before ordering his troops to fire on the Bud Dago Moros. To substantiate his claim, he cited the fact that "four days were occupied sending prominent chiefs into the fort to induce women and children to come out." However, as was previously noted by Captain Reeves in a letter to Captain Langhorne on March 1, none of these "prominent chiefs" had any knowledge of the Bud Dago Moros, as they had informed Scott when he was there at the time. Consequently, whether a good faith effort at negotiation was extended to these dissidents prior to the use of overt force is open to question. Nonetheless, Scott wanted his readers, primarily Roosevelt, Taft, and congressional Republicans, to believe that it had been.[73]

Although he implied in his autobiography that his memorandum was drafted when he arrived at the War Department on March 20, one can reasonably assume that he spent time while he was unavailable to the press writing the tightly worded and well-constructed draft. Evidently, he was prepared to bend the truth in documenting a pattern of mediation and pacification in Wood's policy of dealing with Moros. However, Scott would not place himself in a position where he would appear to second-guess Wood's decision to use overt force. In his autobiography, he refused to speculate as to whether his presence would have made a difference, expressing doubt that it would have changed the outcome.[74]

The truth is that military strategy had nothing to do with it. It would not have made a difference. Scott's objective was to save Moro lives; Wood's objective was to destroy them! Over the last six years, Wood had played an important role in advancing Scott's military career. Despite his personal feelings regarding the use of overt force, Scott, with a strong sense of loyalty, was willing to return the favor.

It is difficult to determine how effective Scott's defense of Wood was in refuting his critics' accusations. Scott did his best to dampen and undermine the claims of Wood's critics in the firestorm that immediately followed the Battle of Bud Dago. Whether his memorandum gave Wood an aura of credibility and legitimacy and blunted the accusations of those who sought to destroy his career, the passage of time ultimately made the matter a moot point. The earthquake in San Francisco on April 18 took the nation's attention away from what, to most Americans, was an obscure occurrence in a distant part of the world to a catastrophic event much closer to home.[75]

The racial dimension to Scott's pacification program with the Moros in the southern Philippines was similar to that in his dealings with Indians in the American West. He viewed both as "primitive" races that manifested childlike behavior, guided by emotion and with a limited ability to reason. Gaining their trust by acknowledging the importance of their culture and patiently listening to their concerns brought at least limited success, as he defined it. Scott was equally prepared to advocate for both groups when he could, though his advocacy was predicated on what *he* believed their needs should be.

Brig. Gen. Albert Mills's retirement as superintendent at West Point finally paved the way for Scott's new posting. It provided him with several advantages. After approximately eight years of personal stress and anguish, with a precarious future in his stateside venues and the loss of intimacy with his family when stationed abroad, Scott could now enjoy a period of stability in his home life. He could enjoy the companionship of his wife on a regular basis and care for her when she was faced with health challenges. He could join in the celebration of the marriage of his oldest daughter and the birth of his first grandchild. With a more stable posting stateside, he could now entertain his numerous friends, both in and beyond the military, and share memories together. Because of his position of authority, he could assist them, many from his Fort Sill days, in obtaining pensions, acquiring new postings, and soliciting letters of recommendation. Significantly, too, proximity to the sources of power in the executive branch and Congress facilitated his ability to orchestrate the elevation of his professional career. To be sure, Leonard Wood still played a major role in furthering his career, but Scott would not, at least temporarily, have to endure the daily stress of being under his immediate command. Even as Wood continually sought to micromanage Scott's administrative affairs, dealing with the constraints of a desk job at the Academy was a challenge of a different sort for an officer who had thrived on the frontier.[76]

CHAPTER 5

▼ ▼ ▼

UP THE ADMINISTRATIVE LADDER

A Star at Last

It has been a long time in coming but they say everything comes to him who waits provided he waits long enough. You certainly merit this billet with your family and now an easy stride to a star.
—*Capt. O. J. Charles to Scott, September 5, 1906*

In September 1906, Scott assumed the post as the twenty-sixth superintendent of the United States Military Academy at West Point. Few major modifications in policy occurred during his four-year tenure. Developmental change was generally evolutionary rather than abrupt, and Scott, a West Point graduate steeped in the institution's traditions, was not about to steer an unchartered course. Changes in curricula were directed, however slightly, more toward instruction in the liberal arts and, perhaps most significantly, in the military sciences that were now required by an American army with overseas possessions to guard against incursions by foreign powers. Some additional changes were physical. Scott inherited from Gen. Albert Mills, his predecessor, a capital construction program that included the erection of a chapel, an administration building, a dormitory, and a powerhouse. The renovation of artillery placements was also part of the plan. On a more societal level, Scott had to address yet another hazing scandal, six years since the last one. The earlier one involved the death of a cadet, a subsequent congressional investigation, and all sorts of public ill will toward the Academy. Perhaps because of West Point's tarnished reputation, Scott undertook what was perhaps the greatest contribution of his tenure: opening the Academy up to public display and scrutiny.[1]

Hazing in one form or another was customary at West Point, where upperclassmen could make irrational demands on plebes, testing anything from their physical endurance to their mental aptitude. In his years attending the Academy, Scott himself had been on both the receiving and giving end of the practice, and although he denied suffering any physical or psychological harm from it as a plebe, he was held back a year as an upper-class cadet for hazing others. The death of Oscar Booz, a plebe admitted to West Point in June 1898, created a shadow on West Point's reputation. His family claimed that Booz was a more vulnerable target for harassment owing to his devout daily Bible reading. Following a congressional investigation, efforts were made to abolish the practice, but it was not ended at the time. Another case occurred under Scott's watch, though the consequences on the plebes were not dire. A group of upperclassmen were tried and found guilty of the practice and dismissed from West Point. They went to their congressional representatives, who in turn sought reinstatements from the secretary of war. Although they admitted their guilt, family influence, much to Scott's dismay, raised the case to its highest level, ultimately the president of the United States. Allegedly, according to his autobiography, Scott warned Roosevelt that "if you and the secretary [of war] do what you are now contemplating [reinstating the cadets], you will do the greatest damage to the discipline of the Military Academy that anybody has done in this generation." Although the president accepted Scott's argument, the families of the dismissed cadets turned again to Congress, where a bill was introduced in the Senate to reinstate the students. Nothing came of it in a hearing, and presumably the matter was dropped. The irony is that if it was not for the intersession of Scott's grandfather, the Reverend Charles Hodge, when cadet Scott was in the same situation in 1872 as these dismissed students were now, he would not have gone on to become a superintendent of West Point![2]

Scott used the adverse publicity engendered at West Point as a result of the hazing scandal as an incentive to belay its critics by making the Academy more accessible to the general public. He modified the physical plant with paths and water fountains to accommodate visitors. Members of civic clubs were always welcome, and if his schedule permitted, he would conduct a personal tour of the campus grounds. Many foreign dignitaries visited the Academy, enjoying photo opportunities with the superintendent. Two groups received special attention: members of the press and of Congress. Scott recognized that reporters were influence builders who could convey a favorable impression of West Point through the press. Consequently, he invited them to the Academy, often for extended periods of time, so that they might acquire a better understanding of how public funds were being used in the education of the army's professional corps. Of course, members of Congress, whom West Point depended on for funding, were always welcomed and encouraged to visit.[3]

Shrewdly, enhancing West Point's public profile through visits from civic groups, the press, and congressional delegations served Scott's professional interest and also helped to ameliorate West Point's previously tarnished reputation. Wood had advised Scott as early as 1904 that his best chances for a star ranking would be in the West Point posting and not in the Philippines. Wood's rationale was certainly convincing, given that Mills was awarded a star in 1904 in the post that Scott, at the time, was seeking. It appeared then that precedent was on Scott's side, or so they both believed. Nonetheless, circumstances had changed dramatically in the three years since Congress, on Roosevelt's recommendation, had offered Wood his second star. Roosevelt was embroiled in the 1904 presidential campaign, and the president had already paid a high political price in pushing Wood's promotion through Congress, given what critics continued to see as the paucity of Wood's qualifications. Roosevelt believed that he had reached the political limit in promoting senior officers based on what he regarded as merit rather than seniority. Expressing his feelings of anger and frustration, he was quoted saying, "My next brigadier-general must be chosen from among the colonels or by those who by seniority should be colonels. The trouble is that the public naturally cannot know who the best officer is, and all the mutton heads in the army equally naturally object to anything resembling promotion by merit." Consequently, Roosevelt would not recommend a coveted star for an officer who was less than senior in a colonel's rank (Scott was a major in 1906). The president claimed at the time of Scott's appointment in August 1906 that it was made in lieu of a star ranking. The best that Scott could attain was a colonelcy, but only one in the reserves, which was, in Scott's case, a rank of consolation.[4]

As on numerous occasions in the past, Scott marshaled his supporters to press those in power for an elevation in rank. He now had two advantages that he did not have before. The first was that he was stateside, and unlike previous ventures in promoting his case, he had geographic proximity to the powerbrokers in the executive and legislative branches of government. The second was in the political and administrative access that the West Point posting afforded him in entertaining members of Congress and others who could influence them. At issue was his alleged paucity of tenure in rank, owing to what Scott and his supporters had previously claimed was the adverse consequence of the regimental promotion rule on their military careers. The decimation of the Seventh Cavalry at Little Bighorn in June 1876 had opened postings to recent Academy graduates like Scott, giving them a favorable cavalry branch venue that would have been traditionally beyond attainment with their mediocre class rankings. Consequently, most of the officers in the reorganized Seventh Cavalry were young like Scott. They had had little opportunity for advancement resulting from retirement within their regiment, given the static growth of the army prior to the war with Spain. The regimental rule, during the time period of its imposition, froze their service grade ranking. Had Scott been awarded a star rank in the regular army in 1908, it would have been granted over the heads of 201 other officers![5]

Scott appealed to influential friends whom he hoped could get him a star and thereby circumvent the issue of his limited tenure, but to no avail. However, although Roosevelt had agreed not to recommend a candidate to the Senate for a star promotion below the rank of colonel, he might once again be receptive to the idea if he knew *in advance* that the Senate Committee on Military Affairs would approve such a request. With little else to go on, Scott seemingly had nothing to lose. Initially he could draw on acquaintances and friends he had met at West Point as a cadet, at posts in the Dakota Territory such as Forts Abraham Lincoln and Totten, as well as at Fort Sill in the Oklahoma Territory. As administrator for the settlement of the Chiricahua Apaches, Scott had had contact with a broad range of personnel, such as contractors for post services, government staff at all levels in the Bureau of Indian Affairs, officials in the War Department, and, perhaps most significantly, members of Congress, whom he relied on to fund resettlement programs. Although his work in Cuba and the Philippines may have limited his sphere of influence since he was not stateside, Mary proved to be an invaluable advocate in furthering her husband's career. Moreover, serving under Wood's command brought his credentials to the attention of the commander in chief. The West Point position, with its administrative and social responsibilities to the army, Congress, and the general public, availed Scott of many opportunities to expand his contacts even further. On an administrative level, his position necessitated direct contact with members of Congress annually if not more frequently. Funding requests for specific projects gave him the chance to interact with numerous congressmen on committees and subcommittees beyond the realm of strictly military affairs. And constituent service extended to informing members of Congress where their sons or those of their constituents stood in terms of admission to West Point. On a social level and with broader implications, he extended invitations to congressmen and their friends to visit West Point and provided associates with tickets to the annual Army–Navy football game. Similarly, during his tenure as superintendent, Scott had the opportunity to join several prestigious civic clubs, thereby loaning his stature as West Point superintendent to their enrollment list, while giving Scott an even broader group of influential people to draw upon in his campaign for career advancement.[6]

The next step was to recruit willing individuals who could formulate a strategy to pressure senators within and beyond the Senate Committee on Military Affairs. Senators Francis E. Warren (Wyo.) and Nathan B. Scott (W.Va.) were both staunch supporters of Scott and members of the Senate committee, with Warren as its chair. Wood was still on the scene assisting Scott and endorsing his promotion. Whether they could sway the committee was doubtful, however, owing to the political risks that both Roosevelt and committee members were faced with in making merit-based promotions. Nonetheless, other old-time acquaintances from his days at Fort Totten now willingly stepped forward, coordinating and broadening his base of support to pressure the committee. John F. McGee and Charles E. Rushmore had settled in the Dakota Territory early in their careers, not far from Devil's Lake, where Scott was stationed in the 1880s. Both had made their fortunes and reputations in commerce or law and were individuals of some renown with many influential friends who were, or knew, members of Congress. McGee was an attorney and a district judge before returning to private practice at the time that he assisted Scott. Rushmore was an easterner by birth but had journeyed west to the Black Hills to assist a client in a mining claim. By 1908, both McGee and Rushmore had successful, lucrative law practices, McGee in Minneapolis and Rushmore on Wall Street. McGee sent letters not only to senators on the military affairs committee but also to others in Congress who knew them and believed that they could exert some influence. The letters were well structured, noting McGee's or the subject's relationship to the senator, how McGee knew Scott, and germane knowledge about Scott's background, ostensibly to justify why Scott deserved a star promotion. The letters were also personalized through the recollection of experiences, as well as relationships, that they hoped would flatter the recipients.[7]

It appeared at first that all was for naught, at least for the immediate future. Three Democratic members of the Senate committee were said to be committed to Scott's endorsement. When they joined the five Republican senators, they made a majority, but few were prepared to state so publicly. And Roosevelt was skeptical that the committee would endorse such a recommendation. The political stakes were high for both the president and the committee members.[8]

In March, Scott was ordered to relinquish his command as superintendent of West Point by the end of the following August. He could point with pride to what he had accomplished there: above all, he had procured almost $2 million for West Point through his contacts with congressmen, while maintaining cordial relations with all the bureau chiefs as well as the secretary of war. His vocational options now included rejoining his regiment in the Philippines or, if requested by Wood, serving as the general's military secretary in Washington. Scott preferred the latter. A Philippine detail with the Fourteenth Cavalry at his present rank of colonel (vols.) he believed would be "practical oblivion," ending the possibility of advancement in his military career. A Washington posting would once again give him geographic and political access to the levers of power in the War Department and in Congress. Wood, as usual, was more than willing to help, assigning him to the general staff in Washington after a three-month leave. Scott was to serve directly under Wood when the latter was appointed as chief of staff in April 1910.[9]

Despite being close to Mary in Washington during his leave of absence in the fall of 1910, Scott felt that he was merely marking time, discouraged over what he felt was a posting that would lead to little or no significant opportunity for promotion. However, Scott's fortunes changed with the new year. A military appropriations measure passed both the House and Senate before Congress adjourned in March, increasing the size of the officer corps and leading, in order of seniority, to elevations in rank for Scott, among others. He only received a lieutenant colonelcy—not the full colonelcy that he hoped for—but he was high on the seniority list. Additionally, a new posting held out the chance for a star by broadening his credentials.

An ongoing civil war in Mexico among rival factions vying for power threatened to spread over the border into the United States, creating fear and anxiety among residents in Arizona, New Mexico, and Texas, with the potential threat that the United States could be drawn into a conflict with Mexico. Scott was sent to command the Third Cavalry at Fort Sam Houston in Texas in the spring of 1911 in order to address these concerns.

It was here that Scott undertook perhaps his most unique and challenging task as a peacemaker. At the time of his initial posting in the Southwest, Porfirio Díaz, Mexico's long-serving dictator, was forced to abdicate his office, resulting in a contentious factional civil war south of the border. In March 1911, President Taft ordered 30,000 troops to the border to protect the 40,000 Americans then living in Mexico and to safeguard America's extensive mining interests, especially in the northern Mexican states of Chihuahua, Sonora, and Durango. The numerous armed factions, none of whom controlled the entire country, splintered and reformed as circumstances dictated, following the overthrow and execution of Díaz's successor, Francisco Madero, in February 1913. Unlike other contentious situations that Scott encountered in his career involving America's military penetration of lands claimed by indigenous peoples, this one involved the possibility of confrontations *on American soil* from opposing factions of armed Mexican forces. Among the more prominent factions vying for power were followers of Gen. Victoriano Huerta, a discredited militarist; Venustiano Carranza, leader of the Constitutionalist movement; Álvaro Obregón, governor of Sonora Province; and the flamboyant Gen. Francisco "Pancho" Villa.[10]

As he had in prior negotiations, Scott sought out leaders of factions with whom he could work to promote stability. He had established a good relationship with Obregón when Scott was initially sent to San Antonio, Texas, with the Third Cavalry in 1911, but it was Villa to whom Scott was ultimately attracted for both strategic and personal reasons. In Scott's negotiating strategy, Villa would serve a role like that of I-See-O from the Kiowa tribe or Raja Muda of the Moros, namely, as a leader of an indigenous people who could be befriended in order to gain a better understanding of the local cultural and political dynamics.

The Scott–Villa relationship was mutually beneficial. Villa's growing military power from 1914 to 1915, particularly in the northern provinces of Sonora and Chihuahua, where most American interests were located, enhanced his prestige and logistic importance to Scott, as commander on the southern border. Moreover, Villa, at least verbally, had relinquished any desire to assume the presidency of Mexico, implying that Mexico's next leader should be democratically elected. Such a view was attractive to Scott, whose objective for peace on the border was premised on the establishment of representative government in Mexico. And given the image in the minds of most Mexicans—that their neighbor to the north had always harbored a desire to aggrandize their territory—Villa proudly proclaimed his affinity and respect for the United States and its interests.

Villa in turn viewed Scott as a vital conduit in Villa's relationship with officials in Washington, given Scott's military authority on the border and his apparent influence with congressmen and those in the executive branch. Scott's importance to Villa took on an added dimension when Scott was given an enhanced command for maintaining border security from Texas to California in March 1913. Politically, Villa believed that he could drive a wedge between Carranza supporters in the United States and his own followers. So, too, the size and geographic location of his force would guarantee him an ongoing supply of the arms and coal that he needed from American suppliers, both north and south of the border. Both men shared a desire for frankness in their discourse and shared respect for the other's talent for strategic military command.

On a more personal level, befriending Villa gave Scott some sense of security regarding the safety of his son Merrill, who was employed as a mining engineer for an American firm in northern Mexico, where Villa's forces were in command. In addition, although difficult to calculate, Scott may have been attracted by the general's ability to orchestrate himself as a social reformer and "man of the people." For example, Villa always had a group of loyal

American reporters with him to enhance his image in the U.S. press. While Scott considered Villa as inferior, given Scott's perception of race, it appears he may have felt flattered by the attention that Villa paid him.[11]

Scott used his strategic position with Villa to send reports of ongoing activities in the civil war to the secretaries of war and state. Nonetheless, despite their high regard for one another, diplomatic success between them proved elusive, owing ultimately to the instability of Villa's forces. Scott and Villa met personally on several occasions to address issues of concern to the United States. One involved an ongoing danger to U.S. citizens because of conflict between rival Mexican factions in the border town of Naco, Sonora. In the summer of 1914, a military struggle occurred between two opposing groups, one quartered at a garrison in this northern Mexican town, led by supporters of Venustiano Carranza; the other, which sought to displace them, being followers of Villa. As an example of the political instability that existed in Mexico at the time, both forces had been allied in the past but were now bitter enemies. Gen. Jose Maytorena led the offensive force of *Villistas*, as supporters of Villa were known, against the garrison. Indiscriminate gunfire across the border into Naco, Arizona, killed four Americans and wounded twenty. Scott was ordered to the border to negotiate an agreement with Villa for the mutual withdrawal of forces from the town. Although Villa was reluctant to do so, given Maytorena's military advantage, he did not wish to alienate what support he had among American authorities. The plan brought peace to the region for six months. However, the Scott–Villa relationship was not a viable instrument to achieve permanent border security.[12]

Scott's efforts to bring a permanent peace to the border was initially contingent on Villa's ability to maintain the level of strength that he had enjoyed at the time of his capture of Juárez and the entire province of Chihuahua in January 1914. Unfortunately, his forces had been greatly reduced as a consequence of the warfare occurring south of the border by the late spring of 1915. By that time, the Villistas were desperate enough to undertake what amounted to an act of extortion against American mine owners in northern Mexico. Villa needed coal for his troops and cash to pay in advance for arms from Texas merchants. Consequently, he called representatives from the American mining companies to meet with him and demanded they provide him with a $300,000 loan. Once again, Scott was summoned to the border

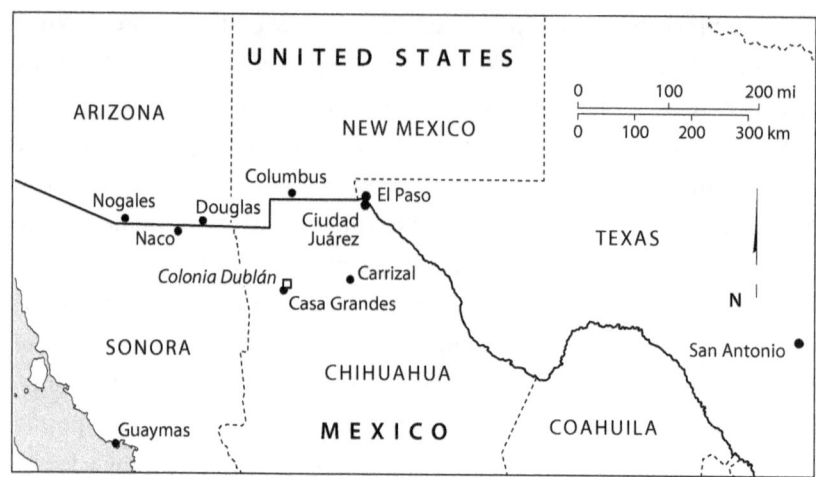

Places in Mexico that Pancho Villa visited or occupied during the Border War, 1914–1916. Reproduced from Katharine Bjork, *Prairie Imperialists: The Indian Country Origins of American Empire* (2018), 204. Reprinted with permission of the University of Pennsylvania Press.

by officials in Washington that summer to secure the safety of U.S. interests. Scott succeeded in negotiating a compromise, whereby Villa would receive a voluntary gift of 100,000 tons of coal from the mine owners in lieu of the mandatory loan. Presumably, he could sell at least some of the coal to raise cash for the armaments he needed. Scott was praised for his negotiation skills in maintaining peace at the border, but the notoriety was temporary. Whatever efforts he could undertake, ultimately decisions were in the hands of the prominent leaders of the Mexican Revolution, and they rejected Scott's efforts to establish a coalition government that would include Villa.[13]

As previously noted, one of the characteristics that Scott consistently manifested throughout his life was his unswerving sense of loyalty to those who assisted him, either directly or indirectly, in his negotiations as a peacemaker or as his advocacy on behalf of indigenous peoples. For example, he campaigned successfully for a pension for I-See-O as an Indian scout in his retirement years and extended to Sultan Raja Muda official recognition of his status when he visited Washington. So, too, Scott demonstrated his loyalty to Villa by denying, for example, the general's complicity in a raid by Villistas in March 1916 over the border into Columbus, New Mexico, that left twenty-four

Americans dead, including nine soldiers and fifteen civilians. Going further, in 1920, Scott sent a note to the secretary of war requesting, unsuccessfully, that Villa be granted political asylum and exile in the United States.[14]

Scott's assignment to the general staff in Washington was not only interrupted by his assignment to the border. On several occasions during this period, he was granted leave to deal with disturbances among the Hopi Indians in the Southwest and, as previously noted, with the resettlement of the Chiricahua Apaches from what was to be their permanent home at Fort Sill. Although, as with his previous pacification assignments, none would add substantial value to his credentials for professional advancement, his regimental command of the Second Cavalry at El Paso under orders from Wood, positioned him in a venue that could lead to a star promotion. Geographically, Scott's command included all American troops stationed on the border from Texas to California. And, as he anticipated, Scott was promoted to the rank of a full colonel in August 1911, following the retirement of several senior officers. Scott served in that posting till April 1914. Then, as he had done so many times before, Wood intended to reward the loyalty Scott had given to his commander. However, ongoing contentiousness among senior officers over the restructuring of the military to address the issue of planning, coupled with Wood's uncompromising stand in asserting the prerogatives of a strong general staff, led ultimately to the dissolution of the Wood and Scott's relationship.[15]

Scott was appointed as assistant chief of staff briefly under retiring Gen. William Wotherspoon in April 1914. Wotherspoon had replaced Wood after the latter's four-year term, and Scott followed as chief of staff from November of that year through his formal retirement from military service in September 1917. Many contemporaries were critical of his tenure as chief of staff. William Howard Taft, who knew of Scott's work when Taft was chair of the Philippine Commission and then secretary of war, derided him thus: "as Chief of Staff he is wood in the middle of his head."[16] Lt. Col. Payton C. March, who succeeded Scott in the post following Tasker Bliss's brief term, characterized him as a man who "was over the hill" and "deaf," saying that Scott "preferred to talk in grunts . . . and . . . went to sleep in his chair while transacting official business." The most devastating critique came later from Wood himself, who described Scott as "dull and stupid"; in addition, Wood criticized Scott for having "dropped off about eighty percent in efficiency since he was with me in Cuba," and for being "far from what I had hoped he would be" as army chief of staff.[17]

These criticisms need to be placed in a broader context. Whatever virtues or detriments Scott possessed as the army's chief of staff, his tenure occurred during a transitional period of ongoing military reform that involved the evolution to a general staff structure as a cohesive planning component in the War Department. The Spanish-American War underscored, among other problems, the challenges of mobilizing an overseas army, but the solution seemed elusive. Service bureaus—specialized agencies and departments within the military structure—had evolved over time to fulfill specific functions deemed essential for the army's successful role in the conduct of military affairs. While the Adjutant-General's Office was one of the first, organized within the Continental Army under George Washington, others were established throughout the nineteenth century, to meet the challenges of national defense, military occupation, internal discord, and the settlement of the frontier. The Office of the Adjutant-General was initially charged with keeping military records of recruitment of troops, among other tasks. The Quartermaster's Corps had the responsibility for transport and supply; the Army Corps of Engineers, maintenance of port facilities and waterways; the Ordnance Department, production of weaponry; and the Office of the Surgeon General, the health of military personnel. The service bureaus were entities unto themselves. Bureau chiefs and staff officers often enjoyed the prerogatives of a protracted tenure and promotional advantages within their departments because of the seniority rule. Being in Washington gave them opportunities to form unique relationships with members of congressional committees charged with the financial oversight of the army and of military affairs in general. One of the most powerful bureaus that benefited from the relationship was the Office of Adjutant General, which through its Records and Pensions Division held influence in Congress. Constituents petitioned their congressmen for tenure records to substantiate or enhance their military service pensions. Consequently, both bureau chiefs and senior congressmen enjoyed long-standing relationships, with all the influence that such a mutual association provided.[18]

Secretary of War Elihu Root sought to rectify some of the problems in military administration with the Army Reorganization Act of 1901. The multipurpose measure included a provision to increase the size of the army to meet the unanticipated military challenge of Philippine insurrectionists following the war with Spain. Another sought to address the disparity between line and staff positions in the officer corps by requiring a rotation of officers between the two components. A more sweeping and controversial measure in 1903, known as the Organic Act, promulgated the creation of a general staff. As originally constituted, the general staff consisted of forty-six members to provide for professional military education and training through the Army War College and, concurrently, to serve as a planning body for the army. A chief of staff replaced the independent general of the army. In this new position, he would seek the advice of the general staff and bureau chiefs on policy matters and report directly to, and act under the authority of, the secretary of war. The chief of staff could serve up to four years, but his service tenure was at the discretion of the commander in chief and secretary of war.[19]

Neither reform initially altered the bureaus' authority nor their autonomy within the War Department and vis-à-vis Congress. The Army Reorganization Act of 1901 exempted certain technical bureaus from the line-staff rotation and grandfathered in all current staff officers with the seniority rule, to assure them professional advancement. Moreover, the creation of a general staff, far from mitigating the bureaus' power, underscored the contentiousness between military reformers and the more traditional officers, many of whom were Civil War veterans whose subsequent careers were mostly in frontier service, and had now reached senior command. The Organic Act created an administrative body whose charge was vague and precarious in undertaking strategic planning. Officers appointed to it in the early years had little understanding of what it meant. Moreover, the relationship between the general staff with its chief, on the one hand, and the bureaus that reported to the secretary of war, on the other, was never clearly defined, perhaps owing to the contentiousness that greeted the measure to begin with. Both weaknesses worked to the disadvantage of the general staff while affirming the authority of the bureaus. Specifically, while officers under the command of the chief of staff would rotate on a regular basis, bureau personnel were initially grandfathered into their lines. And although general staff officers did not have a clear idea of their function in strategic planning, bureau personnel had years of experience and a cultural history that defined their specific function. The administrative relationship between the bureaus, the general staff with its chief, and the secretary of war created a bigger problem. Many reformers believed that the chief of staff should be the *only* officer in the military hierarchy to advise the secretary of war, making the bureau chiefs subservient to him. Bureau chiefs were not about to accept the loss of their direct access to the secretary of war. Moreover, none of the three senior officers who served as chiefs in the first three years after creation of the general staff established a precedent that potentially could have strengthened it in its contention with the bureaus.[20]

Such was Scott's challenge when he assumed the office. Compounding his problems, Scott faced congressional acrimony engendered by Leonard Wood, when he was chief of staff, in dealing with a particularly recalcitrant bureau chief. Maj. Gen. Fred C. Ainsworth's career as adjutant general began when he turned the War Department's dysfunctional Records and Pensions Division into a model of efficiency, eventually acquiring greater authority in the War Department commensurate with his increasing responsibilities. To his supporters, both staff officers and congressmen, Ainsworth was a valuable political asset as the most powerful bureau chief. To military reformers, he was one of the greatest obstacles to change needed in the administration of the army. In late December, Wood issued a directive mandating that all communications emanating from the War Department be issued through the chief of staff's office. The directive was preceded by an order from President Taft prohibiting any contact between bureau chiefs and members of Congress. Ainsworth's reaction to Wood's challenge to his authority placed the adjutant general in a compromising position, saying things in a letter that he later regretted. His provocative words led to an early and unwanted retirement when faced with the possibility of a court-martial for insubordination. Unfortunately for Wood, and ultimately Scott by association, Ainsworth would not go away quietly. His allies in Congress, of which there were many, took revenge on Wood through an army appropriation bill in 1912. When enacted, the measure limited the size of the general staff as well as the period that officers could serve on it before they had to return to their regiments, restricting its ability to carry out its original function. A clause in the original bill would also have removed Wood as chief of staff. However, Root came to Wood's defense, as he and Roosevelt had done so many times before, in pressuring Congress at least to delete the noxious provision. Nor did Wood's assault on the bureaus end there. Throughout his term as chief of staff, Wood took every opportunity to demonstrate how and why the structure of the bureaus in the War Department thwarted needed military reform. In 1914, when he assumed command, Scott bore the brunt of both the general staff's ongoing weakness in dealing with the bureaus and the animosity of Congress resulting from Wood's treatment of Ainsworth.[21]

Nonetheless, Scott had three advantages in his favor. The first was the general respect he had earned among the senior military staff for his honesty and integrity. Many might differ with his views or his approach to situations, but few questioned his motives. The second was his reputation as a peacemaker in seeking reconciliation with dissident groups among and between indigenous peoples, both on the western frontier of the United States and in the southern region of the Philippines. The third was his long experience in dealing with the legislative process, including his advocacy for the Fort Sill Apaches under his supervision, the favorable publicity that he sought for the Academy from Congress when he was superintendent, and the influential relationships that he engendered in seeking promotion in rank.

Scott was aware of the importance of the general staff and the chief of staff in promoting military reform without Wood's prodding. However, unlike Wood's frontal attack on the authority of the bureaus in the administration of the War Department, Scott took a slightly different tack. While the National Defense Act of 1916 increased the size of the army over five years, a provision in the measure submitted by Ainsworth's congressional friends all but emasculated the authority of the general staff. The measure reduced it to nineteen officers and limited its work only to military planning. Scott strongly contested the opinion of Gen. Enoch Crowder, judge advocate general of the army, who supported the measure's limits on the general staff. In a spirited and detailed defense of the staff's authority and that of its chief, Scott addressed the intent of the original Organic Act. He noted that while the general staff as a body was restricted in its supervisory duties in relation to those of the bureaus, the chief of staff, as a representative of the secretary of war, had administrative and supervisory authority over the bureaus and departments. Consequently, the chief had the prerogative in his own right to solicit information from the bureaus and review their annual reports before he sent them to the secretary of war.[22]

While he was assertive in promulgating the authority of the chief of staff, he was more conciliatory and deferential to the bureaus and corps in the War Department with respect to the general staff. Unlike Wood, he solicited the views of bureau chiefs as to whether they believed the general staff had infringed upon their administrative prerogatives. Few saw it as an issue, but the fact that he raised the question reveals an attitude different from that of Wood. Ever the conciliator, Scott might well have believed, as he had with dissident tribes on the Great Plains and the Moro datos in the Philippines, that "talking it out" would placate much of the anger and frustration that opposing groups felt toward him or toward their perceived enemies. His unique military career as a negotiator enabled him to search for common ground between those advocating the line and those touting the staff perspective in military organization. So, too, his frontier experience may have made him somewhat sympathetic to staff officers, having served as an acting assistant quartermaster at both Forts Totten (1880–81) and Sill (1890–91) and as a judge advocate at Fort Meade (1883).[23]

One of the most important advantages that Scott brought to the job was influence. As circumstances turned out, when Woodrow Wilson assumed the presidency in March 1913, military affairs took on a different meaning from that of the administrations of Roosevelt and Taft. Wilson "had no interest in military and naval strategy, little understanding of the role that *force* plays in relations of great powers and a near contempt for Realpolitik and the men who made it." The militaristic attitude of Leonard Wood can best be summarized by his description of those who opposed his preparedness campaign. Wood characterized them as "emasculated white rabbit type[s] trying to shape a policy which means the prostitution of the country's best interests on the altar of personal timidity and reluctance to play a man's part." Theodore Roosevelt, with his typical overt bellicosity, also was especially noxious to the new president. Scott was perhaps the most amicable senior military officer that Wilson could tolerate; the president shared with him the idea that overt force should be used only as a last resort. On a more personal level, Wilson had befriended Scott's younger brother, William, who was a professor of paleontology at Princeton University, when Wilson had served as its president, prior to his term as governor of New Jersey. In 1910, Scott was awarded an honorary doctor of laws degree from Princeton and presumably had the opportunity to meet Wilson if they were not previously acquainted. The commonality of thought on the use of military force, and the familial relationship, gave Scott unprecedented access to the White House, certainly as much as he had enjoyed during the Theodore Roosevelt administration. And equally significant, Scott was rewarded with a brigadier generalship by his new commander in chief within a month of Wilson's assuming the presidency in 1913. Moreover, Scott's professional position in the War Department was enhanced with the appointment of Newton D. Baker, formerly mayor of Cleveland, as the secretary of war in March 1916. Both men shared an ideological affinity with Wilson on the limitations of overt warfare. Baker's respect for Scott's honesty and integrity further strengthened their relationship. Equally important, Baker's exceedingly deferential attitude toward Scott bordered on veneration, given Scott's age, his army service, and the paucity of Baker's military experience. Ultimately, after reviewing Scott's defense of the powers of the chief of staff, Baker accepted his interpretation of the National Defense Act over that of Crowder.[24]

Scott's tenure as chief of staff led to an irreparable break in his relationship with Wood. Given Wood's controlling and acerbic personality and Scott's aversion to desk work and tendency to resort to diplomacy when confronted with a contentious situation, a falling out between the two was perhaps inevitable. Wood frequently micromanaged Scott's administration throughout his entire term as chief of staff. Some interventions included unsolicited advice on military contracts, the assignment of personnel, and relations with any organization opposed to Wood's army preparedness campaign for a potential European war. Wood also felt the need to remind Scott often about the importance of maintaining the size and focus of the general staff and its authority over the bureaus in the War Department. The irony of this is that if it were not for Scott's effort, his mentor would not have enjoyed a four-year term as chief of staff. Wilson had no love for Wood and was prepared to end his tenure when he took office in March 1913. Scott had used his influence with Wilson to prevent that from happening.[25]

On a substantive level, and in addressing his preparedness campaign, both contemporaries and historians generally credit Scott with advancing the initiative of conscription as a method to mobilize forces in preparation for the possibility of a war. In a report to the secretary of war in 1916, he advised:

> In my judgment, the country will never be prepared for defense until we do as other great nations do that have large interests to guard... where everybody is ready and does perform military service in time of peace as he would pay every other tax and is willing to make sacrifices for the protection he gets in return. The volunteer system in this country, in view of the highly organized, trained, and disciplined armies that our possible opponents possess, should be relegated to the past.[26]

Scott had good reason to denigrate the efficacy of a volunteer state militia in a battlefield setting, an opinion shared by many officers in the regular army at the time. His experience with the training camps in Georgia and Kentucky during the Spanish-American War era, as well as the paucity of volunteer enlistments during the more recent Mexican border campaign, gave him little hope that such a force could even serve as a second line of defense in a national emergency. Training these would-be soldiers in discipline and basic tactics was perhaps one of the most frustrating experiences in his military career. And although adept at playing a political role with state governors in order to enhance his own career, he recognized that the claims of preparation by these state officials who directed their militia units were often dubious at best. Moreover, in asserting the primacy of conscription, Scott initially had to contend with the most powerful bureau chief, and in some ways the most obstructionist, since Ainsworth: Enoch Crowder. Crowder was initially opposed to conscription, but Baker's influence and the erosion of diplomatic relations between the United States and Germany pushed the Wilson administration to consider the draft.[27]

Scott saw other virtues in the utilization of a national draft beyond its use in a European war. He believed that conscription was a necessary commitment for any military confrontation that the nation would face. But it was more than that. It imposed on the citizenry a recognition and an obligation: a recognition that the freedoms Americans enjoyed were not free; and an obligation and responsibility on the part of each male citizen to protect those freedoms. And given America's new role in the emerging world order, Scott believed that the recognition and obligation extended beyond America's shores "as the exponents of democracy that should regenerate the political systems of the world." To him, this obligation assumed that the draftee would have undergone universal military training, whether war was imminent or not. Such a regimen was significant in its own right. He believed that adolescent males and those in their early twenties lacking vocational focus could best deal with a disruption to take time for military training. The rigor, Scott believed, would build character through the "stabilizing effect of military discipline . . . (and) would become an asset of incalculable value to the nation, not only in time of emergency but in the recruitment to industrial life." Returning to his theme of universal public service, the military experience would "inspire them with the spirit of patriotism and sense of duty and responsibility with which each generation must be imbued if we are to continue our high mission as a nation."[28]

His success in imposing conscription, if not universal military training, was only one major decision that most historians credit Scott with in his role as chief of staff. Another was the recommendation of Maj. Gen. John J. Pershing to lead the American Expeditionary Force in assisting Great Britain and France in defeating Germany and the Central Powers. Pershing was a logical choice for Scott. The two men had interacted when both were stationed in the southern Philippines—Scott in Sulu, and Pershing in the Lake Lanao District to the east on the mainland of Mindanao. Both employed pacification first, rather than overt force, in dealing with dissident Moros. Pershing followed Wood as governor of Moro Province and, ultimately, as commander of the Philippines Division. Scott and Pershing came into contact again when both were dealing with the possible ramifications of the Mexican civil war, initially at El Paso, Texas. During Scott's tenure as chief of staff, Pershing was placed in command of U.S. forces in the Mexican Punitive Expedition. Baker supported Scott's recommendation with Wilson's approval and gave Pershing broad authority in his conduct over American troops, evidence of the high esteem in which Scott held both the secretary of war and the president.

Scott's endorsement of Pershing's military command was yet another reason for the dissolution of the relationship between Wood and Scott. Pershing's selection was a bitter blow to Wood, creator of the preparedness movement and the Plattsburg training camps. Henceforth, Wood looked upon Scott with scorn and feelings of anger and ingratitude, having used his influence to advance Scott professionally throughout his career and to address his many personal concerns. The adjutant general directed both senior officers, along with the commanding generals of each National Guard division, to tour Allied headquarters in Europe as well as the battlefields in France. This was to allow them to gain a better understanding of the training regime needed in the camps they would shortly command when they returned to the States. The two never traveled or worked together again.[29]

Although he officially retired from the army at the mandatory age of sixty-four in September 1917, Scott's last posting in military service began in January 1918, when he was in command of the Seventy-Eighth Division at Camp Dix, New Jersey, in one of the many hastily constructed containment camps for training troops to be sent to Europe. Established in July 1917, pursuant to the National Defense Act of 1916, the camp had some of the unpleasant conditions that Scott had encountered at the training facility in Chickamauga Park, Georgia, during the Spanish-American War. Both camps, hastily constructed without much thought to inclement weather, incurred major challenges from disease. Although the New Jersey encampment had barracks of wood with floors, while the Georgia camp had tents with no undercover to house the recruits properly, the uninsulated and inadequately heated dwellings undoubtedly proved equally uncomfortable to the recruits that were cycled through the camp. Illnesses like pneumonia and influenza were increasingly rampant. Although, unlike Chickamauga, Dix had had a hospital from the beginning, sanitary conditions there were deplorable. As a result of latent planning for mobilization, the regular army had confronted a shortage of trained military officers. Compounding the problem was what Scott regarded as the limited time allowed for the training of recruits before their embarkation to the battlefields of Europe. Nonetheless, Scott was well treated and respected by the officers and recruits under his command. Perhaps most significantly, the camp's location gave him proximity to Mary and their numerous relatives and friends, and now with the use of a telephone as an instant means of communication![30]

Scott served his command at Camp Dix through May 1919 and was awarded a Distinguished Service Medal upon his "unofficial retirement," for his work as chief of staff in "advocating and persistently urging the adoption of the selective service law" as well as for his efforts as commander at Camp Dix "in organizing and training the divisions and miscellaneous troops committed to his care." The final year at Dix was bittersweet. The Scotts purchased and renovated a farmhouse in Kingston, New Jersey, not far from their many relatives and friends in Princeton. Like many families then as now, Scott had a yearning to live with his family as a gentleman farmer. The farm would be their first permanent home beyond the constraints of military service. Despite his initial desire to raise pigs, he possessed little in the way of knowledge of the care and feeding required.[31]

Nonetheless, in his final months at Camp Dix, tragedy struck the Scotts. When he toured the European front in the fall of 1917, Scott took pride in the fact that three of his five children were overseas contributing to the effort to defeat Germany. Blanchard was a nurse in the Red Cross at the French front; Merrill, or Pudd, as he was called, was a machine-gun instructor at Langes; and Hunter, Scott's oldest son, served in battles at Château-Thierry, Soissons, and the Argonne, remaining in France after the armistice was signed in November 1918. Scott enjoyed visiting with them, touring the Verdun battlefield with Hunter, and especially delighted in how his eldest son, the source of much stress and anguish for his parents in reaching adulthood, had "the right spirit and (was) making of himself a fine soldier." Little did he know that Hunter would soon be lost, not in battle as a casualty of war, but as a victim of the rampant influenza pandemic devastating Europe and the United States. Evidently, he had become ill on the transport ship taking him home in March 1919. His condition worsened as he reached New York, so much so that he was immediately transferred to a hospital when the ship landed. Hunter was conscious when his family was at his bedside, then died shortly thereafter. Aside from his parents, and siblings, he was survived by his wife and their son.[32]

Although he could not know it at the time of his military retirement, Scott was about to embark on an active and challenging career. He would be doing what he enjoyed best: advocating on behalf of tribal groups; returning to his research on American Indian culture, including use of the sign language among western tribes; and enjoying the adulation of a nation that venerated his courage and conviction in a generation looking for its roots as a nation in the glorification of the frontier experience.

CHAPTER 6

▼ ▼ ▼

A FULL AND ENRICHED RETIREMENT

Tribal Groups First and Foremost

I am afraid I am going to mind it like the devil. It is not so much the actual retirement as the cessation of ambition. I feel just as young and able as I was fifteen years ago, and will not want to go on the shelf.

—*Scott to H. J. Slocum, March 12, 1917*

If such were Scott's feelings in 1917, he had nothing to worry about. Far from going "on the shelf," Scott would be blessed with a relatively long, active, and productive retirement. From the time of his official mandatory detachment from military service in 1917 to almost the end of his life in 1934, Scott engaged in years of advocating for American Indians on the Board of Indian Commissioners and pursued scholarly endeavors on the origins and application of cultural symbols of North America's indigenous peoples to enhance the use of the Indian sign language. He also invoked and cultivated a nostalgic image of Indians as part of a nineteenth-century adventurous American frontier heritage, to a nation confronting overseas challenges in the early twentieth century. His many years in military service, involving intimate contact with tribal groups, provided a foundation in cultural understanding that served him well in his retirement.

When Edward Ayer, director of the Field Museum in Chicago and an old friend of Scott's, wrote him about an appointment to the Board of Indian Commissioners in November 1918, Scott immediately accepted the offer. Scott's nomination had the board's and the interior secretary's full support. In joining the board, Scott associated with a distinguished group of reformers from a broad spectrum of American society, including the press, clergy, cultural affairs, education, law, the arts, and politics. Among the more regular members he would interact with in his tenure were George Vaux Jr., a Philadelphia attorney and board chair till his death in 1927; Samuel Eliot, D.D., a prominent Unitarian minister and board chair from 1928 until the board's termination; Malcolm McDowell, a journalist with the Chicago Daily News, who served as board secretary during Scott's tenure; and Warren K. Morehead, a curator of anthropology at Phillips-Andover Academy. Flora Warren Seymour, a Chicago attorney and author of works on historical subjects relating to American Indians, was an active ally of Scott on the board.

The board was organized in 1869 under the Grant administration as part of his "peace policy" for dealing with tribes, and in response to the extensive corruption in the federal administration of Indian affairs. From its origins, board members were prominent individuals from the professions. Aside from travel expenses, members received no compensation for their service. In the first letter of what would be voluminous correspondence between the board's secretary and Scott, McDowell outlined its functions and responsibilities: "We take up the larger problems affecting Indians, such as health, morals, education, progress, industries, material and social development, tribal affairs, farming, stock raising, forestry, the relations of Indians to their white neighbors, the exploitation of Indians by white men, and the relation of the Indians to the states and nation." The board implemented this solemn responsibility of federal guardianship or wardship to tribal groups through annual visits of its members to reservations as far west as California. Subsequent reports on these visits were then submitted to the secretary of the interior. McDowell noted that although the board often took matters up with the commissioner of Indian affairs, "he has no control over us in any way; the Secretary of Interior is our door to the President, Congress and the Department."[1]

Scott believed in the board's mission that the administration of tribal groups was a federal responsibility. He also regarded federal wardship as a solemn trust. He had zealously guarded the interests of his Chiricahua Apache charges at Fort Sill from white ranchers who aimed to steal their cattle and aggrandize the lands that they occupied, and he protected them from traders who sought to exploit them through commercial transactions. He was always solicitous of congressmen and other government officials who could safeguard the interests of Native peoples, and in reaching the goal of being economically self-sustaining. And early in his career, when he acquired an understanding of how the Bureau of Indian Affairs functioned, he was equally critical of those administrators whom he believed lacked the experience to know, or the interest to understand, what he believed to be best for tribal groups.

To Scott and most Friends of the Indian, federal wardship implied a view that defined Christianity and civilization as synonymous. Consequently, he shared the biases of many of his denominational Presbyterians and other Christians in their view of tribal groups. He believed, as did they, that Indians possessed a primitive culture, and that by embracing assimilation, they could advance to a state of sophistication equal to the level of their Euro-American neighbors. Moreover, federal wardship was not simply ethnocentric; it was paternalistic as well. Scott shared the view of most Indian reformers that they had a moral obligation to lead tribal groups on what they believed to be the path to civilization.[2]

Where reformers differed—and the differences were profound—was in the interpretation of salvation. Orthodox Christians considered tribal groups as the epitome of a lost people. The doctrine of original sin and the Gospel mandated that tribes repudiate their "primitiveness" before they could "journey" on the "road" to salvation. There was no middle ground. To remain in their present state of "sin" was to regress down the road to hell. Tribal chiefs who were "unrepentant sinners," according to these more orthodox Christians, undermined their followers' chances of salvation. They saw the spiritual world in absolute terms. Although Scott was generally skeptical of this view of man's relationship with God, his widowed mother embraced the orthodoxy, as a devout Presbyterian and the daughter of the Reverend Charles Hodge, one of the most renowned theologians of the nineteenth century. She repeatedly chastised her son for his skepticism regarding his salvation, warning him that repentance was essential and his time on Earth to do so was finite.[3]

Consequently, both had a different view of the efficacy of tribal cultures. To more-orthodox Presbyterians, tribal cultures had no redeeming value whatsoever. Scott's view was both more nuanced and complex as well as more tolerant and pragmatic. Unlike his coreligionists, he treated the distinctive ways in which Native peoples organized their lives, and defined themselves and the world around them, with both reverence and respect. And he was critical of more-orthodox Christians who denied them any cause for cultural pride. For Scott,

> one of the greatest mistakes made by our missionaries in our Indian country is their opposition to everything native—the notion that everything peculiar to the Indian must be broken down and destroyed, and their pride in the achievements of their ancestors must be preached against, derided, and wiped out. . . . It is not possible to raise up any people who are destitute of pride; and pride once lost is one of the things most difficult to restore; it lies at the root of all formation of character; its possession is a priceless gift; and no effort should be spared to save it.[4]

As a youth, he emulated those who could test their endurance and master an adaptation to the natural world. Consequently, Scott could embrace, both intellectually and emotionally, indigenous peoples who attained a similar goal in their lives. He gained such an understanding as a result of his fluidity with the Indian sign language and used it most effectively in a critical and turbulent period in Euro-American and tribal relations.

However, while he believed that their culture should be a legitimate source of pride to them, he did not believe that it could sustain them amid the dramatic changes in their physical environment brought about by Euro-American incursions on their lifestyle. His solution was to prepare them, with empathy and understanding, for the tangible rewards of what he defined as civilization: an economic system that gave every individual American Indian family an irrevocable tract of land for farming or ranching. Scott never wavered in his belief that land ownership was the essential prerequisite for assimilating into American society. The imposition of the Dawes Act in 1887, with its consequent and dramatic loss of tribal lands through severalty in the early twentieth century, made him even more determined to preserve what tribal allotments individual families could retain or hold in common, by using federal wardship to protect them in their individual and collective holdings.[5]

Nonetheless, his ethnocentrism and paternalism had unforeseen consequences. The ideal farmer-rancher community to which he was leading tribal groups was not always economically sustainable. Nor were many of these tribal groups culturally amenable to the kind of economic arrangement Scott and others thought best for their ultimate survival. Moreover, his view of tribal groups on reservations as wards negated meaningful relationships that he might have developed with a broader range of Native American organizations and individual Indians who celebrated their cultural aspirations and broader vocational goals. Pan-Indian movements flourished in the early twentieth century, though Scott had few contacts with the leaders who organized them. Educational training for Scott's reservation wards took place on a ranch or farm or in a trade school—but not on a college campus![6]

Scott was aware of the board's work prior to his tenure in 1919 and shared its mission. He had worked with some of the board members in the relocation of most Fort Sill Apaches to the Mescalero tribal lands in New Mexico. Therefore, Scott felt comfortable in utilizing the board's resources to do what he could only partially accomplish when preoccupied with advancing his military career. Owing to his work with tribal peoples, he was called on to undertake special assignments. Specifically, he settled disputes involving adversarial tribal groups as well as confrontations between tribal peoples and white settlers. And it was through these venues that Scott gained a more comprehensive understanding of the important role that field personnel, such as agency supervisors, played in implementing the mandate of federal wardship. In this context, his paternalism extended beyond tribal groups to field service personnel whom he fought to protect.[7]

Such was the case with Frank Thackery, posted at the Shawnee agency in Oklahoma, in 1908. Thackery's immediate predecessor had attempted to defraud the Kickapoos at Shawnee of their tribal lands and to profit from the oil leases on their holdings. The Kickapoos initially acquiesced to the scheme of the former agent, with the understanding that lands would be available to them in Sonora, Mexico. While posted at the Academy, Scott was ordered by the secretary of war, through a request from the Interior Department, to investigate the Kickapoos' situation. He assisted Thackery in convincing the Kickapoos that their interests would be best served by remaining on their lands, while both Scott and the agent exposed a land fraud involving collusion with several senators. Many similar scenarios occurred on reservation lands between dedicated agents and others who often represented adverse economic and political interests. Scott was impressed by Thackery's integrity, which led to a personal as well as professional relationship between them.

Consequently, Scott willingly and actively defended Thackery, with both ongoing praise to his superiors and resistance against threats from opposing interests to terminate his service.[8]

A similar situation occurred when Scott was sent on another special assignment to quell unrest among a dissident group of Hopis in their pueblo, Hotevilla, at the Moqui Indian Agency in Keams Canyon, Arizona. Yukeoma, a medicine man with a strong following among more conservative members of the tribe, had succeeded over the years in intimidating numerous agents and government officials by his defiant behavior. The latest episode occurred in the fall of 1911, when he countered any attempt to send Hopi children under his control to schools on the reservation. Scott patiently listened to him over ten days, giving him the opportunity to express himself as he had done numerous times with other tribal leaders and indigenous groups in the past. Yukeoma's ranting and raving convinced Scott that he was delusional, and that he would raise other issues simply to assert his authority, as he had in the past. An amicable arrangement was worked out whereby the children would attend boarding school at Keams Canyon until a day school could be constructed near their pueblo.

The incident led to a long-standing mentoring relationship between Scott and Leo Crane, a young, newly appointed, conscientious agent. Crane, on his first field assignment outside of Washington, was initially reluctant to assert his authority, fearing that it would be contrary to the direction of his superiors. Scott challenged him to maintain what he saw as his prerogatives. As with Thackery and others, Crane provided Scott with eyes on conditions at his reservation, affording an opportunity to monitor developments over time. Board membership gave Scott an added constituency in his role as advocate; he used his standing to protect the positions of reservation agents when threatened by forces within and beyond the bureau.[9]

Consequently, at the time that he joined the board, Scott could look back on a roster of agency supervisors some of whom, over the years, he had placed directly, and others who already had established reputations in their dedication to serve the interests of their tribal groups. They included but were not limited to Fred C. Campbell, Ernest Stecker, and James McLaughlin, the latter having already performed nearly forty-five years of service by the time Scott joined the board. Some were military personnel with whom Scott had worked during his career. When called on or when he personally saw an injustice in their treatment, he actively defended them, utilizing the influence of his friends in the federal government, both prior to and increasingly during his tenure on the board. Intrusions on their prerogatives included obstructive commercial activities on reservation lands, inequitable transfers and terminations by Washington administrators in the Indian Service, and failure to record their service time accurately. His defense of their tenure intensified when cuts to service budgets increased with the onset of the Depression, as did his determination to preserve their field autonomy.[10]

Moreover, board membership gave Scott the opportunity to renew relationships and establish new ones with members of Congress and officials in the executive branch who in the past had furthered his military career and assisted him with tribal groups. The board's delegated authority gave it immediate access to the secretary of the interior, and ultimately to the president and Congress. Scott used it to obtain funding for projects to improve access to health care and education on reservations, and to enhance the economic viability of lands allotted to individual tribal families.

In Scott's fourteen-year tenure on the Board of Indian Commissioners, he visited at least twenty-four agencies, encompassing nineteen tribes and embracing an area from the northern and central Great Plains to the Pacific Northwest. He did this on an annual basis, generally from May to September. Moreover, the field reports provided a forum for him to comment on the condition of reservation inhabitants and the impact of the BIA's policies on them. The content of the forty-two reports that Scott wrote during his tenure reveals that he took full advantage of his position on the board, with a clear set of criteria to assess an agency's resources for meeting tribal needs. He was equally cognizant of the condition of given agencies in previous years, so he was able to examine and comment on their progress.[11]

One of the most ambitious undertakings in the early years of his tenure on the board, one that most clearly illustrates how he used his congressional influence, was in his ongoing assistance to the Mescalero Apaches, along with the Chiricahuas that he persuaded to move from Fort Sill. In 1916, Senator Albert Fall (N.Mex.) pressed for the passage of a bill to use part of the Apache reserve on the Mescalero reservation for the creation of a national park. However, Fall was not concerned with tourism that could economically benefit the Apaches. Fall's ranch was adjacent to the area, and he stood to profit considerably if the measure became law. The designation of a national park would potentially increase the value of Fall's landholdings, since the measure called for the allotment of adjacent lands that Fall owned. Another provision potentially favored those who purchased the land from Fall, by extending the mineral rights to the park, allowing claimants to pay the Apaches only one hundred dollars per claim, regardless of the profits that accrued to the claimants in the sale of the minerals. Of concern to the Apaches was the absence of any provision allowing them to sell their abundant timber reserves; they feared that this resource would be taken from them without compensation. The tribal chiefs appealed to Scott, and he attempted to enlist the support of Interior Secretary Frank Lane. Scott countered Fall's measure with a proposal that the Indians be given an interest-free loan from the federal government to enhance their cattle herds, using the timber as collateral for the loan. In this way, he reasoned, they would soon be self-supporting and "no longer the subject of anxiety to the Indian Bureau." As to the proposal for a national park on their reservation, he believed that there was a great deal of desirable land beyond its borders, "without molesting these Indians who should be allowed to work out their own salvation."[12]

Along with his congressional allies, Scott engaged the assistance of both the Indian Rights Association, a group with a long-standing history of advocacy for the protection of Indian resources, and the board itself. It took four years for the Bureau of Indian Affairs to obtain a bona fide estimate of the timber's value, which was calculated at $500,000. Ernest Stecker, then superintendent at the Mescalero Agency, proposed that half of the funds be used to purchase six hundred cattle, with the yearlings sold to generate an annual income of $180,000. The other half would be invested in houses and barns. Stecker believed that the BIA commissioner, Cato Sells, was deliberately stalling the transaction owing to his anger over Stecker's reaching out to Scott and the board concerning sale of the reservation's timber. By December 1920, Stecker wrote Scott that "things really look discouraging. If you can help out, please do so and in your own way and without delay." Scott's "own way" was to contact McDowell, the journalist; Senator Charles Curtis (Kans.), an old friend; and Representative Homer Snyder (N.Y.), chairman of the House Committee on Indian Affairs.[13]

All appeared to be going well, at least at first. Sells informed the Mescalero Apaches in January 1921 that their contract for the loan on their timber was approved. Nevertheless, owing to a national recession, the amount requested by Congress would be only $250,000. Although Stecker wrote Scott that the Apaches were quite pleased with his efforts, the stumbling block was Senator Fall's nomination as secretary of the interior in the new Harding administration. The bill was approved by the House Committee on Indian Affairs in early June 1922, but it languished in the Senate committee, perhaps owing to the displeasure of their former colleague, Senator Fall. By December, Scott was running out of patience. He asked Curtis to intercede with his senatorial colleague Seldon Spencer (Mo.) to get the bill reported out of committee. Scott had also lined up the support of New Mexico's two senators, Holm Bursum and Andrieus Jones, and urged the new superintendent at Mescalero, Fred C. Morgan, to put additional pressure on them and on Representative Carl Hayden (Ariz.) as well. "Nothing talks like votes to the ears of a congressman," he wrote, "and the more pressure you get from New Mexico to pull over the bar the better[,] and impress upon them if this appropriation for New Mexico is lost[,] it will be their fault since it is so close to success." The efforts proved successful. The final hurdle was getting the measure approved by the appropriations committee once again, but now as part of a general deficiency bill. To ensure its funding, Scott called on Herbert Lord, director of the budget, "to let him know," as McDowell reported to Morgan "that some rather influential people were interested in your Indians."[14]

On a more intimate level, membership on the board provided Scott with yet another opportunity to visit old friends in places where he had been stationed during his military career in the American West. Touring Forts Totten, Lincoln, and Sill, where he and Mary had spent their early married life when they were fortunate to be together, engendered nostalgia and sadness, as when they beheld barren foundations where dwellings they had once lived in stood. Equally sorrowful was seeing the places where Scott had Hunter with him alone to instill discipline in the rebellious youth. In a more positive way, his annual agency tours gave him the opportunity to renew old friendships with Indians, such as scouts and tribal chiefs, as well as soldiers and post traders that he had worked with where he was stationed. Seeing I-See-O, the Kiowa scout, whom Scott credited with preventing a violent reaction to the

Ghost Dance religion among the Kiowa, Comanche, and Apache peoples, was a great source of satisfaction to Scott. In other places he was pleased to see some of the old soldiers from the Seventh Cavalry, and in another venue he was pleasantly surprised by his reception, commenting to his wife that "it is really touching the way I am received everywhere by the Indians."[15]

While membership on the board brought advantages to Scott, other members came to have mixed feelings about his participation. His criticisms of the treatment of tribal groups and the agency personnel guarding their welfare was increasingly directed toward the bureaucracy within the Bureau of Indian Affairs, and ultimately at the Department of the Interior. Specifically, he believed that they were at best indifferent to what was going on in the field, and at worst implicit in encouraging the corrupt practices of special interests on reservation lands.

Examples of corruption were not difficult for him to find. Capt. Ernest Stecker initially served under Scott's command at Fort Sill, assisting in the settlement of the Chiricahua Apaches in the 1890s. Subsequently, and on Scott's recommendation, he was appointed as agency superintendent of the Apaches at Anadarko, Oklahoma Territory. His seven-year tenure ended when he was transferred to the Mescalero Agency (in New Mexico), where most of the Fort Sill Apaches were eventually relocated. It was here that Stecker, a dedicated agent who took his responsibilities to protect these tribal groups quite seriously, ran afoul of those with different agendas. Senator Fall, in addition to his attempt to undermine the economic viability of the Mescalero Apaches by the creation of a national park abutting his ranch, also initially sought to insert a provision in the original Mescalero funding bill to divert the Apaches' water rights to his own land. Fall's acrimony toward the agent intensified when Stecker expressed vocal and public opposition to the provision. Consequently, when Fall left the Senate and assumed the management of the Interior Department in the Harding administration in 1920, he was prepared to take his revenge out on Stecker by terminating his tenure at the Mescalero Agency. When he was transferred to the San Carlos reservation in Arizona, Stecker chastised a group of white cattlemen who were illegally grazing their herds on reservation lands. The cattlemen complained to the Interior Department, and Stecker was subsequently furloughed from the Indian Service without just cause.[16]

Stecker's removal was not a unique event. Other agents were frequently selected based on partisan politics and subject to congressional influence tied to local interest groups, often at the expense of tribal peoples. Perhaps not as pernicious but equally disheartening was what a longtime reservation supervisor in California, J. Jenkins, identified for Scott as one of his ongoing problems: "First one Administration and then another comes in, with new ideas (at least they think them new) and various inspectors happen along each with his own opinion largely influenced by dyspepsia or what he had been 'told' to report, and the result is that we have no settled policies, no outline of work, no definite information as to what we are trying to do or whither we are drifting." Jenkins also surmised that few BIA officials in the senior ranks "ever had experience on an Indian reservation." Jenkins concluded that what was required was what Scott already knew: "put men in charge there who have five, ten, or more years of actual experience in the field handling Indians—men who know Indians and have demonstrated their capacity for handling them."[17]

If Stecker's experience with Albert Fall was not a reminder of the deficiencies in the Indian Service, Scott soon had his own in one of his first annual visits as a board member, in this instance to the Blackfeet Agency in Browning, Montana. He noted that conditions there were "very deplorable." Specifically, he reported to a board member on his return that

> there have been seven incumbents [agency supervisors] in charge in the past five years. There are but two regular men in the office and seven temporary. Only one man who has been here one year and he has not been here two. The accounts of the last four Superintendents have not been settled, and no one here knows anything about them. The current work is more than the inadequate force is able to accomplish, and there is a constant change of policy.

The rapid turnover in field service personnel was often indicative of low morale. Other detriments eroding their morale included major disparities in pay regardless of assigned duties, although all were subject to civil service regulations. Equally demeaning, field personnel were frequently reassigned regardless of their administrative skills, and often without their input.

The dilemma led Scott to sharpen his focus on what he regarded as the BIA's shortcoming—namely, its administrative hierarchy in Washington.

Authority was so concentrated there that field supervisors could not make basic decisions without first getting the approval from the commissioner's office. Scott's aversion to bureaucracy stemmed from his experience in Washington while working up the administrative ladder to chief of staff. Military bureaus were entities unto themselves with staffs who enjoyed, among other perquisites, opportunities for professional advancement that were not as readily available to field service personnel if at all. His misgivings moderated to some extent when the bureaus were nominally placed under the chief of staff, during a period when the army administration reorganized. Such was not the case with the administrative structure of the Interior Department, and specifically the Bureau of Indian Affairs, at least according to Scott. The adverse consequences for reservation agents in the field was a manifestation of Washington bureaucrats who were threatened by coordination and change. A parallel situation occurred when Scott served as director of the New Jersey Highway Commission, a position he held concurrently with his membership on the Board of Indian Commissioners. And when change was ultimately forced on both bodies as a result of the Depression, each party moved quickly to protect its own interests.[18]

The initial challenge, however, lay in gaining consensus for his position among board members. Although they shared his views on federal wardship and assimilation, and even recognized the deficiency in the bureau's administration of Indian affairs, it was doubtful that they saw or were primarily concerned with the consequences of the bureau's structure on the field supervisors, and if they did, they deemed it not within their purview to alter the channel of communication. Scott included his criticism of the bureau in his report to the board but conceded that the policy of the BIA, or Indian Office, toward its employees "may be outside my province, as I am too new as a Commissioner to know my limitations." However, that did not stop Scott from pressing his case in a report on the condition of the Mescalero Apaches in 1920, written directly to the board to correct what he regarded as the injustices agency superintendents incurred on the reservation under the authority of the BIA and ultimately the Department of the Interior.[19]

All did not go well, however. Scott's strongly felt assertion of what he believed were the board's prerogatives to investigate the treatment of agents led to a cautionary rebuke by Malcolm McDowell, its secretary. McDowell warned Scott that as a board member he needed to be more discreet in his criticism of the Indian Service:

> You will pardon me for suggesting that printed words appear much stronger than off-hand observations as spoken or casually written in a personal way. . . . Your phraseology would seem, to most people who read your report that the [Indian] Office deliberately turned down [an agent] without justification or good reason. Also, that it has done this in other cases. The Office would certainly come back with a justification which to most people would be sound and proper.[20]

Scott went even further that same year, authoring a resolution, which was passed by the Lake Mohonk Conference on the Indian, protesting the apparent Indian Office policy of ignoring the recommendations of the Board of Indian Commissioners. The resolution's passage, and Scott's insistence that it be sent to the interior secretary *from the board*, drew the attention of the board's chairman, George Vaux Jr. He, in turn, warned Scott that such a move might prove counterproductive, claiming that the secretary would not have the time to read all the reports submitted by board members. A more telling response was Vaux's assertion that "with due respect to your judgment . . . [w]hilst I do not think that we should be lacking in backbone, my past experience on the Board have seen such absolute failure, resulting from lack of diplomacy in methods of presentation, that I should not want to unnecessarily antagonize the officials of the Interior Department."[21]

Consequently, after less than two years on the board, Scott was determined to assert what he saw as its prerogatives and to use it to impose major reforms in the way that the BIA conducted its affairs. Vaux's cautionary tone did not dissuade him. Writing two years later in upholding the integrity of an agency supervisor, Scott sought to bolster the prerogatives of the commissioner of Indian affairs, Charles Burke, by noting to him that "I am on very good terms with the management of several influential dailies and would consider it an honor to support you against the predatory interests and if you give the word will go with you to the mat in your defense of those Indians."[22]

In other ways as well, Scott's ongoing and assertive advocacy on behalf of tribal groups placed the board in an awkward position, enraging the board's chairman. In 1915, prior to joining the board, Scott was sent to settle a dispute among a group of Paiutes in Utah. Hatch, a son of one of the chiefs, was accused of murder in Colorado. Because of the accusation, the U.S. marshal in Utah organized a posse of seventy-five men, surrounded the Paiute encampment, and, without warrant, demanded the surrender of Hatch. Shooting followed, with each side claiming that the other fired first. Scott claimed that the unrest was the result of the frustration over ongoing squalid conditions on the reservation, and he blamed the BIA and ultimately the Interior Department for their failure to address them, despite the fact that these conditions were noted in Scott's annual reports to the board from 1915 to 1923. Scott's assumption was that the board should have notified the Interior Department regarding the BIA's failure to address the matter. An article he wrote, published in 1923, was prefaced with a statement that not only noted Scott as a member of the board but referred to the board as a group of "highminded impartial men who have tried vainly for many years to bring about an improvement in the nation's wards, but their recommendations were usually relegated to the waste basket by the Indian bureau." Vaux, the board's chairman at the time, was incensed by what he saw as Scott's usurpation of his prerogative: "The General forgets that he is no longer Chief-of-Staff grand-high-executioner, and a few other things in the United States Army. Surely, as an Army man in active service, had he written with regard to the Secretary of War and Major-General of the Army what he has put in this article, he would have been no doubt court-martialed in short order."[23]

The manner if not the substance of Scott's advocacy was not the only contentiousness that the board encountered during the early 1920s. Indian rights advocates had enlisted legislative support from Scott, among others, and thereby prevented passage of a measure, the Bursum Indian Land Bill, which, in its original form, would have undermined the land claims of Pueblo Indians in favor of white squatters.[24]

Its defeat, however, far from uniting the Friends of the Indian, underscored disparate approaches to what should be the future direction of Indian reform. Traditional reformers, including Scott, most members of the Board of Indian Commissioners, and many members of more conventional advocacy organizations favoring tribal assimilation were challenged by a growing group of American Indian reformers who believed that the distinct cultures of tribal groups should be encouraged. However, unlike Scott and other assimilationists, these cultural pluralists believed that Native American civilizations could endure and prosper in an Anglo world. They were led by John Collier, a trained sociologist and social worker. Collier had taken a personal interest in the land disputes between New Mexican Pueblos and white settlers and was very critical of the self-serving agenda of Bursum and his followers. He claimed that more-traditional reformers did not go far enough or act soon enough in opposition to the Bursum Bill. The board manifested the same reticence in initially opposing the Bursum Bill that it did with Scott over direct advocacy for field personnel, and for the same reason: a reluctance to offend the BIA. Ultimately, compromise legislation was negotiated, the Lenroot Bill, to protect Pueblo land titles while recognizing the legitimate claims of some non-Indian titles on Pueblo lands. While most reformers embraced the compromise, Collier, who saw the board's acquiescence as selling out, remained adamant in his opposition, suspicious of the board's intentions and unwilling to work with it in promoting reform. That Scott was a lobbyist pressing for the compromise Lenroot measure on behalf of a broad range of Indian reform groups did not augur well for any accommodation with Collier. Although the bill was ultimately defeated in the House, Collier's anger led him to form his own group in 1923, the American Indian Defense Association.[25]

The near passage of the Lenroot Bill and a speech by the Indian bureau commissioner, Charles Burke, hardened the philosophical differences between the assimilationists and the cultural pluralists. In February 1923, in a public address, "Message to All Indians," Burke chastised Indians for engaging in dances and other traditional cultural practices that he felt were antithetical to the Christian faith and that, he believed, impeded their economic progress. Although many anthropologists, artists, writers, and western chambers of commerce that were dependent on the tourist industry, and not strictly Indian reformers, were shocked by Burke's position, Vaux defended Burke when he was criticized for his views. The board's implied endorsement put some of its members, such as Scott, in a precarious position, since they did not share the view that Indians' retaining their traditional cultural practices impeded their ability to assimilate. Nonetheless, Collier, somewhat impetuous and quick to act, not only painted his opponents with a broad brush, but was even more emphatic in his views on the importance of preserving tribal cultures. He advocated "a basic policy of recognizing and building on the Indians' native energies, their . . . inherited craft and art forms, their very real inherited moralities, and their group-consciousness."

While both men sought to reform the Indian Service, in temperament and ideology, Collier, as a cultural pluralist, and Scott, as a more traditional Christian assimilationist, could not come to an accord. And as far as Collier was concerned, the existence of the board, which Scott was struggling to use as a mechanism to promote necessary change as *he* saw it, was increasingly an impediment to needed reform.[26]

Fall resigned from the Interior Department in March 1923 under a cloud of scandal, ushering in Hubert Work as his successor. Work was aware of the shortcomings in the Indian Service and made a conscious attempt to build consensus among Indian reformers in the direction of change. To accomplish this, he convened the Council of One Hundred, what amounted to a summit of eclectic and diverse advocates of American Indian welfare. All was for naught, however, perhaps because most attendees were hard-core assimilationists.[27]

While Collier was attempting to garner support among reformers who might share his point of view, including a Progressive Republican attorney, Harold Ickes, Scott was compiling a comprehensive plan to reorganize the Indian Service, turning to his military experience for guidance. Basically, he viewed the bureau as being in the same position as the U.S. Army immediately prior to the Spanish-American War. Similar problems—the concentration of authority in Washington, and a lack of coordination among departments (bureaus in a military context)—plagued both, he believed. To alleviate them, he proposed the creation of a general or administrative staff of trained men with experience in the techniques of all departments—education, finance, health, and others—but possessing no bureaucratic allegiance. This body would formulate policy subject to the commissioner's approval. Under Scott's plan, channels of communication would be clearly drawn between the commissioner and the field supervisors, with a greater degree of discretion given to reservation agents in conducting routine business. Scott believed that the commissioner and a corps of inspectors could verify that the superintendents were doing their job in implementing policy.[28]

Scott worked actively for the approval of his plan, speaking before groups of reformers throughout the period when he was not in the West on reservation visits, and pressing successfully for its consideration before the board. He even went so far as to enlist the military's support to study the Indian bureau to determine the feasibility of implementing his plan. His annual reports frequently and increasingly referred to problems faced by agency personnel, and he was quick to point out how his recommendations would remedy these issues.[29]

In 1928, he won the initial support of Charles Rhoads, then president of the Indian Rights Association. Rhoads was sufficiently impressed with his recommendations that, early in 1929, he wrote President-elect Herbert Hoover concerning Scott: "It seemed to us, that he, of all persons, could carry out views to you, reinforcing them by his long & intimate experience with the subject." By March 1929, McDowell informed Scott that his plan was "working through" the Indian Office, with letters sent to superintendents asking their views on the matter of greater latitude. Eventually, this aspect of Scott's plan—giving agency personnel greater discretion in the decision-making process—was implemented through a formal directive by the agency.[30]

However, perhaps owing in part to the failure of the Council of One Hundred to provide constructive avenues for reforming the Indian Service, Secretary Work commissioned his own independent investigation under the nonpartisan Brookings Institution. Lewis Meriam, a lawyer with a doctorate in the study of bureaucratic structures, and his group worked for two years analyzing the Indian Service. They published their findings in 1928 as *The Problem of Indian Administration*, which came to be known as the Meriam Report. In contrast to Scott's report on the reform of the Indian Service, the Brookings commission ignored any investigation of the Indian Office in Washington, which Scott believed had hindered, through its cumbersome bureaucracy, the ability of field service personnel to carry out their functions. Moreover, although the report recognized the importance of agency personnel, it did so in a way that redefined the kinds of agency supervisors that could best serve the needs of tribal groups. Professionalism was interpreted in the context of experts who had studied tribal matters more from the perspective of a social scientist than someone who had spent many years on the reservation. Other conclusions in the Meriam Report were equally ominous from Scott's perspective. Meriam, who had no personal experience in Indian affairs, believed that the administration of field personnel should evolve in the direction of states' control, on the assumption that local officials would have a better understanding of the needs of reservation families in their own locale. This position essentially repudiated the concept of federal wardship. Scott believed that such a move would expose Native peoples to incursions by elements that would undermine their welfare.[31]

Initially, the positive professional relationship between Scott and Rhoads did not change following Rhoads's appointment as commissioner of Indian affairs under the new Hoover administration. As previously noted, he was extremely receptive to Scott's plan, and his prominent role in the Indian Rights Association was seen at the time as the dawn of a new day among reformers. Increasingly, however, acting in what he regarded as the Indians' best interest, Rhoads began implementing many of Meriam's recommendations, particularly those relating to the upgrading of professional qualifications of field service staff. He set a deadline of March 1931 for his reorganization of the Bureau of Indian Affairs. Under the overall direction of the new interior secretary, R. Lyman Wilber, Rhoads reorganized the bureau into five divisions: health, education, agricultural extension, forestry, and irrigation. Each division had a technical supervisor, with the authority to direct the agency superintendents on matters within the supervisor's area of specialization. Scott saw this as yet another level of redundant bureaucracy, particularly when the bureau initially hired over two thousand people, increasing their salaries by 25 percent more than those long-standing in similar rank in the service. Despite the deepening depression, the Hoover administration raised appropriations for the Indian Service from $15 million to $28 million by 1931. By 1932, when it became obvious that the economy was not going to improve, furloughs and retrenchments became the bureau's policy.[32]

Older, more traditional field service personnel were particularly vulnerable to the bureau's reorganization plan. Many often felt pulled in two opposing directions in dealing with tribal administration: what the so-called experts were telling them to do, on the one hand, and the course that their long experience in tribal administration suggested they should follow, on the other. Moreover, the increase in college-educated personnel, many of whom held salary grades above traditional staff, compounded a serious morale problem. To make matters worse, when retrenchment became the general rule in 1932, many senior superintendents were forced to retire.

Rhoads, perhaps out of deference to Scott's plan that had been supported by the board, wrote a seven-page letter to its chairman, Samuel Eliot, in December 1931, defending his implementation of the Meriam Report. In it, Commissioner Rhoads went out of his way to explain how Scott's plan was given "the most thorough consideration" by the bureau, describing it as "a friendly and sincere indictment of our administration." While recognizing the problems with personnel, the commissioner believed that though some complaints may be justified, they were insufficient to warrant changes to what the Meriam Report proposed.[33]

Diplomacy and tact aside, Scott was both frustrated and disheartened. A ruling by the solicitor general in the office of the interior secretary denied Scott's assertion that the board had the prerogative to recommend the selection and compensation of field service personnel—what he had advocated for, shortly after joining the board. Consequently, he was unable to protect many of the agents that he had worked with and who had gained documented improvement in the welfare of the tribal families that they supervised. Among them were Fred C. Campbell, who initiated a five-year economic development program on the Blackfeet Agency in Montana, and John Buntin, at the Kiowa reservation in Oklahoma. Both were forced out after forty years of useful service, "a vital loss to the Govt and to the Indian that cannot be replaced for many years if at all, a loss for which there is no excuse." On a more general note, Scott bemoaned the fact that "the men of experience are rapidly going out of the service who are without college diplomas. There is a general feeling that experience is a detriment to success with this administration, which places an inordinate value upon college diplomas. . . . I have never seen such bitterness before in the field service, which feels that . . . there is no one in power who is interested in their welfare."

The board's ultimate attack on the Meriam Report in 1929 further alienated both John Collier and prominent members of Congress, such as Senator Lynn Frazier (N.D.), chairman of the Senate Indian Investigating Committee, a body convened in 1927 to provide the groundwork for a new Native American legislative program, and Senator Burton K. Wheeler (Mont.), who would serve on the Committee on Indian Affairs beginning in 1933.[34]

Moreover, the board became an easy political target. The ongoing depression forced the new Roosevelt administration to impose severe constraints on federal spending, and the very existence of the board, despite its modest expenses, was called into question. Scott, on the request of the board's new secretary, Earl Henderson, appealed directly to his friends in Congress for the reinstatement of funds stricken from the 1932 appropriation. Although the appeal was successful, the victory was a temporary one. The board was abolished the following year, thereby defeating assimilation as a goal of Indian reform. John Collier and his sponsor and advocate Harold Ickes, the new interior secretary, redefined federal wardship to embrace the integrity of tribal cohesion. Whether the legislation imposing the new reform goal, the Indian Reorganization Act of 1934 (also known as the Wheeler-Howard Act), would be successful remained to be seen.[35]

Consequently, many of Scott's working assumptions over his long career advocating on behalf of tribal groups now seemed anachronistic. The sanctity of individual landownership as an essential prerequisite for a stable American Indian society no longer seemed a viable option. The subsequent loss of approximately two-thirds of all tribal holdings following the passage of the Dawes Act may have convinced Scott and more-traditional Indian reformers that it was imperative to preserve what was left for distribution to individual Native American families. However, the problem was not simply the prevalence of incursions by pernicious interests defrauding tribal families of their individual allotments to farm or graze their lands. Although the inclination now to embrace farming or cattle raising varied with a tribe's culture, many tribal families were more than willing to lease or sell their holdings to non-Indians, rather than work the land themselves, using the lease money or proceeds from the sale, however minimal, to sustain them in increasingly hard times. The same scenario had been played out in the late nineteenth century among the Comanche and Kiowa tribal groups—in some cases, even prior to the Dawes Act. Droughts and economic challenges faced by farmers and ranchers at the end of World War I, both tribal and nontribal, and the consequences of the economic depression may not have caused these reformers to waiver in their belief in federal wardship, but it encouraged others to challenge their assumptions. At the age of seventy-seven, and at a time when years of frontier service were taking a physical toll on his body, Scott was prepared to accept the inevitable rejection of his agenda for Indian reform.[36]

During this period, the Scotts sought to enjoy what they never had before: a permanent home together. The family farm that the Scotts purchased in 1918 through the estate of Charles Hodge, Mary's father, in Kingston, New Jersey, near Princeton, was to serve that purpose. Their expectation was that with additional acreage and needed renovations, it could become a place of refuge and relaxation from the demands of the board's work that he was then about to undertake. Nonetheless, Scott primarily saw its purchase as a financial investment that could sustain his wife should she be left a widow. She was thrilled with the idea of living a life in a rural setting, where their extended family could visit. The Scotts were especially pleased with what they believed to be its commercial potential, situated as it was with access to electricity, water, and transportation. Scott had plans to cultivate and harvest the oak and hickory trees on the property and plant vegetable crops on four hundred acres of flatlands. More esoteric plans included an orchard of English walnut trees, the raising of Duroc-Jersey pigs, and Angora goats for mohair.[37]

Sadly, as with other financial endeavors in which the Scotts engaged over the years, including their earlier purchase of western lands, farming proved to be an unprofitable avocation for them. The basic problem seemed to be a lack of sound business sense: they invested heavily in stock, equipment, and renovations without a comprehensive understanding of the vicissitudes of market fluctuations. Within two years of the farm's purchase, it was apparent that it would not bring them the security that they had hoped for. Efforts to enhance revenue from the farm, such as by leasing some acreage for pasture to other farmers, failed to diminish its financial liability. Perhaps equally frustrating to them both, Scott seemed to place responsibility for its upkeep squarely on Mary's shoulders, given his frequent trips west to visit reservations. When the Scotts finally sold the farm in 1928, it was a great relief.[38]

Nevertheless, other aspects of life from his years of military service and on into retirement ultimately proved enriching and self-satisfying. Prior to and concurrent with his tenure on the Board of Indian Commissioners, Scott was engaged in an extensive period of research, writing, and speechmaking on tribal cultures, both for scholarly audiences and for the general public. These outlets gave him the opportunity to share his intellectual interests in the cultures of indigenous peoples and to convey images of American Indian tribal societies to those who never experienced life on the late-nineteenth-century western frontier. Ultimately, Scott enjoyed the attention and adulation he received relating his knowledge and experience of the adventurous frontier life that was now part of America's past.

Scott's introduction to a study of indigenous cultures was inspired by his desire for excitement as a newly commissioned second lieutenant on the late-nineteenth-century western frontier. Consequently, learning and utilizing the sign language, a long-practiced means of intertribal communication, was initially a pragmatic necessity to further his quest for adventure. He soon embraced its study as an intellectual pursuit that went well beyond his initial incentive to learn it. As early as 1892, Scott was asked by Fletcher Barrett, chair of a forthcoming folklore conference to be held at the Columbian Exposition in 1893, to prepare a paper on American Indian signs "in which many persons tell me you are an expert." And, in the fall of 1897, prior to the buildup of military forces for the Spanish-American War, Scott was detailed to the Bureau of Ethnology in the Smithsonian Institution in Washington to research and write a book on the Indian sign language. Although diverted from the posting to train recruits for anticipated combat, he never lost his intellectual curiosity about Native Americans. Indeed, his interest was whetted and broadened when he was exposed to different overseas cultures in his postings in the early twentieth century.[39]

Throughout the period of his military service and beyond, Scott communicated with a diversity of scholars, both soliciting information and offering it when asked. Many of these scholars, along with Scott, published articles in scholarly journals such as the *American Anthropologist* and delivered papers at numerous conferences on American Indian customs and traditions. Scott's correspondents also included museum directors and individuals who were starting academic programs on tribal cultures or seeking to sustain them. He was generous with his time and expertise when they solicited suggestions or general information. Conversely, they provided Scott with information helpful to his own research.[40]

Other useful sources of information gathering in his studies included those provided by tribal leaders, either directly when he visited their locations or through agents whom he either placed or befriended on reservations administered by the BIA. The agents often interviewed elders of a tribe to gather information about cultural symbols and signs. They would provide Scott with their notes when he visited the reservation. Although not unique, perhaps one of the most significant examples of information gathering occurred through the long-standing relationship between Scott and I-See-O. Scott worked with the Kiowa scout while handling the assimilation of the Chiricahua Apache prisoners of war who were to be settled on the Kiowa reservation. Scott credited I-See-O, whom he appointed as a sergeant in the all-Indian Troop L that he created, with preventing his tribe from embracing the more bellicose aspects of the Ghost Dance religion. Most significantly perhaps, I-See-O provided Scott, often through sign gestures, with invaluable sources on the tribe's cultural history that he later used to broaden his understanding of not only the legends and myths of other tribal groups but also how such information was transmitted through sign language. I-See-O received in return a lifetime commitment of financial security from a military establishment that otherwise showed little recognition for the invaluable service that American Indian scouts provided on the late-nineteenth-century American frontier.

Ben Clark, an Anglo scout initially in one of Custer's early campaigns, was another indispensable source for Scott's scholarship. Married to a Cheyenne wife, Clark spoke the tribal tongue and was recognized by military officials as an expert on Cheyenne history and culture. Scott considered him a mentor because of his knowledge of the sign language. John B. Dunbar, a Civil War veteran, was another source; he explained to Scott signs that were unknown to him at the time.[41]

Scott's extensive scholarly research, produced in both articles and speeches, can generally be analyzed in terms of what he studied and how he studied it. His interests included tribal customs and traditions, such as myths and sacred stories, generally on the origins of a people on the earth. Legends—that is, stories from the past associated with a specific event, such as a war or famine—was a related field of study. His fields of inquiry often included but were not limited to the origins of tribal names and ritual practices in a tribe's culture; comparisons of such practices among different tribal groups; the significance of specific geological features in a tribe's settlement patterns; and similarities and differences in the origins and development of verbal language groups. To summarize, Scott was concerned with the components of a tribe's cultural history, and he used their customs and traditions as a method to garner additional information about their evolution and development.[42]

The sign language, as a means of intertribal communication, was just as important to study in gleaning an awareness of the culture of individual tribes as a study of their dances and legends. In mastering the history of the use of the sign language through correspondence and interviews with tribal members and others, Scott was able to discern subtle differences in hand gestures related to the dialects of specific tribal groups. Consequently, Scott was able to demonstrate these differences in "the first known use of motion picture film to create a language dictionary."[43]

Throughout his active military career, Scott continued his research on the Indian sign language and was urged many times to publish a dictionary based on his findings. An obvious reason for his tardiness in doing so was his preoccupation with the demands of military administration. In theory, his retirement would give him the opportunity to organize his materials and arrange them in a form for publication. However, Scott did not live to publish his dictionary. Part of the problem may well have been a need to glean the *final word* on a particular sign or symbol, in order to be assured that he had all the information for a comprehensive reference. Nonetheless, linguists and phonetic scholars were rewarded with a more vibrant product of his scholarly research on signs—the production of a film with synchronized sound that showed Scott and tribal sign talkers *actually* performing the ancient custom of intertribal communication.[44]

Bringing the production to fruition was not without its challenges. As early as 1913, Scott explored the possibility of having his hand gestures filmed, but arranging financing for the project was an ongoing concern. Scott had a devoted ally in Representative Scott Leavitt (Mont.), chair of the House Committee on Indian Affairs, whom he had worked with and assisted in his efforts to protect reservation lands. In 1930, Leavitt used his influence to provide a congressional appropriation of $5,000 for the film's production and took an active role in its completion. Malcolm McDowell, then secretary to the board, described Scott's elation to a fellow board member: "He is as inthusiastic [*sic*] about this as a sixteen-year-old kid is about going to camp. I have never seen him in better health. He sure is a wonder."[45] A three-day conference on the Plains Indian Sign Language was held in Browning, Montana, at the Blackfeet Agency during the first week of September 1930. Both the event and the filming went well, and Scott was pleased with the outcome, at least initially.

He was proud of the camaraderie among the tribal council that represented fifteen bands and thirteen dialects, among whom were groups that had been "bloody enemies until compelled to stop fighting by the White man." The tribal groups suggested that a memorial of the occasion be constructed, with each man's name and footprint engraved in concrete. Nonetheless, a shortage of funds continued to plague the successful completion of the project. Leavitt tried to secure an additional $4,000, but the fiscal exigencies of the Depression and Leavitt's ultimate defeat in the Roosevelt landslide made further public funding impossible. A private donation covered the production costs of six reels, with Scott demonstrating the signs, but funds were inadequate to film an additional one thousand signs beyond the four hundred originally recorded. The situation was financially dire enough that Scott's friends on the board and others contributed enough that he could have a record of the fruits of his labor. Sadly, as late as a month before his passing in April 1934, Scott was still pleading for additional funding to complete the project and provide proper archival management by the Smithsonian Institution before knowledge of the language was lost to posterity. Nonetheless, the extant film provided a unique legacy for a soldier who devoted his intellect to the study of western tribal cultures.[46]

Aside from the movie on the sign language, Scott used other forums to reach a broader audience in his effort to convey an aura of adventure and fascination to a generation far removed from a time and place on the nation's western frontier when hand gestures were used to prevent bloodshed. The statistical closing of the frontier in 1890 now seemed more traumatic than it did at the time, signaling the passing of what many now regarded as a simpler way of life, and what it meant to be an American.

The indigenous inhabitants of the nation's western frontier took on an often reconstructed image for Anglo-Americans in the search for authenticity. Whatever the views of more culturally astute scholars, the generic Indian, whether noble or savage or both, was a major actor in the performance of a nation seeking to relive its past.[47]

Scott both contributed to and profited from the aura and mystique that many Americans saw or wanted to see in reassessing their nation's western frontier experience. Popular audiences enjoyed the narration of his early military experiences, especially the dangers that he confronted while negotiating with hostile tribal leaders through a unique form of communication; his seemingly inexhaustible understanding of eclectic tribal cultures; and his knowledge of major battles among tribes and between them and frontier soldiers. Scott conveyed his knowledge, always with enthusiasm, through speeches delivered to diverse audiences; articles written for the popular press; a radio show on which he spoke about his frontier career; illustrations of tribal signs that he helped produce for the Boy Scout Handbook; the publication of his autobiography, *Some Memories of a Soldier* (1928); and even the commercial exploitation of his experience to encourage tourism to the northern Great Plains.

A cursory examination of the archives on Hugh Lenox Scott at the Library of Congress reveals that he gave at least seventy-five documented speeches during his active career and into retirement. To be sure, not all were related to American Indian subjects. Some pertained to his role as superintendent at West Point, where he addressed the graduation of Academy cadets and the dedication of a new chapel; as army chief of staff, noting the importance of preparedness on the eve of the nation's entrance into World War I; as a member of the Root Commission, articulating the failure to save Russia; and as chair of the New Jersey Highway Commission, on the condition of roads in the state. With increasing frequency in the last decade of his life, his speeches addressed topics relating to the Indian sign language and Native history. At one point, Scott utilized the services of a speakers bureau to hone his skills at public speaking. He gained increasing confidence in gearing his talks to the level and interest of his audiences, which included civic groups, chambers of commerce, fraternal lodges, and celebrants commemorating specific events in the nation's western frontier history, as well as Boy Scout and Girl Scout troops fascinated by tribal rituals, symbols, and signs.[48]

The medium of radio allowed Scott to reach an even broader and more diverse audience. Ralph Budd, president of the Great Northern Railway, created an extensive publicity campaign in the mid to late 1920s to exploit commercially the aspects of American Indian cultures in various northwestern localities on the railway's right-of-way to the Pacific. As early as 1925, Scott's tribal knowledge was incorporated into the railway's publicity campaign, which included, along with Scott, presentations by the Great Northern Songsters and the Great Northern Railway orchestra. Subsequent presentations included a radio broadcast where Scott spoke about the Blackfeet Indians and another on Chief Joseph and the Nez Percés, as part of the railway's *Empire* series.[49]

Perhaps Scott's greatest literary triumph, one that underscored his contemporary popularity, was the publication of his lengthy autobiography, *Some Memories of a Soldier*, in 1928. At 673 pages, it addresses all phases of his career in field assignments and in Washington, with the first third dealing directly with his experiences with tribal groups on and off the reservation, and other sections touching on the disputes he settled and the reservations he visited while a member of the Board of Indian Commissioners. As early as 1919, Scott had been approached by a publisher to narrate his military experiences in a volume for the general public, but he noted his need for relief from his administrative responsibilities at Camp Dix. Although several publishing firms expressed an interest in a manuscript on Scott's life, Scott chose the World Publishing Company for its publication.[50]

In addition to articles he penned for popular journals, the bulk of feature articles that appeared in print on his ventures during his lifetime were written by others and indicate that he was regarded by editors as good copy. In addition to the popular press, contemporary periodicals such as *Illustrated World*, *The Outlook*, *Literary Digest*, *Mentor*, *The Nation*, and *Current Opinion* appealed to a more general audience, while more selective periodicals such as *The Red Man* and *World's Work* appealed, respectively, to tribal groups and their advocates and to leaders of commerce and industry. Although many stressed different themes in Scott's life according to when they were published and what were the anticipated interests of their readers, all noted his work with tribal groups, both on and off the reservation; how he utilized the sign language as a tool of pacification; and the courage he demonstrated in confronting danger.[51]

The articles about Scott and his autobiography alike garnered a great deal of praise. Newton D. Baker, the former secretary of war under whom Scott served as army chief of staff, was especially effusive in his description of the latter, so much so that its publisher wanted to use Baker's words in promoting sales. Others, too, praised Scott's accomplishment.[52]

Scott enjoyed the adulation that he received, which came perhaps at an opportune time in his life, concurrent with the Roosevelt administration's rejection of federal wardship for tribal groups. In one visit to Lawrence, Kansas, Scott was scheduled to speak at no fewer than four events—at a masonic lodge, a Boy Scout troop, a women's club, and Haskell Institute, now known as Haskell Indian Nations University. Enjoying his reception, he noted to Mary that he had "many adventures to relate—I have enjoyed the friendship displayed so abundantly and the kindness of everybody." At Glacier National Park in Montana, where he met agents and friends, Scott claimed, "It seems like coming home to come here where everything is done for me in a wonderful way." Accolades continued with honors bestowed upon him by western-oriented fraternal organizations.[53]

Scott had enjoyed generally good health throughout much of his life, considering the demands on his body from the physically challenging postings where he was stationed. Aside from the loss of several fingers in the Philippines, several cases of mild influenza over the years, an enlarged prostate, and toothaches, Scott seemed to be physically fit for a man approaching his eightieth year of life. In 1933, however, his energy and stamina diminished to the point where he could no longer manage the speaking schedule that he so much enjoyed in the latter part of his life. Scott entered Walter Reed General Hospital in early April 1934, after suffering a stroke, and died on the last day of that month. After a well-attended service at Washington National Cathedral, Scott was buried at Arlington with full military honors. Tributes to his life came from many geographically and culturally different quarters of the nation from the many eclectic groups of friends he had made over a lifetime of public service. The inscription on the gravestone overlooking the Potomac River where he is buried succinctly sums up his life with the partial verse: "*Blessed are the peacemakers.*" A perhaps equally fitting tribute was inscribed on the memorial plaque placed in the Washington National Cathedral at the time of his funeral:

> A soldier valiant in action, wise in counsel, he successfully waged war to bring peace. By a rare combination of simplicity, integrity and courage, he was able to know the hearts of alien people and turn suspicious enemies into trusting and loyal friends.[54]

▼ ▼ ▼

CONCLUSION

The Legacy of a Reluctant Warrior

As a career army soldier on the American frontier at the end of the nineteenth century, Hugh Lenox Scott wanted to be characterized as a reluctant warrior. Throughout his numerous years of service in various capacities, he believed that violent, aggressive military action should be used only as a last resort. He relied on his skills as a negotiator to avoid military conflict whenever and wherever he could to minimize what he believed to be unnecessary bloodshed. Scott was no pacifist, however. As chief of staff in Washington near the end of his career, Scott proposed a plan of conscription, advocated a compulsory draft for all young men above the age of eighteen, organized training camps, and even directed one on an interim basis immediately following his mandatory retirement in 1917. He was acutely aware that the war in Europe would eventually involve the United States, and hence he believed that the country must be prepared for its defense.

Scott's reluctance to engage in aggressive warfare evolved as a consequence of his belief in and dedication to the preservation of American Indian tribes in the United States and the Moro groups in the southern Philippines. As a graduate of West Point and a a soldier on the American frontier, he eagerly learned about the cultures of the numerous tribes he encountered. His initial interest became a fascination that led to service as a negotiator, promoting peace and stability, avoiding overt military conflict, and advocating for the interests of the people in his charge.

Loyalty can be defined as devotion to a cause, commitment to a belief. Related qualities include trustworthiness, honesty, dependability, and reliability—all of which were used to describe Hugh Lenox Scott's character by those who knew him either personally or through the work he sought to accomplish within and beyond his military career. Both as a negotiator preventing bloodshed among tribal groups and between American Indians and their Anglo neighbors, and as an advocate seeking to protect tribal integrity, Scott manifested and engendered in others a strong sense of loyalty. During negotiations, he befriended specific tribal members not only to enhance his cultural understanding of a tribal group, but also to use the knowledge that they could provide from their interactions with other tribal members to anticipate and hopefully prevent conflict. For example, Scott befriended the Kiowa native I-See-O, whom he credited with preventing the more bellicose manifestations of the Ghost Dance religion among his tribe and among the Comanches. Scott repaid his loyalty to him, as well as others who served in the all-Indian Troop L that Scott organized at Fort Sill, by successfully lobbying government officials for equitable pensions based on their years of service. His correspondence with I-See-O through the Kiowa's nephew continued until the Indian's death in the mid-1920s.

Scott showed his loyalty, as well, to many datos in the southern Philippines, rewarding their willingness to maintain peace by advocating for their interests from his post in Jolo and with the Philippine Commission in Manila. Others whose service benefited from Scott's loyalty included numerous agents assigned to reservations by the BIA whom Scott befriended and assisted as early as his posting at Fort Sill, when he was charged with the care of the Chiricahua Apaches in the late nineteenth century. Such was the case with Ernest Stecker. Others such as Leo Crane, Frank Thackery, and Fred C. Campbell were befriended by Scott shortly thereafter. He recognized that they were the frontline workers, as it were, who monitored that tribal groups were receiving what was allocated to them in terms of economic assistance and health care. The efforts of these men to safeguard the tribes in their care were rewarded by Scott's determination to protect their tenure of employment.

However, Scott's loyalty to tribal integrity was tested by his fidelity to the military structure. As an ambitious junior officer in a highly competitive vocational environment in the late nineteenth and early twentieth centuries, Scott had to choose between advancement in his military career and assisting the tribal groups whose welfare he desired to protect. Compounding Scott's problem was his reluctance as a warrior. When the U.S. Army evolved into a professional fighting force to safeguard the nation's new overseas possessions with the objective of preparing for war, Scott was ill-suited as a candidate for military advancement.

When Scott was first commissioned, the army's primary function was to promote stability on the western frontier and avoid conflict between American Indians seeking to preserve their tribal holdings and Anglo settlers and commercial interests determined to exploit their lands. Given the army's limited size and the vast area of the American West, it was difficult to maintain adequate outposts for defense. In this environment, Scott had to hone his skills as a peacekeeper and peacemaker. He learned the Native sign language that enabled him to communicate among a number of different tribes. While his negotiating skills were appreciated by his commanders at the time, military authorities all but relinquished any interest in tribal affairs once these groups were no longer deemed a military threat. The twentieth-century army was structured to guard and protect America's new empire beyond its shores, and in doing so, to prepare for war. Seniority was no longer the prime criterion for advancement in rank, supplanted by the subjective one of merit, which was defined by one's battlefield experience. Consequently, Scott's résumé was scant when it came to his postings on the western frontier.

Scott deferred to military authority over tribal advocacy on several occasions. One example involved the Chiricahua Apaches, who were displaced from Fort Sill in the early twentieth century despite assurances from Scott and senior military officials that lands near the post would be their permanent home. With those assurances and Scott's assistance, these Apache families had made significant improvements on these lands. However, when the army decided to turn much of the land near Fort Sill into an artillery training school, Scott, as a career officer owing paramount allegiance to the military, believed he had no choice but to comply with his superiors' wishes. He therefore did so, to the extent of lying to the Apache families that he had ever told them that their occupation of those lands would be permanent! To his credit, at a later time, he formally apologized to the Chiricahua elders who had been all but coerced into accepting resettlement with the Mescalero Apaches in northern New Mexico.

Other incidents tested Scott's loyalties as well. His relationship with Leonard Wood, and Wood's friendship with Theodore Roosevelt, provided Scott with the recognition that ultimately led to his posting in the War Department as the army's chief of staff and a star ranking near the end of his career. Wood was initially attracted to Scott because of Scott's loyalty—his trustworthy, dependable, and reliable character. Equally important to Wood was an officer's willingness to assume the rigorous schedule that Wood imposed on himself and on the staff under his command. In turn, Wood earned Scott's loyalty through not only the vocational opportunities he provided but also the personal assistance he extended to Scott's family. Unlike Scott, however, Wood believed firmly in the use of overt force and used it to garner acclaim among the army's senior military command. Scott's service as military governor of the Sulu Archipelago in the southern Philippines under Wood's command placed Scott in a precarious position: he was challenged to work with the Moros and their leaders to promote peace and stability over against Wood's ongoing assertions to use overt force. Wood's bellicose posturing tested Scott's diplomatic skills on numerous occasions, not just with the Moros but with Wood himself. Once again, Scott was faced with having to choose between conflicting loyalties—to the Moros he sought to pacify, and to Wood, who was indispensable in the elevation of Scott's career. Specifically, the circumstance involved his defense of Wood's aggressive actions following the Bud Dago massacre in the Philippines. While Scott was on leave in the States, Wood and the officers under his command took preemptive military action against a number of Moro families who refused to come down from the mountain they occupied, where they had retreated in part because of their opposition to the cedula tax. When confronted with what had occurred, Scott refused to second-guess Wood's action, although it represented a complete repudiation of Scott's own determination not to use overt military action except as a last resort.

While a desire for adventure initially brought him to the northern Great Plains in 1876 with a commission as a second lieutenant, Scott was eager to learn the cultures of the numerous tribes he encountered. Such an understanding of tribal culture would serve a pragmatic purpose in negotiation. His embrace of the tribes' sign language garnered the respect if not the accord of the diverse dissident groups with whom he conducted negotiations. Learning the unique characteristics of a tribe's culture, such as their hierarchical structure, enabled Scott to identify how to initiate negotiation and with whom to negotiate.

More than his Anglo contemporaries, he recognized the importance and the value of the cultural pride of tribal groups and indigenous societies. To deprecate their values and traditions would negate any trust that tribal groups would have in Scott's ability to serve as an impartial arbiter. For example, although the practices of slavery and polygamy were personally repugnant to Scott, he was not prepared to chastise indigenous peoples for these practices, whether American Indians or Moros in the southern Philippines. His initial respect for their cultural practices was coupled with an ability to listen. Scott believed that tribal leaders and their followers who felt aggrieved should have the opportunity to "talk it out," knowing that in simply listening to them he was showing respect for their position and giving them an opportunity to dissipate their anger. Moreover, building confidence in tribal leaders through negotiation enabled Scott to befriend individuals within the group who could provide him with invaluable intelligence and thus prevent potential conflicts.

Scott's interest in tribal cultures was an intellectual pursuit as well. He corresponded with cultural anthropologists, sharing insights on the use of symbols by eclectic tribal groups; presented papers at scholarly conferences; assisted students in Native American studies; and used the press and public speaking engagements to promote an understanding of tribal lore and legend.

However, as an Indian negotiator and advocate, Scott was confronted with critics who deprecated the practices of indigenous groups, viewing them as heathen and uncivilized. Tribal dances, religious rituals, and institutional practices such as slavery and polygamy were castigated by many federal officials, and even by Anglo religious leaders devoted to tribal reform. Many critics believed that these ongoing practices by indigenous peoples inhibited their ability to attain salvation, while others felt that they could never be saved under any circumstance and would always remain as heathens.

Scott shared the views of those who believed that these practices were manifestations of primitive cultures. He, too, was patronizing from the perspective of a member of what he regarded as the highest form of civilization. Similar to many in his time and in the present, Scott believed in racial marginalization, defining people of different races as inferior according to a scale of social development relative to the so-called Anglo race. His perception of indigenous peoples was an important component in understanding both his need to negotiate with them as well as his rationale to assist them.

When writing to his friends and acquaintances about the character of American Indians and the Moros of the southern Philippines, he frequently noted both their savagery and their childlike behavior. Even what he saw as their favorable virtues—their sense of trust and loyalty—he attributed to a kind of innocence. His role as both a negotiator and an advocate manifested his racialist views.

The techniques he developed over time in the negotiating process were predicated on the belief that indigenous peoples were prone to war, and that such a tendency defined their primitiveness. Therefore, Scott, the reluctant warrior, honed skills that he hoped would mitigate their tendencies toward overt conflict.

While he respected tribal groups and was duly impressed with how their beliefs enhanced their dignity as people, he never believed that their cultures could sustain them in an Anglo-dominated world. As the buffalo were decimated on the northern Great Plains near the end of the nineteenth century, so, too, might a culture tied to the animal's existence disappear. And, to Scott, a Moro who believed that nothing of significance had occurred in the world since the death of Muhammad could not long survive in a civilized society as Scott defined it. The challenge Scott faced was how to provide both indigenous groups with something tangible to replace what he believed their cultures could not provide: the essential prerequisites of a viable society.

Scott was not overtly spiritual. Nonetheless, given his Presbyterian upbringing, he felt bound by God to help those on what he regarded as the road to salvation. While acknowledging the injustices inflicted on indigenous groups, from the invasion on their lands to the denigration of their culture, he could rationalize to himself that what he was offering in exchange was a lifestyle that he believed would bring them peace and prosperity. Hence, negotiation was critical in dealing with peoples who were prone to warfare and thus would be destroyed by waging it. Advocacy was necessary for those who he believed were in no position to defend themselves.

It may seem that there is little in Scott's legacy that would have meaning and significance for the present generation. The Indian sign language that he sought to promote did not become an enduring, viable means of communication among tribal groups. Nor did the assumptions he made about assimilation of American Indian tribes prove true. His desire for every tribal family to have a plot of land to farm and graze their livestock as a foundation for economic security was anachronistic even at the time the offer was rendered. Many tribal American Indians did not embrace farming or ranching as a feasible foundation for economic security. The Moro datos and their followers that he attempted to pacify never abandoned their belief in a religious code that embraced every aspect of their lives.

Nonetheless, Scott's legacy may be meaningful to our generation in several ways. By example, Scott developed negotiating skills that are universally applicable to many groups confronted with adversarial situations. Although not always successful, as his encounter with the Moros demonstrated, Scott mastered a technique for compromise among disparate groups. He was certainly not the first to use it, but he proved its value on numerous occasions, avoiding unnecessary bloodshed in the process. Scott was unique among those who advocated for tribal groups in the early twentieth century. Few utilized the levers of power and authority in campaigning for the protection of his tribal constituents as successfully as did Scott, who marketed his credentials as a frontier soldier through speeches, news articles, and radio programs to promote awareness of tribal matters.

A troubling aspect of Scott's legacy is the pervasiveness of racism in his generation. Scott's view of indigenous peoples as products of primitive societies was emblematic of a broader concept of racial marginalization, involving African Americans as well as immigrants flocking to America's shores in the early twentieth century. Other, more subtle forms of racism are also destructive of social norms and values. All too frequently, viewing the actions of people from other races or cultures engenders in us stereotypes that guide our behavior in interacting with them, as did Scott in assuming that indigenous people were prone to warfare in settling disputes. Although American Indian tribes were fortunate to have Scott as their advocate at critical junctures in their confrontation with the westward expansion of the United States, one must recognize the subtle currents of racism, not to mention its more virulent manifestations. Our generation faces a similar dynamic in racial marginalization to that of Scott's.

Vision maker is another descriptor that may be used to portray Scott. The journalists who wrote obituaries for Scott in April 1934 described a subject who enjoyed the adulation that he helped to create and perpetuate. Many articles by and about Scott appeared in the popular press. He spoke to civic clubs and participated in radio programs. He gave his audience what they increasingly craved following the end of World War I—a vision of an adventurous western frontier that would never appear again. He encouraged a sense of curiosity and fascination about indigenous inhabitants whose lives were dramatically different from those of ordinary Americans. Undoubtedly, Hugh Lenox Scott's legacy was that of a negotiator, advocate, vision maker, and reluctant warrior.

▼ ▼ ▼

NOTES

Abbreviations

BLC   Papers of Newton Diehl Baker, Manuscript Division, Library of Congress
BP   John C. Bates Papers, Army Military History Institute
CLC   Papers of Henry Clark Corbin, Manuscript Division, Library of Congress
FSM   Fort Sill Museum Archives, U.S. Army Field Artillery Center
NA   National Archives
NAA   National Anthropological Archives, Smithsonian Institution
PLC   Papers of John J. Pershing, Manuscript Division, Library of Congress
RLC   Papers of Elihu Root, Manuscript Division, Library of Congress
SFP   Smiley Family Papers, No. 1113, Quaker Collection, Haverford College
SLC   Papers of Hugh Lenox Scott, Manuscript Division, Library of Congress
TBLC Papers of Tasker Howard Bliss, Manuscript Division, Library of Congress
TLC   Papers of William Howard Taft, Manuscript Division, Library of Congress
USMA Library Archives, United States Military Academy
WLC   Papers of Leonard Wood, Manuscript Division, Library of Congress
WMCP Walter Mason Camp Papers, Box 3, Lilly Library, Indiana University

Preface

1. Among the earliest historians to demonstrate a more positive role for the military in Indian affairs in the late nineteenth century, see D'Elia, "Civilian or Military Control," 207–25; see also Ellis, "Humanitarian Soldiers," 53–66, "Humanitarian Generals," 169–78.
2. See, for example, Ostler, *Plains Sioux and U.S. Colonialism*; for a more general construct of the imperial relationship, see Holm, *Great Confusion in Indian Affairs*. Holm cites Robert K. Thomas, a cultural anthropologist, who claims that colonization is "the deprivation of experience" in which "the colonized are never allowed to experience change on their own. Colonization is the ultimate form of trespass which represses the ability to act without reference to colonial terminology, paradigms, and symbols" (ix).

3. See, for example, Hannah, "Space and Social Control," 412–32. Hannah demonstrates how the burden of reservation life with the imposition of fixed addresses undermined Oglala-Lakota culture; Means, "Indians Shall Do Things in Common," 3–21. Means demonstrates how the Native practice of breeding and herding cattle in common was undermined by federal officials and private interests.
4. Williams, "United States Indian Policy," 810–31; Bjork, *Prairie Imperialists*.

Introduction

1. The inscription on Scott's grave marking at Arlington National Cemetery reads as follows: "His great service to the country was in the remarkable control and influence which he exercised in dealings with the Moros, Mexicans and Indians which was invariably used in promoting peace. By personal effort he prevented many hostile outbreaks on the part of Indians. Blessed are the peacemakers." See Section East Site, S-12, Arlington National Cemetery.
2. Scott was one of only two individuals with military backgrounds noted in the last Lake Mohonk Conference, and the only one to address the group. See Lake Mohonk Conference, *Thirty-Fifth Lake Mohonk Conference*, 175–78.
3. General histories of the period noting the decimation of tribal lands include Genetin-Pilawa, *Crooked Paths to Allotment*; Otis, *Dawes Act*; and Washburn, *Assault on Indian Tribalism*. Thornton, *American Indian Holocaust and Survival*, estimates that the population of Native Americans in what is now the contiguous United States declined from 6 million in 1492 to 250,000 in 1890 (xvii, 43, 91, 133). Berthrong, "Legacies of the Dawes Act," notes that by 1921 more than half of tribal members affected by the Dawes Act lost their holdings (336).
4. LaPotin, *Native American Voluntary Organizations*. The author notes forty-seven Pan-Indian (nontribal) organizations that were formed between 1880 and 1928 with agendas that included advocacy for the welfare of Native reservation inhabitants. See "Chronological List of Organizations with Key Historical Events" (171–74); twenty-eight out of ninety-five attendees at the last Lake Mohonk Conference were clergy or representatives of churches or missionary organizations. See Lake Mohonk Conference, *Thirty-Fifth Lake Mohonk Conference*, 175–78.
5. See Scott, *Memories*, in which Scott affirms his convictions to his Presbyterian faith (6, 7, 256).
6. Guterl, *Color of Race in America*, 15, 16, 18. The author describes the efforts of advocates of racial marginalization "to establish national unity in the face of cultural fragmentation" (5). An illustrative example of a popular study espousing the theory of scientific racism is Grant, *Passing of the Great Race*; a more impressionist example, using the evolution of world history, is Adams, *Law of Civilization and Decay*.
7. On the similarities of logistics that Scott used in his process of pacification, see Bjork, *Prairie Imperialists*, 48, 59. On the similarities of Scott's racial perceptions of both groups, see Scott, *Memories*, 320.

Chapter 1

Epigraph: Scott Papers, box 1, USMA.
1. Folder: *Manuscript—Boyhood Youth*, boxes 80, 103, SLC.
2. *Hugh L. Scott—Genealogy*, box 103, SLC; *Diary of William McKendree Scott*, box 65, SLC.
3. *Diary of William McKendree Scott*, 1–60, box 65, SLC; the quote is on 2–3.
4. The definitive biography of Hodge is Gutjahr's *Charles Hodge*; the quote is on 3.
5. Folder: *Manuscript—Boyhood Youth*, box 80, SLC; Scott, *Memories*, 9; Gutjahr, *Charles Hodge*, 323.
6. Scott, *Memories*, 7; Robert S. Dod to Scott, 9/11/1871, and Postscript, 9/17/1871—both in Scott Papers, box 2, USMA; Scott, *Memories*, 8.
7. Scott, *Memories*, 11; Writing to his brother Len, who was overseas, Charles noted at the time of their mother's passing why she showed a deeper affection for her children than most mothers, "because her thoughts and interests were all centered on us." Charles Scott to Hugh Scott, 1/21/1899, box 1, SLC. As an example of her ongoing concern for her son, see Mary H. Scott to Hugh Scott, 2/19/1872, Scott Papers, box 2, USMA.
8. "Genealogy—Family Group Sheet—Maj. Gen. Hugh Lenox Scott US Army," *Biographical information on General David Hunter*, box 103, SLC; Charles Scott to Mary H. Scott, 7/27/1870, Scott Papers, box 1, USMA; letter to Armand LaPotin from Kenneth W. Rapp, assistant archivist, USMA, 3/13/1985.
9. Hugh Scott to Tom Ricketts, 6/4/1871, Scott Papers, box 1, USMA.
10. Ambrose, *Duty, Honor, Country*, 213–14, 196–97, 212, 203–4; 193. Significantly, Ambrose entitled his chapter on West Point's history in the post–Civil War period "Stagnation."
11. Ambrose, *Duty, Honor, Country*, 192, 193, 197, 201, 206–7.
12. The extensive quote is in Hugh Scott to Mary H. Scott, 10/26/1871, Scott Papers, box 2, USMA; see also Ambrose, *Duty, Honor, Country*, 204.
13. Both older brother Charles as well as their mother were concerned about Len's mastery of the subject. See Charles Scott to Hugh Scott, 1/11/1872, and Mary H. Scott to Hugh Scott, 2/11/1872, Scott Papers, box 2, USMA. For his tendency to procrastinate completing assignments, see Hugh Scott to Mary H. Scott, 12/1875, box 1, SLC.
14. *Register of Delinquencies*, Scott Papers, box 17, USMA. Scott's records are on 54, 111, 191, 224; see also Hugh Scott to Mary H. Scott, 11/28/1875, box 1, SLC.
15. Examples from different family members include Mary's letters to her son on 2/19/1872, 6/9/1872, 2/11/1872, 1/14/1872; see also Charles Scott to Hugh Scott, 12/27/1871; Charles Hodge to Hugh Scott, 6/7/1871; David Hunter to Hugh Scott, n.d., 1871—all in Scott Papers, box 2, USMA; Scott, *Memories*, 4; Hugh Scott to Mary H. Scott, 3/26/1876, box 1, SLC.
16. Robert Dod to Hugh Scott, 6/7/1871, 7/27/1871. Mary noted to her son that young Ricketts, one of her son's peers whose friendship she wanted him to cultivate, was in college at Troy and would love to hear from him. See Mary H. Scott to Hugh Scott, 9/19/1871. In a subsequent letter to her son, she noted how Ricketts took a first in French: "and I know from what you used to do that you could take higher if you tried[.]

[P]lease do me the pleasure of having you high in *one thing* [emphasis in original] & try your best to get out of the 6th section[.] I tell you that there will be Thanksgiving in this house." See Mary H. Scott to Hugh Scott, 1/14/1872—all in Scott Papers, box 2, USMA.

17. Edward Rankin to Hugh Scott, 7/26/1871; the quote is in letter of 10/23/1871; see also letter of 1/13/1872, where Rankin ties hunting to intellectual development, refers to how learning leads to spiritual enlightenment, and to how Scott's mother considered Rankin her son's mentor—all in Scott Papers, box 2, USMA.

18. Early in his freshman year, Scott confessed to his younger brother, William, or Wick, as he was called: "Know my letters from home are about all the fun I have." Hugh Scott to William Scott, 9/11/1871. Mary informed her son that "it [going to West Point] was your own choice—& if I had for one moment thought that you did not want to go you should not have gone. But now that there had been such an amount of trouble to get you an appointment, I do not think you can leave with *honor*" (emphasis in original). Mary H. Scott to Hugh Scott, 6/11/1871. Scott responded that "if hard study will do it I am going to stick." Hugh Scott to Mary H. Scott, 7/5/1871. All are in Scott Papers, box 2, USMA.

19. Mary H. Scott to Hugh Scott, 4/21/1872, Scott Papers, box 2, USMA.

20. Ambrose, *Duty, Honor, Country*, 222, 223, 224.

21. Ambrose, *Duty, Honor, Country*, 225; Reed, *Cadet Life at West Point*, 88.

22. Scott noted to his mother that "the deviling as they call it does not amount to anything at all and I cannot help laughing when they do it to me." Hugh Scott to Mary H. Scott, 6/2/1871, Scott Papers, box 2, USMA. Mary noted in her scornful letter to her son, "I believe you would have been home long ago if your grandfather had not happened to be there at the time." Mary H. Scott to Hugh Scott, 6/30/1871, Scott Papers, box 2, USMA.

23. Hugh Scott to Mary H. Scott, 10/26/1871; Mary H. Scott to Hugh Scott, 11/5/1871—both in Scott Papers, box 2, USMA.

24. Hodge chastised his grandson: "I am greatly surprised and grieved, that after the serious warning given your class you should have done such a thing." Charles Hodge to Hugh Scott, 6/10/1872, Scott Papers, box 2, USMA. Mary blamed the class of plebes "with a very low sense of honor . . . a wretched platoon for I know that a man who would tell tales in that way must be a coward." Mary H. Scott to Hugh Scott, 6/21/1872, Scott Papers, box 2, USMA.

25. Suspension noted from 7/12/1872 to 7/12/1873. See *Register of Delinquencies*, 17:111, Scott Papers, USMA; Reed, *Cadet Life at West Point*, 287; Scott, *Memories*, 17, 18; Ambrose, *Duty, Honor, Country*, 276.

26. Hugh Scott to William Scott, 11/10/1871, Scott Papers, box 2, USMA. Although he was working off demerits he had incurred in a previous period, the number of demerits that he received in his senior year were about 30 percent less than in his junior year. See *Register of Delinquencies*, 17:191, 224, Scott Papers, USMA; and Hugh Scott to Mary H. Scott, 9/12/1875, box 1, SLC. When an officer had his class doing double-time for an hour in the hot sun, Scott described it as "the worst exhibition of senile

imbecility & travesty of everything military that I ever saw." Hugh Scott to Mary H. Scott, 5/28/1876, box 1, SLC.
27. Scott, *Memories*, 18; Hugh Scott to Mary H. Scott, 10/24/1875, box 1, SLC. In a subsequent letter to his mother Scott noted that "the sense of mastership and exultation of sitting on a *handsome mad* [emphasis in original] horse is perfect bliss to me." Hugh Scott to Mary H. Scott, 4/23/1876, box 1, SLC.
28. Scott pondered all of these factors in letters to his mother during his senior year; see Hugh Scott to Mary H. Scott, 12/24/1875, 5/24/1876—both in box 1, SLC.
29. Adams, *Class and Race*, 7, 8. Although Adams addresses Scott's pragmatism in his willingness to serve as an officer of a black division, he notes that Scott "did not question the period's racial conventions" (182). See also Smith, *View from Officers' Row*, 41. Most officers "betrayed a restraint, a detachment, and an inability to penetrate racial barriers in order to achieve much genuine communication, sharing or understanding" (42). Scott was an exception. Leiker, *Racial Borders*, 11. The author notes that the army "operates as a patriotic symbol of the nation itself" (179).
30. Scott, *Memories*, 24–25.
31. Hugh Scott to Mary H. Scott, 5/24/1876, box 1, SLC; The Seventh Cavalry sustained a loss of 52 percent at the Battle of Little Big Horn on June 25, 1876, with sixteen officers killed in the five companies that were wiped out with Custer. Scott noted that two of his original classmates, John Crittenden and James Sturgis, were among the casualties. Prior to the battle, there was only one opening for his class in the Seventh Cavalry, and it went to Ernest Garlington, Scott's roommate and friend, who was four "files" above Scott. Scott claims that after he learned about the losses in the Seventh Cavalry, he approached his uncle Samuel Stockton, who "told me to sit down at once and write an application and send it through our uncle David [Hunter], in Washington who knew everybody in the War Department." Scott added, "Our uncle got my letter at breakfast, went at once to the War Department, where they were then making out the transfers to the Seventh Cavalry, and saw to it that my name was included in that fighting regiment, much to my satisfaction. Things were now coming my way." See Scott, *Memories*, 26.
32. For example, Garlington wrote at least one letter of commendation for Scott; Slocum would serve with Scott on the Great Plains; in Lexington, Kentucky; and in Cuba. Scott, *Memories*, 89, 102, 222, 265.
33. The quotes are in Hugh Scott to Mary H. Scott, 12/24/1875; for other examples of his thought process, see Hugh Scott to Mary H. Scott, 12/18/1875, 5/24/1876—all in box 1, SLC.
34. Scott, *Memories*, 26–28.

Chapter 2

Epigraph: Scott, *Memories*, 31.
1. References to Scott's assignment to the Seventh Cavalry and his commissioning as a second lieutenant are found in E. D. Townsend, Adj.-Gen., to Scott, 9/7/1876 [copy], box 1, SLC. All quotes on the Laramie Treaty are in Ostler, *Plains Sioux and*

U.S. Colonialism, 50, 52–53. Other sources include Parker, "Military Posts," 8, 10, 11, 13; Hedren, *After Custer*, 18–19; Tate, *Frontier Army*, 253–54; Wooster, *Military and United States Indian Policy*, 159, 161.

2. Ostler, *Plains Sioux and U.S. Colonialism*, 63; Hedren, *After Custer*, 5–6, 133–34; Price, *Oglala People*, 155.

3. Price, *Oglala People*, 155–57. Price notes that some Sioux chiefs such as Red Cloud did not understand that they were negotiating a land cession (157); Hedren, *After Custer*, 8, 19–20; Ostler, *Plains Sioux and U.S. Colonialism*, 77–78. Ostler notes that although the unity among dissidents was broken owing to their inability to obtain a reliable food supply, "the army was never able to score a major victory owing to the Indians' ability to avoid military defeat." Ostler also claims that diplomacy became increasingly important in dealing with the dissident tribal groups (78).

4. Utley, *Indian Frontier*, 41–42; Ostler, *Plains Sioux and U.S. Colonialism*, 54; Wooster, *Military and United States Indian Policy*, 103–4, 178–79; Hannah, "Space and Social Control." Even when corruption in the distribution of allotments and supplies to tribal peoples was not an issue, Hannah claims that the government used the threat to withhold essential provisions previously agreed to as a method to coerce Indians onto reservation lands (416–17). Hannah further notes that although the Fort Laramie Treaty (1868) had stipulated that one pound of beef and one pound of sugar per capita per diem would be distributed to the Oglala, this was never fulfilled in practice (414–15). See also Means, "Indians Shall Do Things." The paucity in the allotment was even worse since the government calculated the poundage of beef on the basis of what cattle weighed "on the hoof" (8). Means also examines the unscrupulous practices of the so-called Indian Ring, made up of reservation agents and their commercial suppliers, in defrauding tribes (8–9).

5. Hedren, *After Custer*, notes that by midspring 1877 "thousands of Sioux were still unaccounted for" (20). Ostler, who generally stresses a theme of unity among various band chiefs in Sioux polity, concedes that "scholars have often emphasized that Indian communities under colonialism were crippled by factionalism" and that "nevertheless, Native leaders were sometimes able to overcome tendencies toward divisiveness" (*Plains Sioux and U.S. Colonialism*, 116). Price, *Oglala People*, documents one example of the contentiousness among bands within the Sioux tribe over the issue of selling the Black Hills to the federal government in 1876 (133–54); the confusion over of the commissioners' perception of Red Cloud's leadership as a tribal negotiator is noted on 174–75.

6. Gutjahr, *Charles Hodge*, 320.

7. Barnes, *Forts of the Northern Plains*, 105–6; Scott, *Memories*, 29–30.

8. Scott to Mary H. Scott, 1/26/1878, Scott Papers, box 2, USMA. Another, perhaps more vivid example of extreme weather conditions was when Scott bemoaned to his sister-in-law, "Lulu," what a Dakota winter could be like, with temperatures twenty degrees below zero, a biting northwest wind, and blinding drifts that obliterate trails, causing disorientation. See Scott to "Lulu," 12/24/1879, Scott Papers, box 2, USMA; and Scott, *Memories*, 31. Scott's frequent letters to Mary, his mother, during his early

post-Academy years on the Northern Plains, were circumspect. He rarely referenced his experience in how he transitioned from an "adventurer" to an American Indian "conciliator." He was well aware that she would worry if she knew the dangers that he confronted. Mary H. Scott to Scott, 1/4/1880, Scott Papers, box 2, USMA; see also West, *Contested Plains*, 58, 71, 115–16, 125, 129.

9. Scott noted that he "did not undergo five years of toil at West Point to come out to the Plains to be a 'wagon' soldier." Scott, *Memories*, 35. See also Dunlay, *Wolves for the Blue Soldiers*, 19. Dunlay also notes that Indian scouts, the majority of whom served as guides, were in high demand by military commanders in Sioux Country in the postbellum period through the 1880s. Their military quota ranged from 100 to 1,000, with that number subtracted from the army's total manpower as designated by Congress (50–51). See also Smits, "Fighting Fire with Fire." Smits notes that among the many benefits in the use of Native scouts as an advanced column was in their knowledge and sophistication of the strategies used by other tribes, both allied to or enemies of their tribe (81). On Scott's sense of observation, see General Samuel D. Sturgis to Scott, 11/15/1885, box 6, SLC. The quote is in Scott, *Memories*, 32.

10. See *Argument to Support S. 106* (1918?), 1, Scott Papers, box 5, USMA. This request on behalf of Scott, to justify additional compensation in his retirement pension for his service in keeping the peace on the nineteenth-century frontier, documented how he learned and used the sign language so effectively; he also notes in his autobiography how he bribed a Cheyenne chief, White Bear, with sugar and coffee, to teach him the sign language (86); the second quote is from a speech he delivered to the Boy Scouts near the end of his career. See Scott, "Sign Language of the Plains Indians," 1/3/1931, box 82, SLC.

11. See, for example, Scott's description of a Crow encampment where "everybody was carefree and joyous in a way we do not comprehend in this civilized day." Scott, *Memories*, 56. Scott was similar to others who encountered Indians during this historical period in embracing the myth of the noble savage, viewing the so-called Indian as a "child of nature." The implication of his beliefs, and the foundation of his association with tribal cultures on all levels, will be analyzed in chapter 6. Scott, *Memories*, 34–35. The quotes are in Smith, *View from Officers' Row*, 20.

12. Scott's order to assist Miles in the capture of the Nez Percés is noted in Cullum, *Biographical Register*, 3:266. The treaty of 1863 and its consequences are analyzed on 8–14. Fear that Chief Joseph would join with Sitting Bull's band is noted on 165–66, 205. A description of the circumstances leading up to Joseph's surrender and the journey to Bismarck is on 293–324. See also Hampton, *Children of Grace*, 317; and Scott, *Memories*, 83–84; the second quote is on 84.

13. Scott, *Memories*, 51–52; the quote is on 52.

14. Hutton, *Phil Sheridan and His Army*, 35, 131; Ostler, *Plains Sioux and U.S. Colonialism*, 109, 116, 117–20, 121–22, 124–26. The quote, on 126, is from James Irwin, agent at the Red Cloud Agency.

15. Scott, *Memories*, 94. In his autobiography Scott recalls that "it was a good deal of responsibility to throw on a young man only two years out of West Point; I not only

had to act as interpreter, and extricate the commanding officer from the tense situation, but must still preserve his dignity" (96). The two quotes are on 97; for another example, see 112.
16. Recollections of the Crow and Sioux buffalo hunts are noted in Scott, *Memories*, 57–58, 59. Ostler, *Plains Sioux and U.S. Colonialism*, relates one telling of the symbolic origins of the buffalo's introduction to Sioux culture through the story of the coming of White Buffalo Calf Woman, when the Sans Arcs, moving westward, were faced with starvation (26–27). Black Elk, a highly respected Lakota medicine man, had a vision involving the presence of the buffalo, a vision that he believed would cure the illnesses of his people. The vision was acted out at the Pine Ridge Agency in the early 1880s. For Black Elk's description of the ceremony, see Neihardt, *Black Elk Speaks*, 209–12; a description of the ceremony that preceded the chase is noted in Walker, "Communal Chase of the Buffalo," in DeMallie, *Lakota Society*, 74–94. So important was the ritualistic aspect of the hunt that tribal groups, once regimented to the reservation agency, requested and were permitted to hunt and slaughter the animals, initially buffalo and subsequently cattle, themselves. Means, "Indians Shall Do Things," 4; Hedren, *After Custer*, 102–3.
17. Ostler, *Plains Sioux and U.S. Colonialism*, 57. Hedren, *After Custer*, describes the commercial hunt on 96–100, and the trade in hides on 96, 110; Gen. Phillip Sheridan, commander of the Department of the Missouri, noted in the 1870s that "the destruction of this [northern] herd would do more to keep Indians quiet than anything else that could happen." Hutton, *Phil Sheridan and His Army*, 246.
18. Each quote is found in the following: Scott, *Memories*, 123, 124.
19. All quotes are in Scott to Joe Culbertson Jr., 3/24/1920, MSS 57, box 2, folder 8, WMCP.
20. On Scott's detail to rebury the remains of Custer's troops, see Hedren, *After Custer*, 34–35, 180–81; and Scott, *Memories*, 46. On hunting see Scott to Mary H. Scott, 8/4/1879, 8/18/1879, 9/1/1879, box 2, USMA. On lake sailing, see Scott to Mary H. Scott, 5/18/1879, box 1, SLC. On "fishing," see Scott, *Memories*, 103–4. During this time, Scott could comment to his mother, "We live in the style that men of property do in the East." Scott to Mary H. Scott, 9/20/1879, box 1, SLC.
21. Scott, *Memories*, 4–5; The death of Scott's grandfather is noted in Mary H. Scott to Scott, 10/27/1879; on the imminent passing of his grandmother, see Mary H. Scott to Scott, 3/14/1880—both in Scott Papers, box 2, USMA; Examples of his mother's ongoing chastisement of his alleged immoral behavior are in Mary H. Scott to Scott, 1/4/1880, 4/14/1880, 6/1/1880—all in Scott Papers, box 2, USMA.
22. Scott, *Memories*, 86, 109; Scott's mother noted of her son's marriage, "I don't think I shall be weaned from you but I know you will be weaned from me. Life is short and full of trouble. Do let us keep together while we can." Mary H. Scott to Scott, 4/11/1880, Scott Papers, box 2, USMA.
23. References to the survey of a telegraph line and the delineation of a reservation boundary are respectively noted in "Order No. 45, 4/22/1882" [copy]; "Order No. 167, 7/27/1883" [copy]—both in box 6, SLC; "Walter Camp Interview Notes of Hugh L. Scott," October 1915, MSS 57, box 2a, folder 20, WMCP. A description of the circumstances

surrounding Crazy Head's rebelliousness is noted in Col. John P Hatch to [Indian agent] N. J. Armstrong, 4/9/1883, box 6, SLC; Scott's final order noted that "*Under no circumstances* will the commanding officer of the force allow a *collision* [emphasis added] to take place with these Indians." Order No. 93—official copy respectfully furnished to Lt. H. L. Scott, 7th Cavalry for his information and guidance, 4/28/1883 [copy]box 6, SLC.

24. David Hunter was born at Fort Totten in November 1881; Anna Merrill in Allegheny, Pennsylvania, in April 1884; Lewis Merrill at Fort Meade in October 1885, and Mary Blanchard in Philadelphia in July 1887—all noted in *Family Group Sheet* [copy], folder: *Hugh L. Scott—Genealogy*, box 108, SLC; In applying for an extension for leave in the East, he noted that he had a "considerable" family and would not be able to return "for a number of years because of expense." Scott to the Adjutant-General, 9/13/1888, folder 3, ACP 4879, RG 94, NA.

25. Tate, *Frontier Army*, 286–91; on Sturgis see 290–91. Sturgis noted to his junior officer: "There is no man in Dakota, either in the Army or out of it, who is as well posted as you are from personal observation, in the resources and possibilities of Dakota." Sturgis to Scott, 11/15/1885, box 6, SLC. References to Merrill as a source of land investment, given his posting along the construction of the Northern Pacific railroad, the investment in Dakota lands with brother Charles, opportunities for their mother to join the enterprise, and the general perils in such an investment are in Scott to Charles, 6/22/1882, box 1, SLC.

26. Coffman, *Old Army*. Coffman noted that the size of the army during this period ranged from 25,000 to 28,000 men (215); see also 231, 232–33, 234, where he references a restrictive retirement system, the regimental constraints regarding promotions, and the percentage of officers competing for promotions at any given time. Coffman remarked that "the promotion game started when an officer received his initial commission" (230–31).

27. The quote is in Harry Hoyt to President Benjamin Harrison, 6/1/1889. Similar views are noted in Governor James A. Beaver (Pa.) to President Benjamin Harrison, 3/12/1889, and James Losh to the President, 5/28/1888—all in folder 2, ACP 4879, RG 94, NA.

28. Coffman, *Old Army*, noted that during this period, "too many officers showed their understanding of the superiority of civilian power by using whatever political influence they could generate to their advantage in assignment and promotion matters" (368); Gutjahr, *Charles Hodge*, notes that on Hodge's fiftieth anniversary as a professor at Princeton Theological Seminary, more than four hundred of his former students showed up to honor him. He was to serve another six years (359–61); Hodge's work with the Presbyterian Mission and Education Boards is noted on 122–23, 124. See also Kehl, *Boss Rule*. The reference to Anderson Quay's seminary admission is on 4; his work with the Presbyterian boards and the Colonization Society and the quote by the younger Quay on what he inherited from his father are on 5. References to Matthew Quay's political career are found throughout Kehl's biography, with his dedication to tribal peoples specifically noted on 3–4, 248–50.

29. Charles Rushmore to Scott, 11/27/1908, 12/4/1908; John F. McGee to Senator Porter J. McCumber (N.D.), 12/7/1908; John F. McGee to Scott, 12/7/1908, 12/9/1908, 12/19/1908, 1/13/1909—all in box 10, SLC.
30. Scott, *Memories*—the first quote is on 32; the second is on 108–9. See also Cullum, *Biographical Register*, 6/28/1878, 3:266; Notice of appointment to First Lieutenant, War Department, 7/5/1878, folder: *1870–1878*, box 6, SLC; Scott notified his brother Wick of his promotion. Scott to Wick, 8/23/1878, Scott Papers, box 2, USMA.
31. Perhaps typical of a soldier in a battle venue then and now, Scott initially noted to his mother that "fighting for the good of one's country is one thing & fighting to put stars on Gen'l Miles' shoulder is another." Scott to Mary H. Scott, 2/24/1877, Scott Papers, box 2, USMA. Nonetheless, when he first met Miles at Fort Keough, and the colonel recognized him, calling out his name, Scott recalled, "It caused me visibly to swell with pride." Such was the importance of recognition to Scott. He described Miles's capture of Joseph in the northern Yellowstone District as "one of the most brilliant feats of arms ever accomplished by the American Army, considering the immense distance he had to travel through primeval country." Scott, *Memories*, 66; Greene, *Nez Perce Summer*, 334–36; Hampton, *Children of Grace*, 317–18.
32. DeMontravel, *Hero to His Fighting Men*, 62, 99–100, 124, 126–28; the quote is on 357. While DeMontravel stresses the virtues of his subject, Wooster, in *Nelson A. Miles*, emphasizes more of his shortcomings (265–74; see esp. 269).
33. Hedren, *Great Sioux War*, 132–33, 135–36. Hedren estimates, referring to the Standing Rock and Cheyenne River confrontations, that "in all, more than 1200 horses were confiscated at Standing Rock and some 1900 at Cheyenne River, along with a relatively meaningless cache of obsolete weaponry" (133). On the Yellowstone deployment, see 152; Hedren notes that "it was readily apparent to everyone that the Great Sioux War was all but over."
34. Hedren, *After Custer*, judged the cost of the Sioux War to be "astounding," noting that Sherman estimated to Congress that the army had spent over $2.3 million (25). Military forces engaged in the Nez Percé campaign incurred an expense upwards of $1.8 million. Greene, *Nez Perce Summer*, 332. Obviously, any military venture against dissident tribal groups that promised to reduce the financial costs and the loss of lives would be welcomed. Coffman, *Old Army*, notes that 20,300 troops were in the American West to the California coast, 66 percent of the entire federal military force, during this period (254); Hannah, "Space and Social Control," notes that the army did not have the strength to defeat tribal insurgents (421); Hutton, *Phil Sheridan and His Army*, claims that Sheridan lacked the concentration of force to engage successfully in campaigns against insurgent tribal groups after 1877 (332). In his annual report to the secretary of war, Sheridan, commander of the Missouri Division, noted the paucity of military personnel at the various forts, given the vastness of America's frontiers and the responsibilities that the army had to assume. See *Annual Report of the Secretary of War* (1878), 1:33; Scott noted to his mother that there was no money to finance an expedition short of "a regular uprise among the Indians." Scott to Mary H. Scott, 4/6/1878, box 1, SLC. Constraints on the size, tactical dispersion of the

frontier army, and the superiority of American Indians in guerrilla warfare are noted in Birtle, *U.S. Army Counterinsurgency and Contingency*, 58–59; Haines, "Death of Crazy Horse," 54, 58; and Hedren, *After Custer*, 153. Military and civilian personnel in the BIA recognized that depredations against settlers and commercial interests would only end if tribal groups occupied fixed spaces, and the way to enforce that constraint was through, among other practices, a geographic restriction to a designated area for the distribution of food and clothing. Hannah, "Space and Social Control," 412–13, 422. The lack of training of soldiers in frontier warfare is noted in Smith, *View from Officers' Row*, 10–11, 153; Utley, *Indian Frontier*, 95; and Smits, "Fighting Fire with Fire," 73. The military advantage of winter campaigns in general is noted in Hannah, "Space and Social Control," 420; and Smith, *View from Officers' Row*, 72; use of winter campaigning by Sheridan is noted in Hutton, *Phil Sheridan and His Army*, 185; and Haines, "Death of Crazy Horse," 56; a description of a winter campaign led by Crook against the Northern Cheyennes is in Ostler, *Plains Sioux and U.S. Colonialism*, 70–71; Schofield's opinion on "total war" is quoted in Wooster, *Military and United States Indian Policy*, 142.

35. Hutton, *Phil Sheridan and His Army*. The quote is on 254; 261 and 301 reference Sheridan's belief in the efficacy of total warfare. Scott, *Memories*, notes his reaction to the decimation of the buffalo herds (123–24).
36. Scott described himself at the time as "the enemy of the Indian Department and everybody in it." *Memories*, 201. His view on the Interior Department's treatment of the Northern Cheyennes is quoted on 89–90.
37. On the example involving the capture and subsequent internment of Chief Joseph at Fort Leavenworth, see Greene, *Nez Perce Summer*, 310; and Hutton, *Phil Sheridan and His Army*, 333. This quote is noted in Scott, *Memories*, 84.
38. Scott, *Memories*, 87–88.
39. Order No. 37, 4/3/1882, Order No. 3, 11/17/1882, Order No. 232, 11/25/1882, Order No. 24, 1/31/1883, Order No. 181, 8/12/1883—all are copies in box 6, SLC.
40. A fear on the part of military officers that tribal dissidents might flee to Sitting Bull over the border and launch a massive attack in the Dakota or Montana Territories during this time is noted in Hedren, *After Custer*, 153; Hampton, *Children of Grace*, 264, 285, and Scott to Walter Mason Camp, 9/2/1913, MSS 57, box 1a, folder 23, WMCP. Scott maintained that Sitting Bull had "some 1200 lodges . . . just across the border"; Miles's intense ambition to garner further recognition and professional advancement in battle is noted in Hampton, *Children of Grace*, 283, 284; and Greene, *Nez Perce Summer*, 245–47; Miles's rivalry with Howard is noted on 329–31.
41. Greene, *Nez Perce Summer*, 191; a description of Scott's efforts to apprehend Joseph and his band of Nez Percés is on 192–94, 318–19; Scott, *Memories*, 64–65. Scott later reminisced, "I have always felt that I turned back the Nez Perce advance near the mouth of Gardner River" near the north-central boundary of Yellowstone National Park, thus allowing "Miles to capture them in the end." Furthermore, Scott claimed that Joseph told him, following his surrender in September 1877, and during his ride with Joseph from Buford to Bismarck, that Scott's "rapid advance with ten men at

Mammoth hot springs & chase of his advance guard or rather scouts . . . made him think that I had a strong force behind me"; as a result, Chief Joseph "turned off at the Mud Geysers, crossed the Yellowstone there below the lake—went up Pelican Creek & East Fork, then down Clarks Fork, about 100 miles nearer Gen. Miles." Scott to Walter Mason Camp, 9/22/1913, MSS 57, box 1a, folder 23, WMCP.

42. McWhorter, *Hear Me, My Chiefs!*, 441, 442—both quotes are in Camp to Scott, 9/9/1913, MSS 57, box 1a, folder 23, WMCP.

43. Few letters between Scott and his older brother, Charles, are found in relevant sources during Scott's tenure on the northern Great Plains. Although Len and Wick did not correspond on a frequent basis during this period, the letters that they wrote indicate feelings of affection and interests in what each other was doing. See, for example, Scott to Wick, 8/28/1878, Wick to Scott, 11/2/1879—both in Scott Papers, box 2, USMA. Denial of Scott's request for an additional year's posting at Philadelphia is noted in Adjutant General to Senator Matthew Quay, 5/18/1888, box 6, SLC. Notification of several openings in the Commissary Department are cited in Robert Dechert to William Scott, 5/28/1888, box 6, SLC. Examples of letters endorsing Scott's candidacy for the commissary position include John W. Barr Jr. to Col. W. C. P. Burkingham, 6/27/1888, Princeton College president James Losh to President Benjamin Harrison, 5/28/1888, Col. Samuel D. Sturgis to Secretary of War William C. Endicott, 6/5/1888, Governor (Pa.) James A. Beaver to President Benjamin Harrison, 3/12/1889, Harry Hoyt to President Benjamin Harrison, 6/1/1889, and President (Pa. state senate) Boise Penrose (with endorsements from state senators) to President Benjamin Harrison, 3/12/1889. Scott personally asked for a letter of endorsement from U.S. Senator George Gray (Del.) after Gray had offered to write a letter supporting Scott, if requested. Scott noted that he was a lieutenant in the Seventh Cavalry for twelve years "with every prospect of remaining a Lt for twelve years (or more) longer because most of our Captains are young and low down on the list." Scott to Senator George Gray, 10/16/1888—all in folder 2, *General Appointments, 1888*, ACP 4879, RG 94, NA. Merrill's effort to enlist additional support for his son-in-law is noted in a letter to John Wanamaker, the prominent Philadelphia merchant. Merrill noted that Scott had the support of "the whole of the faculties of Princeton College and Theological Seminaries . . . a large body of the most reputable citizens of Philadelphia including the leading members of the Union League and of the Penna R.R." Also noted in support of his candidacy were "nearly the whole Republican delegation in Congress from Pennsylvania and by the whole of the Senior Officers of the Penna. National Guard who came in contact with him during his recent term of duty in Philadelphia." Lewis Merrill to John Wanamaker, 9/27/1889, folder 3, *General Appointments, 1888–1892*, ACP 4879, RG 94, NA.

44. Quay to Reverend Frank B. Hodge, 10/19/1888, box 6, SLC. Quay stated that he had appealed to Benjamin Harrison through the president's dedication to the Presbyterian faith but noted that he was "overwhelmed with applications." More specifically, Quay indicated that there are some old lieutenants of artillery who have been in rank for twenty-five years, and "their claims have made a strong impression." Box 6, SLC. See

also Attorney-General to Scott, 10/11/1888, folder 3, *General Appointments, 1888–1892*, ACP 4879, RG 94, NA; and Cullum, *Biographical Register*, 4:271.

Chapter 3

Epigraph: Report on the status of Apache prisoners of war, box 6, SLC.

1. Hämäläinen, *Comanche Empire*, 346, 347; Gwynne, *Empire of the Summer Moon*, 23–24, 28–29, 32, 58, 59, 60, 68.
2. Gwynne, *Empire of the Summer Moon*, 91, 113, 164.
3. Hämäläinen, *Comanche Empire*, 322, 330–31, 336, 337; Gwynne, *Empire of the Summer Moon*, 4; Hagan, *United States–Comanche Relations*, 23, 29, 30, 31–32.
4. References to the demoralizing conditions on the reservation during this period are in Hagan, *United States–Comanche Relations*, 124–25, 139.
5. Hagan, *United States–Comanche Relations*, 166, 167, 168–70.
6. Cullum, *Biographical Register*, 3:266.
7. James Mooney, a pioneer and renowned anthropologist, wrote extensively about the religious phenomenon called the Ghost Dance. See *Ghost Dance Religion and Wounded Knee*, esp. "Wovoka: The Messiah," 764–76; and "Ghost-Dance Religion and the Sioux Outbreak."
8. The quote is in Cullum, *Biographical Register*, 3:266; Scott's fourteen-page, highly detailed report (in Mooney, "Ghost-Dance Religion and the Sioux Outbreak") indicates that he took copious notes on what he observed and where he observed it. He also provided a narrative of how and where the movement started, how it spread to other tribes, and how each group that he visited interpreted its prophecies. His report also included a detailed description of how the so-called Ghost Dance was performed. His final assessment as to why and how certain tribal groups turned the movement to violence was supported with evidence drawn from his prior experience in working with tribal groups. References to the evolution of the Ghost Dance are noted on 2, 3, 4; references to Ah-pia-ton's disillusionment in discovering that Wovoka was *not* the Messiah can be found on 10–12. See Scott, "The 'Messiah' Dance in the Indian Territory," No. 31, box 3, FSM; Scott, *Memories*, 157–58; Hagan, *United States–Comanche Relations*, 189–90.
9. Scott, "The 'Messiah' Dance in the Indian Territory," p. 12, No. 31, box 3, FSM; Seymour, *Indian Agents*, 350; Nye, *Carbine and Lance*, 271; Scott, *Memories*, 147, 148.
10. Swett, "Sergeant I-See-O," 347; the quote is on 348.
11. Swett, "Sergeant I-See-O." Scott's praise of I-See-O's work in the Ghost Dance movement is noted on 351; his view of I-See-O's primitive nature is found on 350.
12. References to I-See-O's role in the incident are in *Sgt. I-See-O, Kiowa Indian Scout*, No. 34, box 3, FSM. On limiting the use of overt military force, Scott noted in his lengthy report to the adjutant general at Fort Sill that the reservation's chief of police was anxious to call in troops and arrest the fugitive and have him tried in an Oklahoma court, "a proceeding I was determined to prevent [because] all of these Indians are uneasy about what is going to happen. The papers are read by the Eastern

Graduates [of the Carlisle Indian School] and are full of stories about the arming of the settlers in Oklahoma and Texas and the disarming of the Indians, the fighting with the Sioux, and they do not know what to expect. It would therefore be, in my opinion, injudicious to the last degree to excite them further." He also noted in his report that "from the assurances of the head men of the Kiowa, I was convinced that this wild act was not sanctioned by them." Both references are in Scott to the Post Adjutant, Fort Sill, O.T., 1/18/1891, box 6, SLC.

13. Washburn, *Assault on Indian Tribalism*; a copy of the Dawes Act is on 68–73. The origin of the "forced allotment" provision is noted on 53–55. On the organization and work of the Lake Mohonk Conference on Native American concerns, see 12–13. Hagan, *Taking Indian Lands*, documents the Cherokee Commission's history and negotiating process with the Kiowa-Comanches as well as other tribes as noted herein. For example, the commission's charge is on 16–17. On the belief that white settlers would serve as an example for their tribal neighbors is, see Otis, *Dawes Act*, 17; references to the Lake Mohonk proceedings are on 36–37. See also Hagan, *United States–Comanche Relations*, 58.

14. Hagan, *Taking Indian Lands*; the quotes are on 184.

15. Hagan, *United States–Comanche Relations*, 201, 205–6, 214–15; Hagan, *Taking Indian Lands*, 184, 185–86, 187, 189.

16. Hagan, *Taking Indian Lands*, 183–84; the quote is on 192.

17. Hagan, *Taking Indian Lands*, 187. On Agent Day, see 193, 202, 204. On Parker see 184–85. Hagan notes that Parker owned a herd of several hundred cattle, 150 horses, and a 40,000-acre private fenced pasturage tract. Jerome even attempted to bribe Scott, noting that his presence was giving "countenance to this meeting." However, when offered an allotment from the commission, Scott responded, "I would rather that I never got a foot of land anywhere than that an Indian be induced to do anything . . . on account of any benefit it might bring to me." Nonetheless, Hagan criticized Scott for allowing his name to be put on a list of allottees creating what he felt was "an appearance of conflict of interest" (*Taking Indian Lands*, 197, 203; Hagan, *United States–Comanche Relations*, 202). On his suspicion of Parker's motives, Hagan observes, "It is hard to avoid the conclusion that Quanah [Parker] was an architect of the Comanche surrender to the Cherokee (Jerome) commission" (*United States–Comanche Relations*, 214). For sympathetic views of Parker's actions in support of his people during this period, see Gwynne, *Empire of the Summer Moon*, 308–15; and Otis, *Dawes Act*, 39, 40, 96. Scott, *Memories*, maintains that Parker was speaking to the Committee on Indian Affairs "only for himself and not for his people, who have not sent him here, and he does not represent their sentiment" (200).

18. Hagan, *United States–Comanche Relations*, 207, 213, 260–61; "To the President of the United States," 5/11/1893, box 6, SLC; Hagan, *Taking Indian Lands*, 203, 205.

19. Hagan, *United States–Comanche Relations*, 210.

20. Scott claimed that President Cleveland was very impressed with Ah-pia-ton, although it might have been more owing to his dress and stature than the cogency of his

arguments. This meeting and his rivalry with Parker are noted in Scott, *Memories*, 200–201; see also "To the President of the United States," 5/11/1893, box 6, SLC.
21. Hagan reveals his equivocation in summarizing Day's tenure at Anadarko. Compare his views in *United States–Comanche Relations*, where he notes that Day "pushed house construction for the Indians," ostensibly to better their lives economically (170). However, Hagan also stated that "the chance that Day would oppose the commission was virtually zero . . . as Jerome well knew. Certainly none of the other agents had been willing to sacrifice their standings with Washington to battle for their tribes" (*Taking Indian Lands*, 193); Although he does not mention a specific date or agent, Scott noted in his autobiography how one agent's "grafting . . . went beyond bounds, and his actions were a demoralizing influence on his Indians. . . . and he became intolerable to everybody." Scott started a petition for tribal members to sign that would be sent to the Indian Office calling for this agent's dismissal, which was ultimately successful. *Memories*, 205. Scott's criticism of such practices underscored a broader debate between the War Department and the Department of the Interior in the 1870s through the 1890s as to which department could better manage the administration of Indian affairs. Scott's position was that if the army were given legal power on the frontier, it would have "enforced our treaties, keeping faith with the Indian, and so avoided our shameful Indian wars." Scott, *Memories*, 135. Similar reasoning was used by Gen. Philip Sheridan. See D'Elia, "Civilian or Military Control," 215n; for an opposing view, presented by Secretary of the Interior Carl Schurz in 1878, see "Army Charges Answered: The Indian Service Upheld by Mr. Schurz," *New York Times*, 12/7/1878.
22. Miles's criticism of the administration of Indian affairs by the Interior Department and his broader sympathies for the plight of tribal groups are noted in Wooster, *Nelson A. Miles*, 191–92, 194. Quay's political standing and his method of enhancing his power at both the state and federal levels are noted in Kehl, *Boss Rule*, 62–64, 84–85, 95; and Scott, *Memories*, 201–2.
23. Feaver, "Indian Soldiers, 1891–1895," 109, 110. With the exception of the Carlisle Indian School "experiment," under its founding principal, Col. Richard Henry Pratt, at the army barracks in Pennsylvania, the recruitment of tribal males in the regular army was the last attempt by the War Department to take an active role in the administration of Indian affairs in its standoff with the Bureau of Indian Affairs. Tate, "Soldiers of the Line," 353.
24. Feaver, "Indian Soldiers, 1891–1895," 111–12; Nye, *Carbine and Lance*, 261. Parker's rejection may have been due to what he believed would be a loss of his power as a chief; Although I-See-O was well past the age for normal recruitment—he was then about forty-two—when he enlisted his age was noted as twenty-nine; Scott appointed him as a first sergeant, an indication of his confidence in I-See-O's influence among his people. Swett, "Sergeant I-See-O," 347; Scott noted that "I-See-O's influence among the Kiowas; his steadfast position and his many trips to the outlying camps of the Kiowas had a large share in the final success . . . of Troop L,

7th Cavalry." *Notes on the Kiowas and Comanches as Regular Soldiers (1892)*, 8–9, No. 32, box 3, FSM.
25. Nye, *Carbine and Lance*, 262; Scott, *Regular Soldiers*, 9–12. On the younger Quay, see also Scott, *Memories*, 138, 206–7; on Senator Matthew Quay, see 201–2, 204–5; and Kehl, *Boss Rule*, 3, 248–50. Examples of Scott's favorable ratings from the extracts of inspection reports include *Extract of a Report of an Inspection at Fort Sill*, made 1/20/1893 by Col. E. M. Hyle, Inspector General, Washington, 4/8/1893, J. C. Breckinridge, Inspector General; Extract from remarks, recommendations, summary, etc., of Report of the Inspection of Post of Fort Sill, O.T., made 7/1/1893, by Major A. S. Daggett, 13th Infantry, Commanding, covering past fiscal year; Extract from Inspection Report of Fort Sill, O.T., by B. J. D. Irwin, Colonel and Assistant Surgeon General, U.S. Army; and Stecker to Scott, 8/26/1894 (Stecker's report to Scott in his absence)—all in box 6, SLC. Daggett noted that Scott "has, during the last eighteen months, transformed a body of blanket Indians into clean, orderly and fairly well drilled and disciplined soldiers."
26. Scott's order to take charge of the Chiricahua Apaches at Fort Sill is found in, Cullum, *Biographical Register*, 3:266. The major references that specifically address the Chiricahua Apaches at Fort Sill include Turcheneske, *Chiricahua Apache Prisoners of War*; Stockel, *Shame and Endurance*; Haes, "Fort Sill, the Chiricahua Apaches," 28–43; Ragsdale, "Values in Transition," 39–105; Utley, *Geronimo*, 249; Debo, *Geronimo*, 359, 360; and Marion Maus to Nelson Miles, 9/1/1894, box 4, FSM.
27. Scott to Col. Ware, 12/23/1895, box 6, SLC; *Vital Statistics of Apache Prisoners of War*, SLC, 46; Turcheneske, *Chiricahua Apache Prisoners of War*, 43–44, 45, 60–66, 74, 116–17, 184–85; Scott to the Assistant Adjutant General, 11/7/1894, as cited in Stockel, *Shame and Endurance*, 105–7 (the quote is in Scott to the Adjutant General, 10/31/1896, *Apache Indians—1896*, box 46, SLC); Debo, *Geronimo*, 359–60; Betzinez, *I Fought with Geronimo*, 166; Scott, *Memories*, 184–85; Boyer and Gayton, *Apache Mothers and Daughters*, 115, 116; Haes, "Fort Sill, the Chiricahua Apaches," 39.
28. Scott, "Memories," 188; Utley, *Geronimo*, 250; Stockel, *Shame and Endurance*, 102; Betzinez, *I Fought with Geronimo*, 166–67, 168; Nye, *Carbine and Lance*, 267, 292–93, 326. The quote is in Scott to William Cameron & Company, 1/21/1896, No. 38, box 4, FSM.
29. Betzinez, *I Fought with Geronimo*, 166–67; Boyer and Gayton, *Apache Mothers and Daughters*, 115; Debo, *Geronimo*, 372; *(Troop) L 7th Cav*, n.d., hand-written two-page note by Scott, No. 32, box 3, FSM; Haes, "Fort Sill, the Chiricahua Apaches," 35; Tate, "Soldiers of the Line," 362; Habgood and Skaer, *One Hundred Years of Service*, 9, 11–12, 18, 19–20. The endorsements are noted from 8/18 through 9/25/1895, the last being the source of Kellogg's quote—in box 6, SLC.
30. Scott to the Adjutant General, 10/31/1896, *Apache Indians—1896*, box 46, SLC.
31. Tate, "Soldiers of the Line," 361, 362, 363. Twenty years later, as chief of staff, Scott claimed that his Indian soldiers had been "cheated out of success by prejudiced minds in the War Department." On the eve of the U.S. entry into World War I, he urged the army to enlist tribal groups and "would sanction their use for immediate action." Scott to E. E. Ayer, 2/19/1917, File 1669226, *Indian Cavalry Regiments*, Records of

Adjutant-General's Office, RG 94, NA; Dunlay, *Wolves for the Blue Soldiers*, 196, 197; Lt. Charles G. Lyman to Scott, 12/30/1894, 1/9/1895; Adjutant-General's Office to the Commanding General, Department of the Missouri, 2/26/1897—all in box 6, SLC.

32. Shortly after Scott left Fort Sill, twenty-one members of the Anadarko Tribal Council signed a petition to the secretary of the interior calling for, among other demands, the retention of army officers as reservation agents for "an Army Officer thinks more of his duty toward we Indians and less of the benefits he may derive from the position." Kiowa, Comanche and Apache Indian Agency to C. W. Bliss, Secretary of the Interior, 12/7/1897; Scott to the Adjutant, Fort Sill, 8/15/1897—both in box 6, SLC; Turcheneske, *Chiricahua Apache Prisoners of War*, 67. Scott reportedly told an agent he had appointed from the military that the Interior Department "was a hard master to serve under." Stecker to Scott, 5/15/1911, box 47, SLC. For an example of Scott's restraint on the use of troops and a determination to work directly with the tribal parties involved in an incident, see Scott to the [Fort Sill] Post Adjutant, 1/18/1891, box 6, SLC; and Steinbach, *Long March*, 162–63, 164, 165; the quote is on 163. See also Scott, *Memories*, 51; for example, Baldwin had accused the inspector who investigated the case of acting in bad faith. Baldwin to the Commissioner of Indian Affairs, 4/9/1897, box 6, SLC.

33. Scott, *Memories*, 178, 197; *Matter of Lieutenant Ernest Stecker, Superintendent, Kiowa Indian School*, 7/1/1910, box 47, SLC. The quote and Stecker's challenges in providing for the tribal groups under his care are noted in Stecker to Scott, 172/28/1910; see also Stecker to Scott, 2/14/1911; 5/15/1911; for a reference to Scott's determination to defend Stecker against charges of dereliction of duty, trumped up by his partisan adversaries, see Francis F. Kane to Scott, 6/23/1911, 7/15/1911—all in box 47, SLC. See also Francis Leupp, Commissioner of Indian Affairs, to Scott, 10/29/1907, box 46, SLC; Scott, *Memories*, 188; Turcheneske, *Chiricahua Apache Prisoners of War*, 67–72; and Quinette to Scott, 4/30/1897, box 6, SLC. Clancey noted that all the Apaches as well as Beach and Capron were doing well. Thomas Clancy to Scott, 5/16/1898. In a letter to Scott on 6/8/1898, Clancy reported that the Apaches were branding four hundred calves, doing well, and harvesting eighty acres of cotton—both in box 7, SLC.

34. Turcheneske, *Chiricahua Apache Prisoners of War*, 72–79, 89.

35. Turcheneske, *Chiricahua Apache Prisoners of War*, 92, 103–4, 105, 116–17, 184–85; Utley, *Geronimo*, 269.

36. Turcheneske, *Chiricahua Apache Prisoners of War*, 54, 56. The quote is in Scott to George Davis, 8/17/1896, box 46, SLC.

37. Turcheneske, *Chiricahua Apache Prisoners of War*, 91, 121, 122, 124; George Scott to Scott, 12/14/1910, box 47, SLC. George Scott (no relation) was a recently appointed officer in charge of the Apaches in the fall of 1910. As previously noted, the status of George Scott's posting at this time was subservient to that of the post commander. Stockel, *Shame and Endurance*, 133; Henry P. McCain to Scott, 7/24/1911, box 47, SLC; Robert Valentine to Scott, 8/8/1911, box 76, SLC. A fourteen-page internal War Department report that attempted to outline the position of both sides, in answering the question of how to address the settlement of the Chiricahuas at Fort Sill, tended

to weigh in the army's direction. For example, it noted the cost involved in preparing the facility to be used as a school for artillery instruction; the alleged desire of the Chiricahuas to move to another location, and the alleged encouragement from their friends who were welcoming the move. Significantly, too, War Department officials hypothesized that if the Apaches were to remain at Fort Sill their lands would be aggrandized by white settlers, and "having spent their money [from the land sales], they [the Chiricahua] would probably soon disappear." Scott's order to go to Fort Sill never indicated that remaining there was an option open to the Apache prisoners of war. Given the chronology of the report, it may be assumed that the War Department was giving Scott talking points to use in his impending conferences with the Chiricahuas. See *Apache Prisoners of War: Order and Memorandum*, 7/20/1911, box 47, SLC; and Haes, "Fort Sill, the Chiricahua Apaches," 35, 37–38.
38. Scott to Walter L. Fisher, Secretary, Department of the Interior, 11/17/1912, box 47, SLC; Turcheneske, *Chiricahua Apache Prisoners of War*, 101–4; 125, 135. Other examples of the acrimony directed against Scott by Chiricahuas present at his conferences are cited on 156; see also Vincent Natalish to Theodore Roosevelt, 1/7/1909, 1/12/1909, box 46, SLC.
39. All quotes are from *Memo for the Chief of Staff*, 11/1911, box 47, SLC; see also Turcheneske, *Chiricahua Apache Prisoners of War*, 136–42, 143–54; Scott Ferris to Scott, 5/20/1914, 5/23/1914; Senator Henry Ashurst to Scott, 5/29/1914—all in box 47, SLC; and Haes, "Fort Sill, the Chiricahua Apaches," 38–39.
40. Haes, "Fort Sill, the Chiricahua Apaches," 40 (quote); Turcheneske, *Chiricahua Apache Prisoners of War*, 165. Turcheneske describes Scott as a "tragic hero" (186); see also Ragsdale, "Values in Transition," 98; and Stockel, *Shame and Endurance*, 146.
41. References to Mary's frail health and Scott's anguish over her condition during this period are in Scott to Mary, 11/5/1889, 11/6/1889—both in box 6, SLC; and 11/29/1895, 12/15/1895—both in Scott Papers, box 2, USMA. Representative references to Scott's plans for their new home at Fort Sill are in Scott to Mary, 10/25/1889, 11/8/1890, 12/4/1889, 12/6/1889, 12/8/1889, 12/16/1889, 12/23/1889, 12/25/1889—all in box 6, SLC; representative references noting the presence of his children at Fort Sill, while Mary was in the East, are found in Scott to Mary, 5/8/1892, 5/10/1892, 5/14/1892, 11/15/1892—all in Scott Papers, box 2, USMA; and representative references to Scott's concern for finances are in Scott to Mary, 12/22/1889, 12/31/1889—both in box 1, SLC.

Chapter 4

Epigraph: Sayre quoted in Turcheneske, *Chiricahua Apache Prisoners of War*, 87.
1. Jerry M. Cooper, "The Army's Search for a Mission: 1865–1890," in Hagan and Roberts, *Against All Enemies*, 184; Weigley, *History of the United States Army*, 267; Coffman, *Old Army*, 222, 232–33. Prior to the end of his tenure as secretary of war in 1908, William Howard Taft noted that an officer initially commissioned as a second lieutenant would spend twenty-nine years as a company-grade officer before attaining a major's rank in the regular army. See *War Department Annual Report (1908)*, 1:87–88. In Scott's case, he spent twenty-seven years as a company-grade officer before being promoted

to major, such was the glacial rate of retirement in the early twentieth century, even with an expanded army at the time.
2. On the eve of the Philippine Insurrection in 1899, and with evident shortcomings in military preparation, Theodore Roosevelt, then governor of New York, noted that the army would need to end the use of *seniority* as a criterion for promotion if it expected to win. "We have got to push up our best men, wholly without regard to seniority" (quoted in Hagedorn, *Leonard Wood*, 1:240). And, as president in 1904, he did just that! Elihu Root, McKinley's innovative secretary of war, noted the advantages of promotions based on merit within a year of his appointment. See *War Department Annual Report (1901)*, 1:538, 539; and Clark, *Preparing for War*, 3, 8. For an example of the differing views of officers who recognized that military education did not end at the Academy, see Clark, *Preparing for War*, 129–30; For examples of subjective biases among officers administering examinations to determine professional competence for promotion determinations, see Clark, *Preparing for War*, 148–49. In his autobiography, Scott claimed that Brig. Gen. Arthur L. Wagner, one of the army's most progressive reformers, told him, regarding efficiency reports, that "not one of those records was called for in making the appointments. Efficiency was of slight weight in those days, when political influence was the main vehicle for advancement"; evidently, Scott's bitterness and frustration endured even twenty-five years later. Scott, *Memories*, 223.
3. Salient aspects of the conflict are noted in Cosmas, *Army for Empire*, 63–64, 66–67, 68, 74–76, 85–86, 88–89, 90, 91, 92, 93, 100–101, 120.
4. Scott's predicament regarding the army's erroneous record of his actual tenure in rank and its consequences as a result of the 1890 law calculating seniority are spelled out in detail. See Mary Scott to President Roosevelt, 11/1/1901, ACP 4879 and 1876, RG 94, NA. Although a cursory analysis of Scott's ACP file reveals numerous letters from military officials and private individuals attesting to his compassion, sympathy, advocacy, and scholarly endeavors with and for tribal groups, as well as his skills as an administrator in supervising them, few attest to his experience in a battle setting. Folders 1–9, *Records of the Adjutant-General*, ACP 4879, RG 94, NA.
5. See Cullum, *Biographical Register*, 3:266, 4:271.
6. Coffman, *Old Army*, 232; Roberts, "Reform and Revitalization," 210; Order No. 37, 4/3/1882, Order No. 3, 11/17/1882, Order No. 232, 11/25/1882, Order No. 24, 1/13/1883, Order No. 181, 8/12/1883—all are copies in box 6, SLC. Scott's promotion to captain in 1895 is in Cullum, *Biographical Register*, 4:271.
7. Cosmas, *Army for Empire*, 88–89, 120; Clark, *Preparing for War*, 99–101, 102–3, 167, 168–69.
8. Russell Alger to Matthew Quay, 10/2/1897, acknowledging his letter in support of Scott; Redfield Proctor to Russell Alger, 6/21/1897; Redfield Proctor to Hugh Scott, 6/21/1897—all in box 6, SLC. Proctor cautioned Scott about the assistant adjutant general's appointment, noting that "these places, as you know, are so much sought after (that) you will need to use all available means to secure the promotion I am sure you so well deserve"; Proctor's high regard for Scott's work with the Indian scouts (Troop L) while Proctor was secretary of war is noted in Coffman, *Old Army*, 259.

9. James Mooney to Scott, 6/6/1897; Special Orders No. 151, Fort Sill, O.T., 11/23/1897 [copy]; Assistant Adjutant General to Scott, 11/12/1897—all in box 6, SLC.
10. Arthur Wagner to Scott, 6/31/1897; Ernest Garlington to the Adjutant-General, 6/19/1897—both in folder: *Records of the Adjutant-General*, ACP 4879, RG 94, NA; the quote is in Scott to Mary, 5/1897, box 6, SLC.
11. Specific references to Miles's direct assistance to Scott early in his career are in Scott, *Memories*, 11, 32, 171, 181–82, 185–86, 214–15; Scott to Mary, 12/1/1896, box 1, SLC; and Nelson Miles to Russell Alger, 11/9/1897, *Records of the Adjutant-General*, ACP 4879, RG 94, NA. Examples of Miles's hospitality to Scott are in Scott to Mary, 11/17/1895, 11/20/1896, 11/30/1896, 12/1/1896, 12/4/1896, 12/12/1896—all in box 1, SLC; and DeMontravel, *Hero to His Fighting Men*, 8, 17, 60. Wooster, *Nelson A. Miles*, presents a more critical analysis of Miles's endeavors than DeMontravel. For example, Miles's opposition to military reform is noted on 214; his increasing acrimony with Secretary of War Alger is noted on 215–16, 220, 232, 234, 235; and his contentiousness and opposition to Root are cited on 238–40. See also Weigley, *History of the United States Army*, 289–90, 311, 316. References to the contentiousness between Miles and McKinley are in Coffman, *Regulars*, 15. By the early spring of 1898, however, Scott learned that McKinley and Corbin's view of Miles would preclude any viable opportunity for a posting that would enhance Scott's chances for a promotion, owing to the general's "political tendencies." See Scott, *Memories*, 221. When Miles requested that his then protégé Leonard Wood join him in Washington, the request was initially rejected. One of Wood's biographers concluded that although "Miles was the ranking general in the army . . . [the administration] had no reason to look with favor on one of Miles's closest associates. In fact, a recommendation from Miles would probably do Wood's cause more harm than good." Lane, *Armed Progressive*, 22.
12. Scott claimed in his autobiography that he was "without political influence" and lamented that "it now appeared [that] soldiers were not wanted in this war." This was an allusion perhaps to *real* soldiers, whom Scott defined as those who promoted peace and what he regarded as "proper professional credentials." Given his feelings, it is probable that he was referring to the poor quality of volunteers. See Scott, *Memories*, 218, 221–22; and Scott to Mary, 3/29/1898, box 1, SLC. For Scott's receipt of his commission and agreement to accept the post at Camp Thomas, see Scott to the Adjutant-General, 5/29/1898, folder 8, *Records of the Adjutant-General*, ACP 4879, RG 94, NA.
13. Scott, *Memories*, 222–23; Scott expressed a similar concern to his sister-in-law, in anticipation of the army's new overseas role: "a garrison must be made for Cuba, Porto Rico and Hawai [sic] & Manila—besides the Indian Country. The army must be enlarged to meet all these conditions—which will probably be done to the detriment of the regular army as always heretofore by pulling in Colonels, etc from these political colonels we see around here without knowledge or experience over the heads of men of long service." He added, "I do not see yet what the outcome will be for us in the least." Scott to Lulu, 8/20/1898, Scott Papers, box 2, USMA.
14. Scott claimed that he had "exhausted every means at my command to get where the war will be—it seems like my fate is to stay out and I cannot alter it." Scott to Mary,

6/5/1898; see also letter of 6/19/1898, box 1, SLC. Scott's reliance on Mary for information on divisional deployments is noted in letters of 9/7/1898, 9/21/1898, 12/10/1898, box 1, SLC. In another letter in the third week of December, after he learned Mary would be leaving Washington shortly, Scott expressed the concern that "as we are both going to be away from Washington when the crush comes. . . . (and) we are not strongly represented[,] we are going to the wall for sure" (Scott to Mary, 12/21/1898, box 1, SLC).
15. Cosmas, *Army for Empire*, 275; G. R. Cecil, Assistant Adjutant-General, Special Orders No. 79, 8/18/1898 [copy], as cited in box 7, SLC; Scott to Mary, 8/28/1898, box 1, SLC.
16. McCallum, *Leonard Wood*, maintains that Wood "maximized his own . . . role in Geronimo's actual surrender" (39). On Wood's military honor, see McCallum, *Leonard Wood*, 45–46; and Lane, *Armed Progressive*, 18. Wood's relationship with Roosevelt is covered in detail in Eisenhower, *Teddy Roosevelt and Leonard Wood*. Wood's contribution to Roosevelt's "Rough Riders" is covered in Roosevelt, *Rough Riders*.
17. W. B. Scott to Hugh L. Scott, 1/5/1899; Scott to Mary, 1/6/1899—both in box 1, SLC.
18. Scott to Mary, 1/25/1899, box 1, SLC; Brigadier-General Theodore Schwan, Assistant Adjutant-General to Scott, 2/8/1899, ACP 4879, Office of Adjutant-General, folder 9 (1900), RG 95, NA.
19. Scott to Mary, 2/8/1899, 3/14/1899, 3/22/1899, 4/8/1899—all in box 1, SLC. The publication of the March ruling regarding the qualifications for advancement of line officers in the Office of the Adjutant General are noted in Headquarters of the Army, Adjutant-General's Office, General Orders, No. 154, Washington, D.C., 8/22/1899, ACP 4879 and 1876, RG 94, NA; Ludlow's endorsement of Scott, dated 4/8/1899, is referenced in Scott, *Memories*, 271. Despite this and other recommendations by senior officers such as Wood, it would take Scott almost five years to attain the rank of major in the regular army. Scott to Mary, 8/2/1899, 8/19/1899. In writing to Mary in August, Scott noted that he had the best place to live and work, 8/10/1899; Scott's leave is noted in Scott to Mary, 8/19/1899, 8/29/1899—all in box 2, SLC.
20. A reference to Mary's pregnancy during this period is in Scott to Mary, 12/2/1899; Scott's ongoing financial duress during this period is noted in Scott to Mary, 12/8/1899. Scott noted confidently that "I am on very good relations with all the gen. offs on the island & if there should be any change here[,] I am very likely to get to be the Adj. Gen. of the island if my promotion is a real fact." Scott to Mary, 8/1899; Ludlow's confidence in Scott is noted in Scott to Mary, 11/4/1899—all in box 2, SLC.
21. On how Wood and Scott initially met, see Scott to Mary, 1/3/1900, box 2, SLC. Wood was described as "a 'man of intense ambition,' hungry for advancement, 'consciously cultivating men who could help him along' . . . 'pushing aside others who stood in his way.'" Lane, *Armed Progressive*, 23 (quoting Gordon Johnson to Hermann Hagedorn, 2/1/1929, Hagedorn Papers, 55).
22. The initial quote is in Scott to Mary, 1/25/1900; the second quote is from a letter to her on 3/10/1900, along with the notification that by early March both Root and Wood expressed the desire for Scott to remain in Cuba—both in box 2, SLC.
23. On his ongoing concern for Hunter, see Scott to Mary, 5/7/1900, 5/21/1900, 6/4/1900, 10/16/1900, box 2, SLC. On the workload of a divisional adjutant general, Scott noted,

"It requires the most constant work—the management is very complicated—and the volume of business is colossal." Scott to Mary, 3/10/1900, box 2, SLC. On Wood's need and desire to prove himself on the battlefield, see Lane, *Armed Progressive*, 126; and McCallum, *Leonard Wood*, 210, 212. For a detailed account of Wood's work in sanitation, education, and the justice system, initially in Santiago and ultimately on the entire island, as well as his vision for Cuba, see Lane, *Armed Progressive*, 56–57, 58–59; McCallum, *Leonard Wood*, 111–12, 114, 118–22, 125–26, 147–96; and Pruitt, "Leonard Wood," 68, 74–75, 146–206.

24. Bacevich, *Diplomat in Khaki*, 9–10, 19–20; Lane, *Armed Progressive*, 88. Palmer, *Bliss, the Peacemaker*, draws a number of parallels between Scott's life and that of Bliss; see 60, 61, 63, 66, 67, 69, 73; see also Pruitt, "Leonard Wood," 150. One of the many letters that Wood wrote on Scott's behalf, noting his qualities as an officer and recommending him for brigadier general in the regular army, is found in Leonard Wood, Brigadier-General (USA) to Henry Corbin, Major-General (USA), *Office of the Adjutant-General*, 7/11/1902, Office of Adjutant-General, folder 12 (1902–4), ACP 4879, RG 95, NA. Wood remarked to a colleague that one of Scott's attributes was his familiarity with conditions in Havana. See Scott to Mary, 2/12/1900, box 2, SLC.

25. Scott to Mary, 5/7/1900, 6/6/1900, 6/8/1900, 10/5/1901, 4/11/1902—all in box 2, SLC; Scott, *Memories*, 246.

26. Scott's ongoing concerns about family finances are noted in Scott to Mary, 6/1/1899, 7/1/1899, 6/13/1901, 6/8/1902, 7/7/1902, 9/2/1902, 10/1/1902, 11/2/1902—all in box 2, SLC. Wood's recognition of Scott's financial situation is noted in Wood to Root, 1/22/1901, 7/24/1901—both in box 30, WLC. The quote is in Scott to Mary, 6/5/1901, box 2, SLC.

27. References to Scott's frustration over Hunter's lack of self-discipline are in Scott to Mary, 5/7/1900, 5/21/1900, 7/8/1901, 9/20/1901, box 2, SLC.

28. Copies of letters that Wood wrote to Lt. Col. William H. Carter and Gen. Henry C Corbin, both in the Adjutant General's Office; Elihu Root, who was serving as secretary of war; and Theodore Roosevelt, who was then governor of New York—all on 12/8/1900—are in box 2, SLC; Corbin wrote directly back to Scott, noting that there were then no presidential appointments that could be made. See Corbin to Scott, 12/15/1900, box 7, SLC. Timing was an important consideration, given Hunter's advanced age. Ultimately, Scott thought it better for his son to wait a year or two before taking the exam, reasoning that to take it and fail would be worse than not taking it at all. See Scott to Mary, 6/30/1901, box 2, SLC.

29. Scott, *Memories*—all quotes are on 253; for examples of his success at diplomacy, see 251, 252, 260, 262–63, 267–68; see also Scott to Mary, 8/30/1901, box 2, SLC.

30. One historian described Scott's physical appearance, even prior to his fiftieth birthday, as looking "much older" than his age. "While just a shade under six feet and having been a powerfully built young man, he now had gone to seed, sporting a noticeable middle-age paunch. He was gray-haired, gray-mustached, balding, and wore large-rim spectacles that gave him an owlish and curmudgeonly appearance," which contrasted with the more youthful appearance of his colleagues. See Fulton, *Moroland*, 159–60. Scott complained to Mary "that now is my opportunity to show off the old age that

has caught me and remain old & older for the rest of my life—not that I am in my first youth now—but since the desk work of the Spanish War I am so much older than my age calls for." Scott to Mary, 9/3/1902, box 2, SLC. On his fiftieth birthday, Scott lamented, "It seems that I am getting very old & losing a great deal of you and the children." Scott to Mary, 9/23/1903, box 3, SLC.
31. Scott to Mary, 6/17/1902, box 2, SLC.
32. Scott sent the letter to his wife indicating the strategy he would use with Wood and his longtime advocate Senator Matthew Quay (Pa.). This quote is in Scott to Mary, 1/20/1903, box 3, SLC.
33. One of Roosevelt's more contentious critics was Thomas C. Platt, boss of New York's Republican political machine. Donald, *Lion in the White House*, documents the origins and contentiousness of Platt's acrimony toward Roosevelt; see 115–17, 122. On the nature of Roosevelt's disagreement with Platt, see Roosevelt to Josephine Shaw Lowell, 2/20/1900, Reel 4, Series 1, RLC. On the contentiousness involving Wood's nomination for a second star, see McCallum, *Leonard Wood*, 177–78, 207–8, 209–11. Lane, *Armed Progressive*, claims that the submission of Wood's request for a second star "set off one of the most explosive debates of Roosevelt's administration" (125); see also 126. Roosevelt warned Wood that "everything must be avoided which will have the least appearance of pushing you at the expense of anyone else." Roosevelt to Wood, 3/19/1904, box 35, WLC. Almost five years after the debate on Wood's nomination, Roosevelt recollected to an associate that "no one incident of my administration has caused me more criticism, more difficulty, more trouble of every kind, than getting Wood made Major General. The Army was against it, Congress was against it, and the people at large were overwhelmingly against it." Roosevelt to Albert Lenoir Key, 4/10/1908, *Letters*, Reel 64, RLC. The details concerning the entire debate are comprehensively covered in McCallum, *Leonard Wood*, 207–11; and Eisenhower, *Teddy Roosevelt and Leonard Wood*, 109–10.
34. On Wood see McCallum, *Leonard Wood*, 206–7, 221; Lane, *Armed Progressive*, 118–19; and Eisenhower, *Teddy Roosevelt and Leonard Wood*, 109, 110. Wood to Roosevelt, 1/4/1902, box 31, WLC.
35. On whether Scott knew in advance that the Senate would approve Roosevelt's offer, see Scott to Mary, 2/5/1903, 2/25/1903; even immediately prior to Roosevelt's offer, Scott rallied his congressional supporters: Senators John Kean and John Dryden (N.J.), noted in Scott to Mary, 1/20/1903; Senators Matthew Quay and Boies Penrose (Pa.), noted in Scott to Mary, 2/8/1903—all in box 3, SLC. These and Senators Henry Cabot Lodge (Mass.) and Francis Cockrell (Mo.) were also enlisted in support of Scott. Scott to Mary, 2/26/1903, box 3, SLC.
36. On the specific military administrative structure in the southern Philippines and Scott's place in it see Pruitt, "Leonard Wood," 225–26. On the challenges that Scott initially faced in Jolo to acquire the important military command that he sought, see Scott to Mary, 7/20/1903, 8/16/1903, 8/23/1903—all in box 3, SLC; the situation was eventually resolved in his favor when he was given military command of the Fourteenth Cavalry, as noted in Scott to Mary, 9/1/1903, 9/23/1903—both in box 3, SLC.

37. McCallum, *Leonard Wood*, 210, 211–12, 216; Lane, *Armed Progressive*, 125, 126.
38. Fulton, *Moroland*, 20–21, 22, 23; Arnold, *Moro War*, 3–4, 17.
39. Arnold, *Moro War*, 4; Fulton, *Moroland*, 25–26.
40. Arnold, *Moro War*, 20; Fulton, *Moroland*, 30–31, 32–33, 35–36.
41. Linn, *Philippine War*, 5–6, 7, 8, 15; Weigley, *History of the United States Army*, 317; Pruitt, "Leonard Wood," 216, 225–26.
42. Byler, "Leonard Wood, John J. Pershing," 89–104. Byler claims that during the Philippine Insurrection, the War Department ordered commanders in the field to do all they could to keep peace in the south. The challenge was to impose American sovereignty in Mindanao without provoking the Moros to armed resistance. Consequently, the commanders kept their troops in the barracks and allowed influential datos to maintain order (90); see also Linn, *Philippine War*, 225–26. Gen. Elwell Otis, military commander of the Philippines, noted that the agreement alleviated the necessity of having to send 15,000 soldiers to fortify the posts in the southern Philippines (Linn, *U.S. Army and Counterinsurgency*, 123). The processes for reaching an agreement are noted in Fulton, *Moroland*, 39–54.
43. Fulton, *Moroland*, 40, 41, 43, 44, 46; Linn, *Philippine War*, 180; Arnold, *Moro War*, 8–9.
44. Fulton, *Moroland*, 41, 181, 224, 227, 240; Arnold, *Moro War*, 9, 12, 13, 14, 15–16, 105; the claim of omission of the word "sovereignty" is on 9.
45. Wood to Roosevelt, 9/20/1903, box 32, WLC. On Wood's initial and unilateral violation of the Bates Agreement and his initial armed meeting with the datos in Sulu, see Fulton, *Moroland*, 177–78—the organization of the Philippine Commission is noted on 177; Bacevich, "Disagreeable Works," 54; and McCallum, *Leonard Wood*, 213–14. On the moderate ruling of the Philippine Commission regarding the "customs of the Moros," see Bacevich, "Disagreeable Works," 52, 55. On the organization of and enactments by the Legislative Council in September 1903 under Wood's control, see Fulton, *Moroland*, 180–81; and Bacevich, "Disagreeable Works," 55. On the cedula and the Moros' response to it, see Fulton, *Moroland*, 41, 181, 224, 227; and Arnold, *Moro War*, 105–6.
46. Arnold, *Moro War*, notes that Wood "showed little interest in Pershing's slow, methodical approach" (87); see also Wood to Roosevelt, 9/20/1903, box 32, WLC.
47. Arnold, *Moro War*, 41, 122–23; Scott's problems with Moros who committed juramentado are noted in Scott to Mary, 9/23/1903, box 3, SLC; Scott's feelings about the matter are in *Memories*, 314–16, 318–19; and his racial attitudes toward the Moros are expressed on 320–21. Other examples include his reaction to their ignorance as to the spread of disease, noting "what a cold hand the religion of Islam puts upon progress; it can see nothing of value that has arisen since the death of Mohammed, some six hundred years ago" (352).
48. On the embarrassment of Raja Muda, see Fulton, *Moroland*, 178–79; and McCallum, *Leonard Wood*, 214–15. Scott's concern for the mortification that he might have caused the sultan is noted in *Memories*, 279–80; the quote citing Scott's response to Wood's command for Biroa's arrest is on 293–94. Furthermore, Scott rationalized his

decision by noting that the demand should never have been made in the first place, but since it was "it must now be upheld and enforced, albeit without legal sanction, if Americans were expected to live in Jolo" (293–94).
49. Fulton, *Moroland*, 185–87; Oscar Charles to Mary Scott, 8/26/1903, 11/28/1903—both in box 3, SLC; Arnold, *Moro War*, 91–92; Scott, *Memories*, 288–89, 298, 304–6; the quote is on 305. Examples noting Scott's respect for the Moros' faith and culture are on 313.
50. In initially dealing with Hassan, Arnold maintains that Scott had "patiently worked through recognized lines of Moro authority to try to apprehend Biroa. Not only had he failed, but he had antagonized a more influential Moro *datu*. To cap it all off, friendly Moros reported that Hassan was plotting a surprise attack against the American garrison" (93). Evidently, Scott did not initially realize the limitations of the sultan of Sulu's power, which was far less than that of an Ottoman caliph. In his autobiography, Scott explained his failure to win over Hassan at the first by noting, "We had been there too short a time for the Moros to have confidence in us." *Memories*, 332. The quote on his reluctance to use overt force against the Moros is in Scott to Mary, 7/6/1903; other examples noted to justify its use are in Scott to Mary, 11/9/1903, 2/25/1904—all in box 4, SLC.
51. On Pershing see Greenwood, *My Life before the World War*. Examples of Pershing meeting formally and informally with Moro datos are noted on 150–54, 156–57; and Arnold, *Moro War*, 88, 103.
52. References to the cedula and its implications when imposed on the Moros are in Bacevich, "Disagreeable Works," 55; Arnold, *Moro War*, 105, 106; and Scott, *Memories*, the first two quotes are on 376, 377.
53. References to Scott's "arms buyout plan" are on 288. References to his advocacy for the sultan's hereditary rights before the Philippine Commission in Manila are in Scott to Mary, 7/3/1904; in a subsequent letter, Scott compared his advocacy to "the very old work in Washington with the Comanche & Kiowa delegations fighting for the rights of the underdog." Scott to Mary, 7/20/1904—both in box 3, SLC. Other measures enacted with adverse effects on the Moros as well as those directed against hereditary title for datos are noted in *Memories*, 370–71; the final quote is on 371.
54. Scott, *Memories*, 382.
55. Pruitt, "Leonard Wood," 128–29; Scott, *Memories*, 307; Birtle, *U.S. Army Counterinsurgency and Contingency*, 164.
56. Scott to Mary, 1/24/1904, 2/4/1904, box 3, SLC.
57. The first quote is in Scott to Mary, 10/28/1903, box 3, SLC; Scott "defined" the guidelines on the use of overt force to include what he regarded as an unprovoked assault on American troops. At an earlier period, in late August, Capt. Oscar Charles, Scott's secretary, outlined to Mary the pros and cons of the use of overt force, noting that "if the Colonel would have attacked immediately, there would have been much bloodshed and the affair would have been reported far and wide and the Col. *would have received much credit*" (emphasis added), the implication being that pacification does not lead to military recognition. Oscar Charles to Mary Scott, 8/26/1903; the quote about protecting Wood is in Scott to Mary, 11/9/1903—both in box 3, SLC.

58. Immediately prior to the confrontation with Hassan, Scott told Mary of his concerns and what he was prepared to do. The "official" interpretation as to why the soldiers remained in their Jolo barracks was that directives from the Philippine Commission required them to stand down and do nothing to provoke the Sulu Moros. Scott claimed that their low morale was due to fear and not to frustration in being kept at their post. See Scott to Mary, 11/9/1903, box 3, SLC.
59. Two weeks following Scott's injury, Captain Charles wrote a lengthy letter to Mary giving her an account of her husband's condition and the circumstances that brought it about. The first quote is from Oscar Charles to Mary Scott, 11/28/1903, box 3, SLC; Scott's recollection of the entire incident, presumably taken from his diary, is in *Memories*, 328–32; Wood immediately cabled Mary Scott to report the encounter and Scott's condition, noting that the injury did not appear to be fatal. See Leonard Wood to Mary Scott, 11/18/1903, box 3, SLC. Scott's detailed description of the injury to his hand and the prognosis for recovery is found in several typewritten and dictated letters: see Scott to Mary, 12/15/1903, for his description of the injury and one on 12/24/1903 and others on 1/20/1904, 1/24/1904 for his further condition—all in box 3, SLC.
60. Scott to Mary, 10/28/1903; Scott noted Tungalan's negative behavior in Scott to Mary, 1/24/1904; the capture of datos Tungalan and Amil are noted in Scott to Mary, 2/4/1904—all in box 3, SLC. Oscar Charles once again gave Mary a detailed account of her husband's field activities, which reads like a progress report on his endeavors. Captain Charles noted how Scott captured Tungalan and Amil without the use of force and with a great deal of patience. See Oscar Charles to Mary Scott, 2/6/1904, box 3, SLC.
61. Examples of Moro leaders providing Scott with intelligence as to Hassan's whereabouts and sending Moros from their cottas out to apprehend him on their own are noted in Scott to Mary, 2/4/1904, 2/25/1904, 2/28/1904; and Oscar Charles to Mary Scott, 3/2/1904, 3/7/1904—all in box 3, SLC. Other pertinent details about the engagement are also noted in Scott to Mary, 2/28/1904, box 3, SLC. Details of the killing of Hassan are noted in Scott, *Memories*, 348–50; Arnold, *Moro War*, 102–3; and Oscar Charles to Mary Scott, 3/7/1904, SLC, 3. Scott's criticism of Wood is from Scott to Mary, 12/1/1904, box 3, SLC.
62. The five letters Charles wrote to Mary, are noted as Oscar Charles to Mary Scott, are dated 8/26/1903, 11/28/1903, 2/6/1904, 3/2/1904, 3/7/1904—all in box 3, SLC. The quote is in Frank McCoy to Mary Scott, 2/22/1904, box 3, SLC. Wood sent Roosevelt a strong recommendation on Scott's behalf; see Wood to Roosevelt, 1/7/1904, box 3, WLC. Scott's speculation on the West Point position is noted in Scott to Mary, 5/14/1904, box 3, SLC.
63. One of many examples noting Scott's strategy for elevation in rank is in Scott to Mary, 11/30/1905, box 3, SLC. On Wood's recurrent illness, see McCallum, *Leonard Wood*, 1, 223–25, 226; and Arnold, *Moro War*, 147, 174. On Langhorne see Cullum, *Biographical Register*, 6:527.
64. On Scott's illness, see Fulton, *Moroland*, 256. On Scott's feeling that it was time to move on, see Scott to Mary, 4/22/1905, box 3, SLC. The depth of his loneliness and

despair can be characterized by the following: "It would seem that our long separation or something else has caused you to lose interest in me." Scott to Mary, 6/2/1904, box 3, SLC. Hunter's successful pursuit of a military career as noted by his father's praise of his progress is found in Scott to Hunter, 3/25/1904, 4/26/1904; and Scott to Mary, 8/13/1904—all in box 3, SLC.

65. Scott's criticism of the method of taxation is in Scott, *Memories*, 376. As early as April 1904, Scott was concerned about threats to the safety of those Moros who had paid the cedula in good faith from those who adamantly refused to pay it. See Scott to Mary, 4/23/1904, box 3, SLC. The incident involving Pala is noted in Fulton, *Moroland*, 242–43; the quote expressing his concern that the imposition of the cedula could destroy his work toward Moro pacification is in Scott to Mary, 4/22/1905, box 3, SLC.

66. Descriptions of what would be the first of two military campaigns on Bud Dago and its aftermath are in Arnold, *Moro War*, 139–77; Bacevich, "Disagreeable Works," 58–61; Byler, "Leonard Wood, John J. Pershing," 95–97; Fulton, *Moroland*, 249–312; McCallum, *Leonard Wood*, 227–31; and Pruitt, "Leonard Wood," 275–77; Fulton's is the most detailed account, and the most critical of Wood's actions.

67. Scott's confidence in his ability to negotiate with the Bud Dago Moros and his view that their occupation of the mountain posed no immediate threat to American forces are noted in Arnold, *Moro War*, 145, 146. Conditions under which Scott would refrain from the use of overt force are noted in Reeves to Langhorne, 3/1/1906, box 37, WLC.

68. Scott to Wood, 6/16/1905, box 36, WLC. Moros loyal to Scott were instructed to observe the dissidents as best they could and ascertain their number, food supply, armaments, and reason for encamping on the mountain. As to the latter, Scott was informed "that they are afraid to go down, as they would have to take out cedulas" (Jolo, 6/12/1905), noted as *Exhibit "B"* [typed copy appended to the Report on the investigation of the Bud Dago incident] in box 37, WLC. Scott's concerns and plans involving Bud Dago are noted in Scott to Wood, 12/4/1905; the first two quotes are in Scott to Wood, 12/7/1905, 12/31/1905; and the third quote is noted in Scott to Langhorne, 12/5/1905—all in box 36, WLC.

69. References to the military force to be sent to Jolo are in Wood, Diary entry: 3/3/1906, box 37, WLC.

70. The quotes are in Reeves to Langhorne, 3/1/1906, box 37, WLC. As previously noted, a detailed description of the battle is in Fulton, *Moroland*, chap. 16; see esp. 267, 271, 281, 284–85. See also Arnold, *Moro War*, chap. 11, esp. 148–68.

71. Fulton, *Moroland*, 292, 294, 296, 297–99; Arnold, *Moro War*, 171–75. On how Wood structured his defense, see Arnold, *Moro War*, 175; one tactic that Wood used was to feed comments from interested parties who were allegedly witnesses to the press in the form of official telegrams sent through the Army Signal Corps. These messages generally noted the logistic challenges that American forces faced and provided detailed descriptions of the wounds and fatalities incurred by the troops (but not those suffered by the defenders), while noting the overtly aggressive behavior of the

Bud Dago Moros. One example of the latter is cited by a "Thomas Kinghorne," who claimed that the Moros "repeatedly charged troops singly and in bogies sprang upon them from fortifications and brush. Wounded Moros killed and injured many soldiers. Other Moros feigned death and attacked soldiers." See "Commercial Pacific," 3/10/1906; the quotes are in Wood to the Military Secretary, 3/13/1906—both in box 37, WLC. Wood's claims were affirmed by the civilian deputy governor of the Philippines. See Henry C. Ide to the Secretary of War [cablegram], 3/20/1906, box 3, WLC.

72. The episode involving his living incognito and his interchange with Taft in Washington following news of the battle are noted in Scott, *Memories*, 384–85. All quotes are in *Engagement of American Forces with Moros on Mount Dago*, U.S. Senate, 59th Cong., 1st sess., Doc. No. 278, 3; see also Scott to Wood, 12/4/1905, 12/7/1905, 12/31/1905; and Scott to Langhorne, 12/5/1905—all in box 36, WLC.

73. James H. Reeves to George T. Langhorne, 3/1/1906, box 37, WLC. Near the end of his memorandum, and in further support of his mentor, Scott mentions that "it is not conceivable that this policy of humanity [negotiating with one's adversary prior to the use of overt force] carried out in ever[y] case in the past two years and a half should now have been changed, especially as General Wood was there in person, and no one would take more trouble to avoid unnecessary bloodshed than he." *Engagement of American Forces*, 4.

74. Fulton, *Moroland*, questions whether Scott talked with anyone about the battle for those ten days (Scott claimed he did not); the structure of the memorandum and its factual background would seem to indicate that he had (295). See also Scott, *Memories*, 386.

75. An officer who headed the Bureau of Insular Affairs in the War Department and who was an acquaintance of "Old Scott" noted about him that "there is one thing about Scott,—he is one of the most loyal men I ever met in my life, and I esteem him as much for that as for many other things." Clarence R. Edwards to H. J. Slocum, 9/15/1904, box 7, SLC. One way that Wood thanked Scott for his support, perhaps ironically, was by praising his efforts at pacification as he seemingly never had done before. See Wood to Scott, 4/16/1906, box 37, WLC; and Scott to Mary, 5/13/1906, box 3, SLC, with notes Wood's pleasure with Scott's defense of his action.

76. Scott's appointment as superintendent of West Point is noted in Special Orders No. 149, War Department, 6/25/1906, ACP 4879 and 1876, RG 94, NA. Shortly after his arrival at his Academy posting, Scott noted that "one of the greatest pleasures connected with the institution [is] that every few days I see some old friend of other years that my station in other parts of the world has prevented me from seeing heretofore." Scott to James Reeves, 10/29/1906, box 9, SLC.

Chapter 5

Epigraph: SLC, 8. This statement reflects Captain Charles's erroneous assumption that Scott's appointment as superintendent of West Point would garner him a promotion to a general's rank.

1. Scott's tenure as superintendent of the Academy is described in *Memories*, 417–60; and Ambrose, *Duty, Honor, Country*, 227, 246, 250.
2. References to the Booz investigation are in Ambrose, *Duty, Honor, Country*, 276–77, and in Scott, *Memories*, 421, 444. Scott's encounter with hazing is noted in *Memories* on 241–45; the quote is on 443.
3. Scott, *Memories*, 421, 422–25, 426–27, 446–47.
4. Wood's logic is noted in Wood to Scott, 1/23/1904; the quote is in Roosevelt to Wood, 6/21/1904—both in box 35, WLC. Although Wood's promotion to a second star had cleared the Senate, Mills's petition for a first was blocked, necessitating that Roosevelt award a recess commission in January 1904, after the presidential election; On Roosevelt's posting of Scott to the West Point superintendency in lieu of a star promotion, see J. E. Jenks to Captain Joseph Herron, 3/19/1907, box 8, SLC. Roosevelt was also quoted as saying: "The Military Committee of the Senate have had a definite understanding with me that they will be asked to report for confirmation no one below the rank of Colonel for promotion to Brigadier-General. This bars out from consideration a number of very good men." Charles Rushmore to Scott, 12/4/1908, box 10, SLC.
5. Scott noted the advantage of his Academy posting in potentially enhancing his career: "We are getting along very well here. I have accumulated a lot of friends of all kinds, congressional and otherwise." Scott to Wood, 6/14/1908, box 41, WLC. The number of officers over Scott in line for a star ranking is found in *The Army List and Directory*, Office of the Adjutant-General, 11/20/1908 [copy], box 9, SLC. However, Scott maintained that there were 207 officers on the "relative list" above him in rank but below him in length of service; see Scott to Wood, 11/12/1908, box 41, WLC. Clark, *Preparing for War*, refers to J. Franklin Bell, who, though not from Scott's class at West Point, was nonetheless subject to the same restrictions on promotion when he joined the Seventh Cavalry two years after Scott (208).
6. Quinette to Scott, 12/15/1908, 12/24/1908; Grayson Heidt to Scott, 12/16/1908—both in box 10, SLC. Scott met Heidt when he was a lieutenant in the Fourteenth Cavalry in Sulu; that Roosevelt would recommend Scott for a star promotion if he knew in advance that the Senate Committee on Military Affairs would approve the request is noted in John F. McGee to Senator William Warner (Mo.), 12/7/1908, box 11, SLC. See also Frank R. McCoy to Leonard Wood, 1/2/1908, box 42, WLC. Although Scott's longtime supporter and friend Senator Quay of Pennsylvania was no longer around to assist him, Senators Charles F. W. Dick (Ohio) and Nathan Bay Scott (W.Va.), whom he met earlier in his career, were committed to helping Scott gain a star ranking. To illustrate, Senator Scott met Major Scott while accompanying members of Taft's Philippine Commission on a tour in Manila during the time that Wood was on medical leave in the States, and Scott was serving as his replacement at Taft's request. Senator Scott was a member of the Committee on Military Affairs, the West Point Board of Visitors, and an ardent supporter; he took umbrage at Roosevelt's refusal to waive the seniority rule when it came to commending Scott for a star ranking. See Nathan B. Scott to Scott, 2/7/1908, box 10, SLC; and 12/4/1908, box 11, SLC. For

an example of constituent service to a member of Congress, see Scott to Senator Charles Dick, 1/31/1908, box 10, SLC. As superintendent at West Point, Scott could meet people of influence to further his military career through membership in various clubs, including The Boone and Crockett Club, founded by Theodore Roosevelt (see Madison Grant to George S. Anderson, 3/3/1906, box 8, SLC); the Union League Club of New York (see John W. Vrooman to Henry Hayden, 1/17/1907, box 8, SLC; and William Sheldon to Roosevelt, 11/27/1908, box 11, SLC); and the Republic Lodge (see Clarence Sanford to Scott, 3/11/1907, box 8, SLC).

7. Wood's efforts were ongoing and persistent. See Wood to Scott, 12/12/1908, box 41, WLC. McGee's recollection of when he first met Scott is noted in John F. McGee to Senator Porter J. McCumber (N.D.), 12/7/1908, box 10, SLC. Examples of other letters to and from congressmen and others soliciting support for Scott from 1908 to 1909 are found in, box 10, SLC.

8. Grayson Heidt to Scott, 12/8/1908, box 10, SLC; Roosevelt's skepticism is referenced in a letter that Wood sent to Scott, marked "*Strictly Confidential*." The president was quoted as saying, "The Senators themselves must come to me if they wish to alter the explicit arrangement, they made with me, for I would then have to take up Colonel Scott's name and a number of others at the same time. As a matter of fact, they have not the slightest intention of altering their attitude." Wood to Scott, 12/14/1908, box 41, WLC. Wood was not optimistic, noting that the president "is very hot at being tied up in this way"; Scott's standing in rank is noted in Oscar K. Davis to Louis Wiley, 12/23/1908, box 10, SLC. Davis was a senior Washington correspondent for the *New York Times* and a confidant of the president. Roosevelt may also have been turned off to Scott's request as a result of the fact that, at one point, he was receiving fifty requests for an advancement a day! This, and the final decision to honor the elevation of line colonels based on seniority to the brigadier rank, is noted in Davis to Wiley, 12/30/1908, box 10, SLC.

9. Scott to Wood, 3/23/1910, box 49, WLC; Robert Bines to Scott, 7/30/1910, Scott to Mary, 8/22/1910—both in box 3, SLC.

10. Bjork, *Prairie Imperialists*, 208, 218; Clendenen, *United States and Pancho Villa*, 131. Eisenhower, *Intervention*, presents a detailed account of American military involvement on the southern border owing to the fractious situation and constitutional crisis in the Mexican civil war; see Introduction and 1–154. By 1914, Villa had control of Juárez (59). See also Harper, "Hugh Lenox Scott y la Diplomacia," 430.

11. Bjork, *Prairie Imperialists*, 221, 222; Harper, "Hugh Lenox Scott y la Diplomacia," 429, 430, 432, 437; Eisenhower, *Intervention*, 53, 54, 127; Scott, *Memories*, 501. In September 1914, at the height of Villa's power, Scott noted that he was "the real force in Mexico.... Villa seems to have taken a romantic regard for me." Clendenen, *United States and Pancho Villa*, 121.

12. Clendenen, *United States and Pancho Villa*, 142–43. Perhaps as a further example of Scott's willingness to embrace Villa's flattery was when he was summoned by Washington to settle the Naco dispute. Scott noted of Villa that "he came up to Juarez announcing that he had come to meet my wishes.... I watched him ... with

the greatest interest—his intelligence is most apparent—he looks you right in the eye" (143). See also Eisenhower, *Intervention*, 171–72; and Harper, "Hugh Lenox Scott y la Diplomacia," 433, 435–36.
13. Eisenhower, *Intervention*, 58–59; Harper, "Hugh Lenox Scott y la Diplomacia," 437–39.
14. Harper, "Hugh Lenox Scott y la Diplomacia," 439; Eisenhower, *Intervention*, 217–21, 224–27; Clendenen, *United States and Pancho Villa*, 244; Scott, *Memories*, 516–18; Scott to the secretary of war, 6/7/1920, Scott Papers, box 4, USMA.
15. Scott commented to his wife, "I don't see that I am doing myself any good and I am serving away from my Regiment." Scott to Mary, 12/11/1910; see also letter of 12/18/1910—both in box 3, SLC. Special Orders No. 104 notes Scott's promotion to lieutenant colonel (War Department, 5/4/1911, folder 16, RG 94, NA). Scott's concern over the border situation is noted in Scott to Mary, 5/3/1911, 5/7/1911, 5/10/1911, 5/16/1911; in a letter to his wife at the end of May, he noted that additional forces were encamped near the border through the summer and fall of the year, seeking to quell the anxiety of American residents in the area. Scott to Mary, 5/31/1911—all in box 4, SLC. For Scott's assignments during this period with tribes and his military commands on the border at Fort San Houston and at El Paso, see Cullum, *Biographical Register*, vol. 6. References to Wood's professional assistance are noted in Scott to Mary, 6/2/1911, 6/14/1911, 6/20/1911—all in box 4, SLC.
16. Cullum, *Biographical Register*, 6:n.p.; William H. Taft to Gordon McCabe, 9/2/1916, ser. 8, vol. 51, William H. Taft Papers, Library of Congress.
17. Smythe, *Pershing*, 5; Wood to Roosevelt, 8/28/1917, box 101, WLC. For other disparaging references that Wood made about Scott during his tenure as chief of staff, see Wood, Diary entries: 12/28/1916, 5/4/1917, box 8, WLC.
18. Nenninger, "Army Enters the Twentieth Century," 222, 223; Clark, *Preparing for War*, 189, 241, 247–48, 253–54; Weigley, *History of the United States Army*, 288, 316; Coffman, *Regulars*, 186–87; McCallum, *Leonard Wood*, 250.
19. Roberts, "Reform and Revitalization," 210, 212–14; Clark, *Preparing for War*, 194–95.
20. Roberts, "Reform and Revitalization," 210; McCallum, *Leonard Wood*, 250–51; Clark, *Preparing for War*, 240; Nenninger, "Army Enters the Twentieth Century," 222–23.
21. A detailed analysis of Wood's conflict with Ainsworth can be found in McCallum, *Leonard Wood*, 250–55; Lane, *Armed Progressive*, 159–67; and Clark, *Preparing for War*, 241, 244, 253. Root, perhaps exasperated once again by Wood's behavior, wished that among Wood's attributes was "the ability not to make enemies." Morison, *Turmoil and Tradition*, 167. References to Wood's criticism of the bureaus, their congressional supporters, and the secretaries of war who Wood felt should have been more assertive with the bureau chiefs are found in Wood to [Secretary of War] Lindley Garrison, 8/20/1914, box 74, WLC; and Wood to McCoy, 1/14/1915, box 80, WLC. The following is a particularly pointed example of Wood's view of how the bureau chiefs undermined military reform: "They [the bureau chiefs] are always here, and if they do not put it over with one secretary, they do it with the next, or with an intervening Acting Secretary. In other words, they are always here with a concentration of purpose and permanency of location, in close contact with the Committees of Congress; and

I cannot believe, as much as I should like to, that we can ever get the best results for the line as long as this continues." Wood to J. Franklin Bell, 2/13/1914, box 76, WLC.

22. Clark, *Preparing for War*, 253–54. Scott's detailed defense of the general staff and chief of staff in opposition to Crowder's ruling in the National Defense Act (1916) is found in Memorandum for the Secretary of War: Duties of the General Staff Corps as affected by Section 5 of the National Defense Act, 7/27/1916, box 87, WLC.

23. Memorandum for the Secretary of War, 6; Palmer, *Newton D. Baker*, 1:65, 66–68; Opinion of the Secretary of War on the effect of Section 5 of the National Defense Act, 9/13/1916, box 86, WLC. Section 5 addressed the prerogatives of the chief of staff. Baker concluded that "the Chief of Staff, speaking in the name of the Secretary of War, will coordinate and supervise the various bureaus, offices and departments of the War Department; he will advise the Secretary of War; he will inform himself in as great detail as in his judgment deems necessary to qualify him adequately to advise the Secretary of War" [COPY]. Coffman, *War to End All Wars*, maintains that Scott had advocated for a strong general staff to support the chief of staff, where the bureaus would report to the latter. He believed that this would have ended the confusion and delay that characterized the deployment of the AEF in 1917 (52).

24. Millet, *The General*, 249, 261, 484; Smythe, *Pershing*, 5; The quote on Wilson's attitude toward the military is in Link, *Wilson*, 77; the quote on Wood's attitude toward his opponents is in Wood to Sydney Brooks, 10/12/1915, box 80, WLC. Scott's elevation to his first star is noted in Cullum, *Biographical Register*, 6:n.p.; Chambers, *To Raise an Army*, 126; and Palmer, *Newton D. Baker*, 1:11, 14, 122.

25. Wood to Scott, 10/17/1914, 11/5/1914—both in box 75, WL. In one such directive, Wood informed Scott, "Do not be bored by these frequent suggestions. Whenever I see anything you need to know, I am sending it on to you." Wood to Scott, 2/27/1915, box 83, WLC. See also Wood, Diary entries: 10/5/1914, 10/23/1914, 10/26/1914, 11/29/1915—all in box 8, WLC; Wood to Scott, 2/19/1915, box 83, WLC; and Wood to McCoy, 1/14/1915, box 80, WLC. Scott's influence in Wilson's decision concerning Wood's tenure as chief of staff is found in Lane, *Armed Progressive*, 179; and McCallum, *Leonard Wood*, 256.

26. Kreidberg and Henry, *History of Military Mobilization*, 242, 254. Gen. Denis Nolan opined, "General Scott deserves the greatest credit for aiding the Secretary of War and the President to advocate compulsory service for our armies." The statement was made in an interview with Nolan, 11/14/47, Office of the Chief of the Military History Collection, Military History Institute; Coffman, *War to End All Wars*, notes that the War College Division endorsed conscription in response to Scott's solicitation. Scott recommended the policy be implemented at once, and both Baker and Wilson concurred (24–25). Coffman also observes that Enoch Crowder initially opposed the mobilization plan but was promptly overruled by Wilson (25). Even more compelling was War Secretary Newton D. Baker's recognition and praise of Scott for initiating the plan. See Baker, "Legal Phases of the War," 323–24, and "Baker Says Scott Evolved Draft Idea," *New York Times*, 11/15/1927. Clark, *Preparing for War*, claims that Wood preceded Scott in calling for conscription in early 1915 (250). While this may have been the case, Scott strongly infers that *he* initiated the discussion. Scott, *Memories*,

557–58. The discrepancy may be explained by noting a distinction between universal military training and a mandatory draft of able-bodied men. In his autobiography, Scott uses the word "conscription" (559); Palmer, *Newton D. Baker*, implies that Baker, as secretary of war, had access concurrently to Wood's and Scott's advocacy of conscription as a way of planning for mobilization. See 1:184; Chambers credits Enoch Crowder, judge advocate general, "more than any other individual, who created the modern American Selective Service System" (*To Raise an Army*, 180), based on the work Crowder accomplished in the spring of 1917 convincing Wilson of the need for conscription while not ruling out the politically sensitive option of using volunteers (131–34). See also *War Department Reports*, 1:159.

27. The experience of the paucity of state militia units at the border with Mexico in 1916 convinced military planners of the efficacy of conscription when it came to national defense. See Kreidberg and Henry, *History of Military Mobilization*, 200–201. Chambers maintains that Wilson's primary reason for embracing conscription was his distaste for the use of a voluntary reserve, and that was out of fear that Theodore Roosevelt would succeed in raising a voluntary regiment as he had done in the Spanish-American War, one that now he would command in a European war (*To Raise an Army*, 136–37, 141).

28. See *War Department Annual Report (1916)*, 1:162.

29. Pershing was flattered by Scott's recommendation, which he communicated to him by wire on 5/2/1917 and directly on 5/10/1917 (box 181, PLC); see also Smythe, *Pershing*, 4, 5; Cullum, *Biographical Register*, No. 3126; and Wood to Roosevelt, 8/28/1917, box 101, WLC. Scott was in Britain and France from mid-October to the third week in December, 1917. Numerous letters, Scott to Mary, 10/1916–12/21/1917—all in Scott Papers, box 3, USMA. Wood was in Europe from the end of December 1917 to March 1918. Lane, *Armed Progressive*, 219, 223.

30. Cullum, *Biographical Register*, 5:248; Weigley, *History of the United States Army*, 372–73; Coffman, *War to End All Wars*, 64. References to Scott's experience in his first year as commander of Camp Dix are noted in Scott to Mary, 1/3/1918, 1/4/1918, 1/5/1918, 2/25/1918, 3/6/1918, 5/8/1918, 10/11/1918. Scott reported that cases of both influenza and pneumonia were decreasing by the third week in October. Scott to Mary, 10/21/1918. Scott was credited by the surgeon general of the army for his efforts to isolate patients and provide a healthy environment that decreased the number of deaths from both diseases. See Memorandum: To all Camp Surgeons, Office of the Surgeon General, Washington, D.C., 9/30/1918. (All letters and the surgeon general's memorandum referenced above are in Scott Papers, box 3, USMA.)

31. The initial quotes relative to his Distinguished Service Medal are in Cullum, *Biographical Register*, 6:219. References to the purchase and renovation of the farmhouse are in Scott to Mary, 12/3/1918, Scott Papers, box 3, USMA. After years of planning to be together, given the constraints of Mary's health, in addition to Scott's mobility, Scott fondly noted that "it is your house for you to live in and to be as satisfied & happy in as our circumstances will permit." 10/11/1918, Scott Papers, box 3, USMA. Houston, Scott's youngest daughter, quoted her father saying at the time that "Washington

was filled with old generals saying, 'the Army is going to hell!' and he [Scott] wasn't going to be one of them." Author's interview with Houston Scott, Princeton (N.J.), 2/15/1982.

32. Scott, *Memories*, 604–5; Scott to Mary, 10/26/1917, 10/29/1917, 11/17/1917 (quote)—all in Scott Papers, USMA, 3; Major-General J. F. O'Ryan to Scott, 3/17/1919, box 66, SLC.

Chapter 6

Epigraph: Box 28, SLC. Scott wrote Slocum concerning the retirement of their friend and longtime classmate Ernest Garlington.

1. Department of the Interior, *Board of Indian Commissioners*, 4–5; Edward Ayer to Scott, 11/26/1918, Scott to Ayer, 12/2/1918, Ayer to Scott, 2/4/1919, Scott to Ayer, 2/7/1919, and Ayer to Scott, 2/28/1919—all in box 48, SLC; all quotes are in Malcolm McDowell to Scott, 2/28/1919, box 48, SLC; see also *Members of the Board of Indian Commissioners*, n.d., E-1395, RG 75, NA.

2. Some historians question whether the father-child metaphor implied subordination on the part of tribal groups. Viola, *Diplomats in Buckskin*, maintains that the term "Great Father" was a diplomatic device rather than an expression of subservience (94); see also Coleman, "Not Race, But Grace," 43.

3. Coleman, "Not Race, But Grace," 44; Mary H. Scott to Scott, 6/9/1872, 1/4/1880—both in Scott Papers, box 2, USMA.

4. Coleman, "Not Race, But Grace," 45–46, 51; the quote is in Scott, *Memories*, 313.

5. Scott to Major Nelson Miles, 8/17/1896, box 46, SLC; Lake Mohonk Conference, *Thirty-Fifth Lake Mohonk Conference*, 10/16–18/1929, 125; Scott to I-See-O, 2/7/1916, box 48, SLC; Scott, *Report on the Umatilla (Oregon) Agency*, 9/13/1922, box 49, SLC. Scott was so tied to the belief that an indigenous people's culture was the product of their physical surroundings that he attributed what he saw as the negative characteristics of northeastern tribes to the dense forests where they lived (*Memories*, 166).

6. For a listing of the numerous and eclectic Pan-Indian organizations that espoused cultural pride in the early twentieth century, see LaPotin, *Native American Voluntary Organizations*; and Hertzberg, *Search for American Indian Identity*. Scott harbored a disdain for those whom he believed to be abstract and impractical in their views of how or even whether Indian and Anglo societies should coexist, and who lacked the extensive field experience that he possessed. For an early example of this stance in reference to his critique of the anthropologist James Mooney, see Scott to H. C. Phillips, 7/20/1914, box 45, no. 313, SFP. Scott's criticisms increased over time when John Collier and his supporters challenged the assumptions of assimilationists.

7. Fritz, "Last Hurrah," 155, 157–59. On the board's ultimate goal, see *Sixty-fourth Annual Report of the Board of Indian Commissioners, Fiscal Year Ended June 30, 1933*, 6, box 3, Scott Papers, NAA.

8. The incident of fraud against the Kickapoos and the ultimate settlement of their landholdings is noted in Pfaller, *James McLaughlin*, 302–10. See also James R. Garfield, secretary of war, to Scott, 5/7/1908 [telegram], box 46, SLC. Examples of Thackery's

acknowledgment of Scott's assistance to him are found in Thackery to Scott, 6/6/1908, box 10, SLC; 12/6/1908, 6/3/1909, box 11, SLC; and 12/20/1909, box 12, SLC.
9. Seymour, *Indian Agents*, 358–59; Scott to Walter L. Fisher, secretary of the interior, 11/26/1911, Fisher to Scott, 11/20/1911, Crane to Scott, 11/23/1911, F. H. Abbot, acting commissioner, to Crane, 11/ 23/1911, Scott to Fisher, 12/5/1911—all in box 47, SLC; Scott, *Memories*, 472. On the ongoing relationship between Scott and Crane, see Crane to Scott, 9/7/1917, Scott to Crane, 9/21/1917, Crane to Scott, 3/31/1918, and Scott to Crane, 4/6/1918—all in box 48, SLC. The immediate situation involved what Crane believed to be the troubling environment on the Navajo-Hopi reservation.
10. As he noted to Henry C. Phillips, secretary to the Lake Mohonk Conference, "I never give up those old faithful soldiers & civil employees—as long as they are alive—and have fought for every one of them for years." Scott to Phillips, 7/27/1913, box 41, no. 395, SFP; for other examples of Scott's writing recommendations for those he knew and who helped him pursue his goals over the years, see Scott to the Secretary of the Interior, 7/31/1915, Scott to Cato Sells, 1/18/1916—both in box 21, SLC; and Scott, *Report on the Northern Pueblos*, 10/4/1921 [draft], 4, Fort Sill Papers, FSM. On protecting reservation supervisors, see Spencer Hilton to Scott, 8/15/1916, box 24, SLC; Leo Crane to Scott, 5/30/1919, box 49, SLC; Scott to Rex Hubbard, 5/19/1923, box 50, SLC; Scott to Mary, 1/29/1926, Scott Papers, box 4, USMA; Scott to Charles Rhoads, 6/23/1930, box 51, SLC; C. J. Lipps to Scott, 4/8/1932, box 52, SLC; and Scott to Mary, 7/5/1932, 8/22/1932—both in Scott Papers, box 4, USMA. On the importance of the board's maintaining its autonomy and remaining critical of interests that sought to undermine it, he noted in one report to the board that "the inordinate number of letters received during the past year from the Washington Office (1500) shows the effect of undue concentration of authority in Washington, an evil of great magnitude, unnecessarily expensive and productive of all sorts of harmful results." Scott to George Vaux Jr., 7/30/1924, box 50, SLC; see also Stella Atwood to Scott, 3/18/1925, box 37, SLC.
11. Scott visited the agencies or reservations of the following tribal groups: Arapahos, Blackfeet, Cheyennes, Coeur d'Alenes, Crows, Flatheads, Jicarillas (Apaches), Kiowas, Lapwais, Mescaleros, Moquis, Navajos, Pawnees, Pueblos, Quapaws, Shoshones, Sioux, Umatillas, and Utes. See Board of Indian Commissioners, *Indian Service Units Visited between 1915 & 1931*, E-1395, RG 75, NA.
12. Peso, Sanspur, and China (Apache chiefs) to Scott, 1/25/1916; the quotes are in Scott to Lane, 1/28/1916—both in box 48, SLC.
13. Scott to Matthew Sniffen, 7/18/1918, box 48, SLC; Mescalero Apache Committee to Scott, 12/29/1919, *Memo: Mescalero Timber*, 1/26/1920, McDowell to Scott, 5/11/1920, Stecker to Scott, 5/13/1920, 11/23/1920—all in box 49, SLC. The quote is in Stecker to Scott, 12/10/1920, box 49, SLC. See also McDowell to Scott, 1/7/1921, Scott to Homer Snyder, 1/10/1921—both in box 49, SLC.
14. Scott, 2/18/1921, 2/23/1921, Stecker to Scott, 3/17/1921, McDowell to Scott, 5/4/1922—all in box 49, SLC. The first quote is in Scott to Morgan, 12/22/1922; the second quote is in McDowell to Morgan, 2/1/1923—both in box 50, SLC.

15. Scott to Mary, 6/7/1920, Scott Papers, box 3, USMA. Scott told Mary that he never thought he would need a guide to show him around Fort Sill given how long he had been posted there. It had changed so much from what it had been like two decades earlier. It was also in this letter that Scott greeted I-See-O. A visit to the Mescalero (N.Mex.) reservation generated memories of Hunter. Scott to Mary, 6/18/1920; other examples of nostalgia are found in Scott to Mary, 8/7/1919, 9/24/1919—all in Scott Papers, box 3, USMA.
16. A brief description by Scott of Stecker's career in defense of the latter's service is noted in Scott to Charles J. Rhoads, Commissioner of Indian Affairs, 1/30/1930, box 51, SLC. The protracted correspondence between Stecker and Scott, prior to Scott's membership on the board, intensified after he joined. Illustrative letters documenting Stecker's dilemma and an example of Scott's response, are found in Stecker to Scott, 1/5/1923, box 50, SLC; 1/8/1923, 3/9/1924—both in box 36, SLC; 1/9/1927, box 38, SLC; 12/20/1928, box 39, SLC; and 11/19/1929, box 49, SLC; see also Burke to Stecker, 1/29/1923 [copy], box 50; and Scott to McDowell, 11/25/1929, box 51—both in SLC.
17. The extensive quotes are in J. E. Jenkins to Scott, 5/19/1919, box 49, SLC.
18. The quotes are in Scott to Isidore Dockweiler, 8/15/1919 and Scott to Lane, 12/3/1919—both in box 49, SLC. As one student of the Indian Service's history noted, centralization during this period had become a problem of "almost stifling proportions." Stuart, "Administrative Reform in Indian Affairs," 143. On Scott's view of bureaus, see Scott to Mary, 1/19/1922, Scott Papers, box 4, USMA; and 3/24/1933, Scott Papers, box 5, USMA. Scott's political and administrative challenges as chair of the New Jersey Highway Commission when it was created in 1923 are noted in "Senate Now Talks of Lifting Moore's Road Power—Highway Dispute Growing—Rift Becomes More Bitter," *Trenton Evening Times*, 3/21/1933; and Scott to Mary, 3/30/1933, 4/9/1933, 4/11/1933—all in Scott Papers, box 5, USMA.
19. McDowell made it clear to Scott when he joined the board that although the word *inspect* is used in the act of Congress that governs the board's operations, "it is scarcely the correct word to designate the Board's activities; 'survey' or 'examine' would be better[,] for we seldom concern ourselves with 'inspecting' the administrative or financial affairs of an agency or superintendency." McDowell to Scott, 2/28/1919, box 48, SLC.
20. McDowell to Scott, 7/2/1920, box 49, SLC.
21. McDowell to Vaux, 11/3/1920; Vaux to Scott, 11/10/1920—both in box 49, SLC.
22. Scott to Burke, 3/22/1922, box 49, SLC.
23. The article goes on to note that it "throws a significant light on the ossified ineptitude of the Indian Bureau and strengthens the country-wide demand for a thorough house-cleaning in the Indian division of the Interior Department." The subtitle of the article—"The Indian Bureau Is Responsible for the Fighting between White and Red Men in Southern Utah"—added to the erroneous assumption that the board had endorsed its accusatory content. Scott, "Paiute 'Uprising'"; quotes from the article are on 38. Vaux's criticism of Scott is in Vaux to McDowell, 5/28/1923, Vaux, 1922–1923, General Correspondence, 1919–1933, RG 75, NA.

24. Amelia Elizabeth White, a prominent Santa Fe philanthropist and proponent of the preservation of Pueblo Indian culture, enlisted Scott's support. Warren K. Moorehead to White, 12/4/1922; White to Scott, 12/3/1922, 12/5/1922, 12/29/1922; F. W. Hodge to Scott, 12/2/1922—all in box 36, SLC; see also "Robbing the Pueblo Indians," a detailed if biased editorial in *New York World*, 11/27/1922, 12.

25. Kelly, *Assault on Assimilation*, 119–20, 160, 190, 216, 218–22, 245, 253–54, 263–64, 267–68; Fritz, "Board of Indian Commissioners," 8, 9.

26. Fritz, "Board of Indian Commissioners," 8–10; McDowell, the board's secretary, noted of Collier "that there are two sides to every proposition advanced by him[,] but he appears to take the position that if you do not agree with him you are in a conspiracy to ruin the Indians, etc." McDowell to John Sullivan, 3/30/1926, Board of Indian Commissioners, John J. Sullivan, 1924–1928, General Correspondence, 1919–1933, RG 75, NA. (Sullivan was a Philadelphia attorney who joined the board in 1924.)

27. On the origins of the Council of One Hundred, see Kelly, *Assault on Assimilation*, 288–89. Attendance included representatives from the more traditional Indian advocacy groups; religious reformers representing Catholic, Protestant, and Jewish denominations; a distinguished group of assimilated Indians; and several representatives from the board of Indian commissioners, including its chairman George Vaux, secretary Warren Moorehead, and board members Flora Warren Seymour and Scott (289). Scott assumed the role of vice chair of the group (290); its demise as an effective group is noted on 293.

28. The origins of the relationship between Collier and Ickes is noted in Samuel Eliot to Scott, 2/24/1933, Board of Indian Commissioners, Eliot folder, General Correspondence, 1919–1933, RG 75, NA; Kelly, *Assault on Assimilation*, 265–66; and Scott, *On Indian Bureau Re-organization, 1924*, 6, 7, 8–10, box 4, Fort Sill Papers, FSM.

29. For Scott's efforts at soliciting support for his proposal among reformers, see, for example, Kane, "East and West," 473–74; Scott, "Historical Relations of the Indians," in Lake Mohonk Conference, *Thirty-Fifth Lake Mohonk Conference*, 24–26; and Scott to Henry Miner, 9/8/1929, 58, No. 110, SFP. On efforts to enlist the army to study the Indian Service, see Edgar B. Merritt to Scott, 2/3/1929, box 51, SLC. *Report of the Blackfeet Indians*, 8/22/1929, 1, 7, 8, Scott Papers, NAA, illustrates the bureau's problems in Scott's view, and how and why he believed that his plan would solve them.

30. The first quote is in Rhoads to Hoover, 1/28/1929, box 51, SLC; the second is in McDowell to Scott, 3/2/1929, box 3, Scott Papers, NAA. See also *Secretary of the Interior to Indian Bureau Personnel*, 11/6/1930, box 52, SLC.

31. Institute for Government Research, "News Release," 11/9/1926, box 37, SLC. Most of the "special staff" held doctorates and or taught college in the fields of history, sociology, social statistics, medicine, and agricultural economics. Although Scott initially praised the Meriam Report, he soon turned against its recommendations. See Scott, "Historical Relations," Lake Mohonk Conference, *Thirty-Fifth Lake Mohonk Conference*, 25–26. Lewis Meriam's recommendations are in "Organization and Administration," 128–32, box 37, SLC. Scott's initial criticism was over the question of the qualifications of field agents who were then serving (132). Stuart, "Administrative

Reform in Indian Affairs," maintains that Meriam's study ushered in a new type of reformer, "the expert in Administration" (143); Scott developed an increasing antipathy toward what he believed Collier and his fellow reformers represented. Shortly after the abolition of the Board of Indian Commissioners and near the end of his life, in speaking of Rexford Tugwell, a Columbia University economics professor, and his proposal to create a national planning board under Roosevelt's New Deal, Scott opined, "I seem to be fed up with professors & their planning boards and do not like them from Columbia, a hotbed of communism planning boards and technocracy." Scott to Mary, 3/22/1933, Scott Papers, box 4, USMA.

32. Rhoads to Scott, 5/8/1929, box 51, SLC; Scott to Henderson, 8/21/1932, box 52, SLC; Lawrence C. Kelly, "Charles James Rhoads, 1929–1933," in Kvasnicka and Viola, *Commissioners of Indian Affairs*, 268.

33. Calvin H. Asbury to Scott, 7/27/1932, box 52, SLC; examples documenting the low morale felt by field staff include E. D. Mossmon to Scott, 11/16/1932; Rhoads to Eliot, 12/28/1931, 1–2 (quote on 1), 6–7; and C. Asbury to Scott, 7/27/1932—all in box 52, SLC.

34. E. C. Finney, solicitor, to John Edwards, assistant secretary of the interior, 2/3/1932, SLC, 52; the quote is in *Draft Report on (the) Piegan, Blackfeet, Crow, Cheyenne, Shoshoni, Arapahoe, and Flathead*, August 1932, 6, box 1, Scott Papers, NAA. For an additional criticism of the BIA during this period, see Scott to Henderson, 8/21/1932, box 52, SLC. Scott did all he could either to prevent the forced retirement of agents with whom he had worked over the years or to provide for them in some other way. See, for example, Scott to Henderson, 11/28/1932, box 52, SLC, and Scott to Edgar Meritt, 1933, box 53, SLC.

35. Henderson to Scott, 3/5/1932, 3/19/1932, 4/11/1932—all in box 52, SLC. In perhaps a final gesture for recognition of what Scott saw as essential in the Indian Service, he appealed directly to the newly elected president. Scott to Franklin D. Roosevelt, 3/2/1933, box 53, SLC.

36. Carlson, *Indians, Bureaucrats and Land*, maintains that farming was not a viable option following the allotment of lands to reservation families (136); the problems that occurred with the leasing of grazed lands on reservations leading to the alienation of tribal family allotments was an ongoing concern to the Interior Department, the Bureau of Indian Affairs, and the Board of Indian Commissioners. See, for example, Hagan, *United States–Comanche Relations*, 176, 239–40; Otis, *Dawes Act*, 111–12, 118–19, 149–50; and Board of Indian Commissioners, *Comments on the Leasing of Indian Lands*, E-1395, RG 75, NA. Even the process of voluntary dispossession of patented lands held by reservation families in fee simple was a common occurrence. In his *Report on the Flathead Indian Agency, Montana*, 9/19/1920, box 49, SLC, Scott noted that "612 living Indians have patents in fee and it is said they usually sell their lands soon after they are turned over to them" (4). Obviously, then, providing reservation families with their own allotments was not a process that would lead to their economic independence.

37. Scott to Daniel Pomeroy, 6/26/1918, box 32, SLC; Scott to U. S. Stewart, 8/6/1918. Stewart managed the Scotts' investments through a bank in El Paso, Texas. See Scott to C. K.

Morganroth, 8/7/1918, Scott to William Scott, 8/30/1918—both in box 33, SLC; Scott to Morganroth, 4/10/19, box 34, SLC; and A. C. McLean to Scott, 2/17/1928, box 38, SLC. McLean was a county agricultural agent and promoter of woodlots on family farms. W. R. Hegler to Scott, 5/27/1921, SLC, 36. Hegler was treasurer of the National Mohair Growers Association.

38. Perhaps Scott's attitude to farming can be best summed up in what he said shortly after the initial purchase: "I shall enjoy riding my old cavalry horse around over it and watching things grow." Scott to E. S. Godfrey, 4/21/1919, box 34, SLC; see also Scott to Mary, 9/7/1920, 8/27/1921—both in Scott Papers, box 3, USMA; and Scott to Mary, 2/4/1926, Scott Papers, box 4, USMA; A. C. McLean, county agricultural agent, to Scott, 6/23/1925, box 37, SLC; Scott to Mary, 7/6/1926, Scott Papers, box 4, USMA; and Elbert Wheeler to Scott, 5/23/1928, box 38, SLC.

39. The quote is in Barrett to Scott, 12/19/1892, box 6, SLC. Illustrative references to Scott's ongoing interest in tribal customs, while preoccupied on military venues, are in Scott to Mary, 9/15/1902, 4/6/1903; references to Scott's broader interests in the cultures of other overseas groups are noted in Scott to Mary, 5/18/1900, 5/29/1900—all in box 2, SLC.

40. Among the published scholars with whom Scott communicated were Edward Curtis, James Mooney, and George B. Grinnell. See Curtis to Scott, 10/20/1909 and Mooney to Scott, 9/3/1909—both in box 12, SLC; Mooney to Scott, 3/6/1911, box 47, SLC; Grinnell to Scott, 3/2/1911, box 13, SLC, 6/19/1912, box 14, SLC, 6/3/1915, box 18, SLC and Scott to Grinnell, 11/3/1915, box 20, SLC. See also Smith, "George Bird Grinnell," 24-26. Ernest Thompson Seton was another. See Seton to Scott, 5/22/1912, box 47, SLC; 6/14/1912, box 14, SLC; 3/19/1914, box 47, SLC; 9/17/1914, box 16, SLC; Scott to Seton, box 19, SLC; Seton to Scott, 1/24/1916, box 21, SLC; and Seton to Scott, 11/24/1916, box 25, SLC. Seton acknowledged Scott's assistance in the preparation of Seton's publication *Sign Talk* (see title page). Scott's interaction with museum officials include George A. Dorsey, director of the Field Museum of Natural History (Chicago); F. W. Hodge, of the Museum of the American Indian (New York); and W. H. Holmes, chair, Committee of the National Academy on Anthropology and Psychology, United States National Museum, Smithsonian Institution. See Scott to Dorsey, 10/8/1906, box 8, SLC; Hodge to Scott, 1/11/1919, box 31, SLC; and Holmes to Scott, 10/14/1914, box 47, SLC. Scott's efforts to assist academics include Edgar Young, University of Utah, and Joseph B. Thoburn, instructor, University of Oklahoma. See Scott to Young, 1/18/1916; Scott to Thoburn, 1/12/1916—both in box 21, SLC.

41. Examples of direct sources of information that Scott obtained from tribal groups while inspecting reservations for the Board of Indian Commissioners are noted in Scott to Mary, 9/21/1920, 6/2/1920—both in Scott Papers, box 3, USMA. One example of an agent helpful to Scott's research was James McLaughlin. See Scott to Marie Louise McLaughlin, 12/15/1916, box 26, SLC. As referenced here and below, scholars with interests in the American Indian Sign Language are now fortunate to have an edited source of his Kiowa notes created on the ledger boards used by agency clerks,

complete with a comprehensive introduction on the history of the language's use as well as a section on Scott and I-See-O. See Meadows, *Fort Sill Ledgers*. On Scott's assistance to I-See-O, see Scott to Granger Adams, 2/1/1915, box 48, SLC. On Clark see Scott, *Memories*, 176; Clark to Scott, 1/5/1906, box 8, SLC; 3/31/1911, box 14, SLC; and John B. Dunbar to Scott, 12/18/1908, box 11, SLC.

42. Illustrative examples of Scott's fields of inquiry include, from the *American Anthropologist*: "The Early History and Names of the Arapaho" and "Notes on the Caddo or Sun Dance of the Kiowa"; and from *Missionary Review of the World*: "Turtle Mountain: Notable Address at the Jubilee Celebration of the National Indian Association."

43. The quote is in Meadows, *Fort Sill Ledgers*, 32. Meadows also notes that the film, with synchronized sound, "demonstrates the use of phonological, morphological and syntactic patterns associated with the use of a 'full-fledged conventional signed language'" (31). Scott's original notes on the sign language, consisting of approximately seven hundred entries, are filed alphabetically in twenty-nine folders in the Library of Congress (boxes 72–74, SLC).

44. Many of Scott's notes were taken on the letterhead of the New Jersey Highway Commission, which he chaired in the 1920s. Consequently, it is logical to assume that much of his work researching signs was done during his retirement period. See boxes 72–74, SLC; the film can be seen at https://www.youtube.com/watch?v=dMVPfv63OU4 (Indian Sign Language Council of 1930 - YouTube).

45. Buck Connors to Scott, 7/21/1913, box 15, SLC; *Recording of Indian Sign Language*, 71st Cong., 2nd sess., Report No. 182. Leavitt's direct ongoing assistance with the project is noted in Leavitt to Scott, 4/10/1930; and Leavitt to McDowell, 4/7/1931—both in box 51, SLC. Scott credited Leavitt with the idea of also filming "a little Indian council," representatives from diverse tribal groups who would be signing with one another, to indicate the broad application of this means of communication. In addition, Scott formulated a comprehensive and detailed plan of how he wanted the presentation filmed. See Scott to McDowell, 4/20/1930, Board of Indian Commissioners, General Correspondence: Scott, 1924–1932, RG 75, NA; the quote is in McDowell to Flora Seymour, 8/7/1930, Board of Indian Commissioners, General Correspondence: Seymour, 1929–30, RG 75, NA.

46. The quote is in Scott to McDowell, 9/8/1930; see also Scott to McDowell, 8/31/1930, 12/21/1931—all in Board of Indian Commissioners, General Correspondence: Scott, 1924–1932, RG 75, NA; Raymond Evans to Stanley Harris, 4/11/1932, box 52, SLC; McDowell to Lindquist, 11/8/1932, Board of Indian Commissioners, General Correspondence: Lindquist, 1932–33, RG 75, NA; and Scott to Charles G. Abbot, director, the Smithsonian Institution, 3/7/1934, box 53, SLC.

47. Deloria, *Playing Indian*, 101, 105, 106. Hatt, "Ghost Dancing in the Salon," believes that the symbol of "the Indian" has less to do with American Indians as people, serving instead as a "useful medium for the consolidation of whiteness" (96). Dyer, "Fatal Attraction," maintains that nonindigenous Americans were simply pragmatic: "Much of contemporary white society's understanding of Indians and Indianness contains little of real substance" (833).

48. Boxes 81, 82, SLC; James Pond to Scott, 3/13/1922, box 36, SLC James Pond to Mary Scott, 10/3/1922, box 49, SLC; "Contract to engage James Pond," 8/13/1923, BOX 36; SLC. An example of Scott's increasing self-confidence in public speaking is noted in Scott to Mary, 5/2/1931, Scott Papers, box 4, USMA; examples referencing the eclectic range of his audience include *Relations of the American Indians with the United States Government*, before the National League of Women Voters, 5/28/1929, box 82, SLC; Scott's speech as a member of the Root Commission expressing his despair over the failure to free the Russian people is noted in Russian Revolution, n.d., box 79, SLC; *The Indian Sign Language*, the Chamber of Commerce (Great Falls, Mont.), 8/20/1929, Scott Papers, box 4, USMA; Celebration of the passing of the Medicine Lodge Treaty, Medicine Lodge, Kans., 10/12–14/1927, box 81, SLC; and *The Sign Language of the Plains Indians*, before the Boy Scouts, New York, 1/3/1931, box 82, SLC. By 1931, the universal Indian Sign Language was adopted as the international medium for Boy Scouts in a number of different countries. One of its advocates observed, "There is a romance, a witchery about the Indian in tribal costume, for the Boy and Girl scouts." W. H. Sears to Scott, 1/24/1931, Scott Papers, box 4, USMA.

49. One such event in which Scott was an active participant was noted in *Program of Events, Upper Missouri Historical Expedition, Itinerary of Upper Missouri Special via Great Northern Railway, July 16-21-1925*, Record of the Bureau of Indian Affairs, vol. 2, RG 75, NA; and Scott to Malcolm McDowell, 5/31/1929, Records of the Bureau of Indian Affairs, General Correspondence: Scott, 1924–1932, RG 75, NA. Budd's campaign extended to applying the names of prominent army officers, including Scott, to Pullman cars that would operate on the railway's right-of-way. Ralph Budd to Scott, 2/28/1929, box 39, SLC.

50. Scott to John Williams, 3/24/1919, box 34, SLC; speculation on Scott's reasons for going with the World Publishing Company include the following: its intent to publish an autobiography by friend and classmate Tasker Bliss; an advance royalty to Scott of $2,000, given that the Scotts were facing financial challenges at the time; and the possibility for additional syndication, expanding the dissemination of his life experiences to an even broader audience. See Herbert A. Gibbons to Scott, 2/3/1926, W. Morgan Shuster to Scott, 2/6/1926, Lyman Sturgis to Scott, 6/7/1926, W. Morgan Shuster to Scott, 6/17/1926—all in box 37, SLC; W. Morgan Shuster to Scott, 3/7/1927; and Lyman Sturgis to Scott, 5/5/1927, 6/9/1927—all in box 38, SLC.

51. *Reader's Guide to Periodical Literature*, vols. 3–9 (1910–35).

52. Illustrative examples that demonstrate praise and admiration for Scott are found in J. W. Redington to Scott, 1/12/1929, box 39, SLC. In a letter to the Scotts regarding his book, Newton Baker expressed the hope that they could "buy two or three more farms out of the proceeds" (Baker to Scott, 5/25/1928, box 38, SLC). See also Baker to Scott, 7/10/1928, box 38, SLC. Others were just as praiseworthy: see George Bird Grinnell to Scott, 5/24/1928, 6/6/1928; and Herbert Adams Gibbons to Scott, 5/29/1928—all in box 38, SLC.

53. Scott to Mary, 5/2/1931, 5/4/1931 (first quote); and 8/31/1931 (second quote); see also Scott to Mary, 8/1/1932, 8/5/1932—all in Scott Papers, box 4, USMA.

54. Scott to Mary, 3/30/1933, 4/18/1933, 5/11/1933, Scott Papers, box 5, USMA. Examples of the numerous tributes to Scott's life in the newspapers of the day include *Great Falls (Mont.) Tribune*, 5/1 and 5/4/1934; *Trenton (N.J.) Sunday Times-Advertiser*, 6/3/1934, which had a special section memorializing Scott's life; and *New York Times*, 5/1 and 5/2/1934—all in box 90, SLC.

BIBLIOGRAPHY

Manuscripts and Audiovisual Material

Army Military History Institute
 The John C. Bates Papers
Fort Sill Museum Archives, U.S. Army Field Artillery Center
 General Hugh Lenox Scott Collection
 The Diary of Hugh Lenox Scott (1919–1933), Hugh Lenox Scott Papers, box 4, folder:
 The Board of Indian Commissioners
 "A Plan to Re-organize the Indian Bureau." Hugh Lenox Scott (1924)
Haverford College: The Quaker Collection
 The Smiley Family Papers. No. 1113.
Indiana University, Lilly Library
 Walter Mason Camp Papers, box 3.
Library of Congress, Manuscript Division
 Papers of Newton Diehl Baker
 Papers of Tasker Howard Bliss
 Papers of Henry Clark Corbin
 Papers of John J. Pershing
 Papers of Elihu Root
 Papers of Hugh Lenox Scott
 Papers of William H. Taft
 Papers of Leonard Wood
National Archives
 Record Group 75. Board of Indian Commissioners.
 Record Group 94. Adjutant General's Office—Personnel File—Hugh Lenox Scott.
 Hugh Lenox Scott and the Indian Sign Language (1930). Motion Picture, Sound and
   Video Branch: 106:13; 106:14; 106:15. A motion picture with synchronized sound.
Smithsonian Institution—National Anthropological Archives
 Papers of Hugh L. Scott. No. 4525.
United States Military Academy—Library Archives

The Annual Report of the Board of Visitors to the United States Military Academy. 1906, 1907.
The Official Register of the Officers and Cadets of the United States Military Academy. 1908, 1909, 1910.
Hugh Lenox Scott Papers. CU 2628.

Books, Articles, and Dissertations

Adams, Brooks. *The Law of Civilization and Decay.* New York: Macmillan, 1895.
Adams, Kevin. *Class and Race in the Frontier Army: Military Life in the West, 1870–1890.* Norman: Oklahoma University Press, 2009.
Ambrose, Stephen. *Duty, Honor, Country: A History of West Point.* Baltimore: Johns Hopkins University Press, 1999.
Annual Report of the Secretary of War for the Year 1878. Washington, D.C.: Government Printing Office, 1878.
Arnold, James. *The Moro War: How America Battled a Muslim Insurgency in the Philippine Jungle, 1902–1913.* New York: Bloomsbury Press, 2011.
Bacevich, Andrew. *Diplomat in Khaki: Major General Frank Ross McCoy and American Foreign Policy, 1898–1949.* Lawrence: University of Kansas Press, 1989.
———. "Disagreeable Works: Pacifying the Moros, 1903–1906." *Military Review* 62, no. 6 (1982): 50–61.
Baker, Newton D. "Some Legal Phases of the War." *American Bar Association Journal* 7 (July 1921): 321–25.
Barnes, Jeff. *Forts of the Northern Plains: A Guide to Historic Military Posts of the Plains Indian Wars.* Mechanicsburg, Pa.: Stackpole Books, 2008.
Barsh, Russell. "Progressive Era Bureaucrats and the Unity of Twentieth-Century Indian Policy." *American Indian Quarterly* 15 (Winter 1991): 1–17.
Berkhofer, Robert F. *The White Man's Indian: Images of the American Indian from Columbus to the Present.* New York: Random House, 1978.
Berthrong, Donald. "Legacies of the Dawes Act: Bureaucrats and Land Thieves at the Cheyenne-Arapaho Agencies of Oklahoma." *Arizona and the West* 21, no. 4 (Winter 1979): 335–54.
Betzinez, Jason. *I Fought with Geronimo.* Harrisburg, Pa.: Stackpole, 1959.
Biolsi, Thomas. "'Indian Self-Government' as a Technique of Domination." *American Indian Quarterly* 15 (Winter 1991): 23–28.
Birtle, Andrew. *U.S. Army Counterinsurgency and Contingency Operations Doctrine, 1860–1941.* Washington: Center of Military History, 1998 ed.
Bjork, Katharine. *Prairie Imperialists: The Indian Country Origins of American Empire.* Philadelphia: University of Pennsylvania Press, 2018.
Blee, Lisa. "The 1925 Fort Union Indian Congress: Divergent Narratives, One Event." *American Indian Quarterly* 31 (2007): 582–612.
Bonnin, Gertrude. "The Indian Side of the Question." In Lake Mohonk Conference, *Thirty-Fifth Lake Mohonk Conference,* 92–96.

Boxberger, Daniel. "Individualism or Tribalism? The 'Dialectic' of Indian Policy." *American Indian Quarterly* 15 (Winter 1991): 29–31.
Boyer, Ruth M., and Narcissus Gayton. *Apache Mothers and Daughters: Four Generations of a Family*. Norman: University of Oklahoma Press, 1992.
———. "Brigadier General Scott: Pacificator." *Outlook* 105 (December 20, 1913): 823.
Britten, Thomas. "Hoover and the Indians: The Case For Continuity in Federal Indian Policy, 1900–1933." *Historian* 61 (Spring 1999): 519–38.
Byler, Charles. "Leonard Wood, John J. Pershing and Pacifying the Moros in the Philippines: Americans in Muslim Land." In De Toy, *Turning Victory into Success*, 89–104.
Calloway, Colin, ed. *Our Hearts Fell to the Ground: Plains Indian Views of How the West Was Lost*. New York: Bedford Books of St. Martin's Press, 1996.
Carlson, Leonard A. "Federal Policy and Indian Land: Economic Interests and the Sale of Indian Allotments, 1900–1934." *Agricultural History* 57 (January 1983): 33–45.
———. *Indians, Bureaucrats and Land: The Dawes Act and the Decline of Indian Farming*. Westport, Conn.: Greenwood Press, 1981.
Carson, James T. "Ethno-geography and the Native American Past." *Ethnohistory* 49 (Fall 2002): 769–88.
Chambers, John W., II. *To Raise an Army: The Draft Comes to Modern America*. New York: Free Press, 1987.
Clark, J. P. *Preparing for War: The Emergence of the Modern Army, 1815–1917*. Cambridge, Mass.: Harvard University Press, 2017.
Clark, William P. *The Indian Sign Language*. Lincoln: Bison Books, University of Nebraska Press, 1982.
Clendenen, Clarence. *The United States and Pancho Villa: A Study in Unconventional Diplomacy*. Port Washington, N.Y.: Kennikat Press, 1961.
Clifford, John Garry. *The Citizen Soldiers: The Plattsburg Training Camp Movement, 1913–1920*. Louisville: University Press of Kentucky, 1972.
Coffman, Edward M. *The Old Army: A Portrait of the American Army in Peacetime, 1784–1898*. New York: Oxford University Press, 1986.
———. *The Regulars: The American Army, 1898–1941*. Cambridge, Mass.: Belknap Press of Harvard University, 2004.
———. *The War to End All Wars: The American Experience in World War I*. Rev. ed. Louisville: University Press of Kentucky, 1998.
Coleman, Michael. "Not Race, but Grace: Presbyterian Missionaries and American Indians, 1837–1893." *Journal of American History* 67 (June 1980): 41–60.
Cosmas, Graham. *An Army for Empire: The United States Army in the Spanish-American War*. Columbia: University of Missouri Press, 1971.
Cullum, George W., ed. *Biographical Register of the Officers and Graduates of the United States Military Academy*. 3rd ed. Vol. 4, no. 2628. Boston: Houghton Mifflin, 1972.
Davis, Jeffrey. *Hand Talk: Sign Language among American Indian Nations*. New York: Cambridge University Press, 2010.
Debo, Angie. *Geronimo: The Man, His Time, His Place*. Norman: University of Oklahoma Press, 1976.

Delgadillo, Alice, and Miriam Perrett. *From Fort Madison to Fort Sill: A Documentary History of the Chiricahua Apache Prisoners of War, 1886–1913*. Lincoln: University of Nebraska Press, 2013.

D'Elia, Donald. "The Argument over Civilian or Military Indian Control, 1865–1880." *Historian* 24 (February 1962): 207–25.

DeLoria, Philip. *Playing Indian*. New Haven, Conn.: Yale University Press, 1998.

DeLoria, Vine, Jr. "Federal Policy and the Perennial Question." *American Indian Quarterly* 15 (Winter 1991): 19–21.

DeMallie, Raymond., ed. *Lakota Society*. Lincoln: University of Nebraska Press, 1982.

DeMontravel, Paul. *A Hero to His Fighting Men: Nelson A. Miles, 1839–1925*. Kent, Ohio: Kent State University Press, 1998.

Department of the Interior. *Report of the Board of Indian Commissioners . . . for 1869*. Washington, D.C.: Government Printing Office, 1870.

De Toy, Brian, ed., *Turning Victory into Success: Military Operations after the Campaign*. Fort Leavenworth, Kans.: Combat Studies Institute Press, 2004.

Donald, Aida. *A Lion in the White House: A Life of Theodore Roosevelt*. New York: Basic Books, 2007.

Dunlay, Thomas W. *Wolves for the Blue Soldiers: Indian Scouts and Auxiliaries with the United States Army, 1860–1890*. Lincoln: University of Nebraska Press, 1982.

Dyer, Jennifer. "Fatal Attraction: The White Obsession with Indians." *Historian* 65 (Summer 2003): 817–36.

Eisenhower, John. *Intervention! The United States and the Mexican Revolution, 1913–1917*. New York: W. W. Norton, 1993.

———. *Teddy Roosevelt and Leonard Wood: Partners in Command*. Columbia: University of Missouri Press, 2014.

Ellis, Richard. "The Humanitarian Generals." *Western Historical Quarterly* 31 (April 1972): 169–78.

———. "The Humanitarian Soldiers." *Journal of Arizona History* 10 (1969): 53–66.

Faucett, T. Benjamin. "They Call Him 'Mole Tequop.'" *Illustrated World* 38 (November 1922): 419–21.

Feaver, Eric. "Indian Soldiers, 1891–1895: An Experiment on the Closing Frontier." *Prologue* 7 (Summer 1975): 109–18.

Field, Ron. *Forts of the American Frontier, 1820–1891: Central and Northern Plains*. New York: Osprey, 2005.

Fritz, Henry. "The Board of Indian Commissioners versus Lewis Meriam and John Collier." Paper delivered at the Western Historical Association, Twenty-fifth Annual Conference. October 9–12, 1985.

———. "The Last Hurrah of Christian Humanitarian Reform: The Board of Indian Commissioners, 1909–1915." *Western Historical Quarterly* 16, no. 4 (1985): 147–62.

Fulton, Robert A. *Moroland: The History of Uncle Sam and the Moros, 1890–1920*. Rev. ed. Bend, Ore.: Tumalo Creek Press, 2009.

———. "General Scott on Turtle Mountain History." *Indian's Friend* 42 (March 1930): 4.

———. "General Scott, Practical Peacemaker." *Literary Digest* 50 (February 13, 1915): 328–30.
Genetin-Pilawa, C. Joseph. *Crooked Paths to Allotment: The Fight over Federal Indian Policy after the Civil War.* Chapel Hill: University of North Carolina Press, 2012.
Grant, Madison. *The Passing of the Great Race.* New York: Charles Scribner's Sons, 1916.
Greene, Jerome. *Nez Perce Summer, 1877: The U.S. Army and the Nee-Me-Poo Crisis.* Helena: Montana Historical Society Press, 2000.
Greenwood, John T., ed. *My Life before the World War, 1860–1917: A Memoir, General of the Armies John J. Pershing.* Lexington: University Press of Kentucky, 2013.
Guterl, Matthew. *The Color of Race in America: 1900–1940.* Cambridge, Mass.: Harvard University Press, 2001.
Gutjahr, Paul. *Charles Hodge: Guardian of American Orthodoxy.* New York: Oxford University Press, 2011.
Gwynne, S. C. *Empire of the Summer Moon: Quanah Parker and the Rise and Fall of the Comanches, the Most Powerful Indian Tribe in American History.* New York: Simon & Schuster, 2010.
Habgood, Carol, and Marcia Skaer. *One Hundred Years of Service: A History of the Army and Air Force Exchange Service, 1895–1995.* Dallas: Headquarters Army and Air Force Exchange Service, 1994.
Haes, Brenda. "Fort Sill, the Chiricahua Apaches, and the Government's Promise of Permanent Residence." *Chronicles of Oklahoma* 78 (2000): 28–43.
Hagan, Kenneth J., and William R. Roberts, eds. *Against All Enemies: Interpretations of American Military History from Colonial Times to the Present.* New York: Greenwood Press, 1986.
Hagan, William T. *Taking Indian Lands: The Cherokee (Jerome) Commission, 1889–1893.* Norman: University of Oklahoma Press, 2003.
———. *United States–Comanche Relations: The Reservation Years.* New Haven, Conn.: Yale University Press, 1976.
Hagedorn, Hermann. *Leonard Wood: A Biography.* 2 vols. New York: Harper and Brothers, 1931.
Haines, J. D. "The Death of Crazy Horse: Symbol of the Annihilation of a People." *Journal of the West* 41 (Summer 2000): 54–58.
Hämäläinen, Pekka. *The Comanche Empire.* New Haven, Conn.: Yale University Press, 2008.
Hampton, Bruce. *Children of Grace: The Nez Perce War of 1877.* New York: Henry Holt, 1994.
Hannah, Matthew. "Space and Social Control in the Administration of the Oglala Lakota ("Sioux"), 1871–1879." *Journal of Historical Geography* 19 (1993): 412–32.
Harper, James W. "The El Paso–Juárez Conference of 1916." *Arizona and the West* 20 (1978): 231–44.
———. "Hugh Lenox Scott: Soldier Diplomat, 1853–1917." Ph.D. diss., University of Virginia, 1968.
———. "Hugh Lenox Scott y la Diplomacia de Los Estados Unidos Hacia la Revolucion Mexicana." *Historia Mexicana* 27 (1978): 427–45.

Harrod, Harold L. *Becoming and Remaining: Native American Religions on the Northern Plains*. Tucson: University of Arizona Press, 1995.
Hatt, Michael. "Ghost Dancing in the Salon: The Red Indian as a Sign of White Identity." *Diogenes* 45 (1997): 93–109.
Hauptman, Laurence. ""A Harbinger of the Indian 'New Deal.'" *American Indian Quarterly* 15 (Winter 1991): 33–34.
Hedren, Paul. *After Custer: Loss and Transformation in Sioux Country*. Norman: University of Oklahoma Press, 2011.
———. *Great Sioux War Orders of Battle: How the United States Army Waged War on the Northern Plains, 1876–1877*. Norman: University of Oklahoma Press, 2011.
Hertzberg, Hazel W. *The Search for an American Indian Identity: Modern Pan-Indian Movements*. Syracuse, N.Y.: Syracuse University Press, 1971.
Hewes, James. "The United States Army General Staff, 1900–1917." *Military Affairs* 38 (April 1974): 67–71.
Holm, Tom. *The Great Confusion in Indian Affairs: Native Americans and Whites in the Progressive Era*. Austin: University of Texas Press, 2005.
———. "How General Scott Smoked the Peace Pipe." *Literary Digest* 50 (April 3, 1915): 762.
Howard, Helen A. *Saga of Chief Joseph*. Lincoln: University of Nebraska Press, 1968.
Hoxie, Frederick. *A Final Promise: The Campaign to Assimilate the Indians, 1880–1920*. Lincoln: University of Nebraska Press, 1984.
———, ed. *Talking Back to Civilization: Indian Voices from the Progressive Era*. New York: St. Martin's Press, 2001.
Hutton, Paul A. *Phil Sheridan and His Army*. Norman: University of Oklahoma Press, 1995.
———, ed. *Soldiers West: Biographies from the Military Frontier*. Lincoln: University of Nebraska Press, 1987.
James, George Wharton. *What the White Man Has Learned from the Indian*. Chicago: Forbes, 1908.
Kane, Francis Fisher. "East and West: The Atlantic City Conference on the American Indian." *Survey* (January 15, 1929): 472–74.
Katz, Friedrich. *The Life and Times of Pancho Villa*. Stanford, Calif.: Stanford University Press, 1998.
Kehl, James A. *Boss Rule in the Gilded Age: Matt Quay of Pennsylvania*. Pittsburgh: University of Pittsburgh Press, 1981.
Kelly, Lawrence. *The Assault on Assimilation: John Collier and the Origins of Indian Policy Reform*. Albuquerque: University of New Mexico Press, 1983.
Kilpatrick, Jacquelin. *Celluloid Indians: Native Americans and Film*. Lincoln: University of Nebraska Press, 1999.
Kreidberg, Marvin A., and Merton G. Henry. *History of Military Mobilization in the United States: 1775–1945*. Washington, D.C.: Department of the Army, 1955.
Kroeber, Karl, ed. *American Indian Persistence and Resurgence*. Durham, N.C.: Duke University Press, 1994.
Kvasnicka, Robert, and Herman Viola, eds. *The Commissioners of Indian Affairs, 1824–1977*. Lincoln: University of Nebraska Press, 1979.

Lake Mohonk Conference. *Report of the Thirty-Fifth Lake Mohonk Conference on the Indian, October 16 to 18, 1929.* Privately published, 1930.
Lane, Jack C. *Armed Progressive: General Leonard Wood.* San Rafael, Calif.: Presidio Press, 1978.
LaPotin, Armand S., ed. *Native American Voluntary Organizations.* Westport, Conn.: Greenwood Press, 1987.
Leiker, James N. *Racial Borders: Black Soldiers along the Rio Grande.* College Station: Texas A&M University Press, 2002.
Leupp, Francis. "General Scott as Chief of Staff." *Nation* 99 (December 12, 1914): 712.
Levinson, Irving. "From Military Victory to Political Stalemate: The United States and the Mexican Revolution." In De Toy, *Turning Victory into Success*, 105–22.
Link, Arthur S. *Wilson: The New Freedom.* Princeton, N.J.: Princeton University Press, 1956.
Linn, Brian M. "The Long Twilight of the Frontier Army." *Western Historical Quarterly* 27 (1996): 141–67.
———. *The Philippine War, 1899–1902.* Lawrence: University Press of Kansas, 2000.
———. *The U.S. Army and Counter-insurgency in the Philippine War, 1899–1902.* Chapel Hill: University of North Carolina Press, 1989.
Marvin, George. "Scott, U.S.A." *World's Work Magazine* 30 (February 1915): 421–32.
———. "Villa: The Bandit Chieftain." *World's Work Magazine* 28 (July 1914): 268–80.
McCallum, Jack. *Leonard Wood: Rough Rider, Surgeon, Architect of American Imperialism.* New York: New York University Press, 2006.
McWhorter, Lucullus. *Hear Me, My Chiefs! Nez Perce Legend and History.* Caldwell, Ida.: Caxton Printers, 1992.
Meadows, William C., ed. *The Fort Sill Ledgers of Hugh Lenox Scott and Iseeo: 1889–1897.* Norman: University of Oklahoma Press, 2015.
Means, Jeffrey. "'Indians Shall Do Things in Common': Oglala Lakota Identity and Cattle Raising on the Pine Ridge Reservation." *Montana: The Magazine of Western History* 61 (Autumn 2011): 3–21.
Miller, Christopher L. "Indian Patriotism: Warriors vs. Negotiators." *American Indian Quarterly* 17 (Summer 1993): 343–49.
Miller, Edward A., Jr. *Lincoln's Abolitionist General: The Biography of David Hunter.* Columbia: University of South Carolina Press, 1997.
Millet, Allan R. *The General: Robert L. Bullard and Officership in the United States Army, 1881–1925.* Westport, Conn.: Greenwood Press, 1975.
Mooney, James. "The Ghost-Dance Religion and the Sioux Outbreak of 1890." In *Fourteenth Annual Report of the Bureau of Ethnology to the Secretary of the Smithsonian Institution, 1892–93*, by J. W. Powell, part 2. Washington, D.C.: U.S. Printing Office, 1896.
———. *The Ghost-Dance Religion and Wounded Knee.* 1973, reprint; Mineola, N.Y.: Dover Publications, 2011.
Morison, Elting. *Turmoil and Tradition: A Study of the Life and Times of Henry L. Stimson.* Boston: Houghton Mifflin, 1960.

Moses, L. George. *The Indian Man: A Biography of James Mooney.* Urbana: University of Illinois Press, 2002.
Neihardt, John G., ed. *Black Elk Speaks: Being the Life Story of a Holy Man of the Oglala Sioux.* Lincoln: University of Nebraska Press, 1982
Nenninger, Timothy K. "The Army Enters the Twentieth Century, 1904-1917." In Hagan and Roberts, *Against All Enemies*, 216-35.
Nye, William. *Carbine and Lance: The Story of Old Fort Sill.* Rev. ed. Norman: University of Oklahoma Press, 1969.
Ostler, Jeffrey. *The Plains Sioux and U.S. Colonialism from Lewis and Clark to Wounded Knee.* Studies in North American Indian History. New York: Cambridge University Press, 2004.
O'Sullivan, John, and Alan Meckler, eds. *The Draft and Its Enemies: A Documentary History.* Urbana: University of Illinois Press, 1974.
Otis, Delos S. *The Dawes Act and the Allotment of Indian Lands.* Norman: University of Oklahoma Press, 1973.
Palmer, Frederick. *Bliss, the Peacemaker: The Life and Letters of General Tasker Howard Bliss.* 1934. Reprint, Freeport, N.Y.: Books for Libraries Press, 1970.
———. *Newton D. Baker: America at War.* 2 vols. New York: Dodd, Mead, 1931.
Parker, Watson. "Military Posts of the Black Hills." *Journal of America's Military Past* 28 (Summer 2001): 5-20.
Pershing, John J. *My Experience in the World War.* Kindle ed. Pickle Partners, 2013.
———. "Persons in the Foreground: The American General Who Hypnotizes Piutes, Moros, and Mexican Bandits into Good Behavior." *Current Opinion* 58 (May 1915): 322-24.
Pfaller, Rev. Louis, O.S.B. "The Forging of an Indian Agent: James Mclaughlin." *North Dakota History* 34 (1967): 62-76.
———. *James McLaughlin: The Man with an Indian Heart.* Richardton, N.D.: Assumption Abbey Press, 1992.
———. "Portrait." *Outlook* 105 (December 20, 1913): 836.
———. "Portrait." *World's Work Magazine* 28 (July 1914): 278.
Price, Catherine. *The Oglala People, 1841-1879: A Political History.* Lincoln: University of Nebraska Press, 1998.
Prucha, Francis Paul. "America's Indians and the Federal Government, 1900-2000." *Wisconsin Magazine of History* 84 (Winter 2000-2001): 769-88.
Pruitt, James H., II. "Leonard Wood and the American Empire." Ph.D. diss., Texas A&M University, 2011.
Ragsdale, John W., Jr. "Values in Transition: The Chiricahua Apache from 1886-1914." *American Indian Law Review* 35 (2010-11): 141-67.
Reed, Hugh. *Cadet Life at West Point.* Richmond, Ind.: I. Reed & Son, 1911.
Robbins, William G. "Herbert Hoover's Indian Reformers under Attack: The Failure of Administrative Reform." *Mid America* 63 (October 1981): 157-70.
Roberts, William R. "Reform and Revitalization, 1890-1903." In Hagan and Roberts, *Against All Enemies*, 197-215.
Roosevelt, Theodore. *The Rough Riders: Illustrated History.* New York: Fall River Press, 2014.

Russo, Elmer. "John Collier: Architect of Sovereignty or Assimilation?" *American Indian Quarterly* 15 (Winter 1991): 49–54.

Scott, Hugh Lenox. "The Early History and Names of the Arapaho." *American Anthropologist* 9 (1907): 545–60.

———. "Historical Relations of the Indians with the Government." In Lake Mohonk Conference, *Thirty-Fifth Lake Mohonk Conference*, 22–26.

———. "Honor, Duty, Country: A Thought for the Fourth." *American Legion Monthly* 7 (July 1929): 39.

———. "Notes on the Caddo or Sun Dance of the Kiowa." *American Anthropologist* 13 (1911): 345–79.

———. "Pioneer Days on the Plains." *Field & Stream* 33 (November 1928): 36–37.

———. "The Paiute 'Uprising.'" *Sunset Magazine* 50 (June 1923): 38–39.

———. "The Sign Language of the Plains Indians." The International Folk-Lore Congress of the World's Columbian Exposition (Chicago, 1893). *Archives of International Folk-Lore Association* 1 (1893): 206–20.

———. "A Soldier's View of the Philippine Question." *Proceedings of the Twenty-Fifth Annual Meeting of the Lake Mohonk Conference* (1907): 119–22.

———. *Some Memories of a Soldier.* New York: Century Company, 1928.

———. "Turtle Mountain: Notable Address at the Jubilee Celebration of the National Indian Association." *Missionary Review of the World* 53 (April 1930): 280–83.

———. "Wovoka: The Messiah." In James Mooney, *The Ghost-Dance Religion and Wounded Knee.* Mineola, N.Y.: Dover Publications, 2011.

Seton, Ernest Thompson. *Sign Talk.* Garden City, N.Y.: Doubleday, Page, 1918.

Seymour, Flora W. *Indian Agents of the Old Frontier.* New York: Octagon Books, 1975.

Smith, Sherry. "George Bird Grinnell and the 'Vanishing' Plains Indians." *Montana: The Magazine of Western History* 50 (Autumn 2000): 18–31.

———. *Reimagining Indians: Native Americans through Anglo Eyes, 1880–1940.* New York: Oxford University Press, 2000.

———. *The View from Officers' Row: Army Perceptions of Western Indians.* Tucson: University of Arizona Press, 1990.

Smits, David. "Fighting Fire with Fire: The Frontier Army's Use of Indian Scouts and Allies in the Trans-Mississippi Campaigns, 1860–1890." *American Indian Culture and Research Journal* 22 (1998): 73–116.

Smythe, Donald. *Pershing: General of the Armies.* Bloomington: Indiana University Press, 1986.

Sniffen, M. K. [Comments on Hugh L. Scott.] *Indian Truth* 4 (January 1927): 1.

Sonnichsen, C. L. *The Mescalero Apaches.* Norman: University of Oklahoma Press, 1979.

Steinbach, Robert H. *A Long March: The Lives of Frank and Alice Baldwin.* Austin: University of Texas Press, 1989.

Stockel, Henrietta. *Shame and Endurance: The Untold Story of the Apache Prisoners of War.* Tucson: University of Arizona Press, 2004.

Stuart, Paul. "Administrative Reform in Indian Affairs." *Western Historical Quarterly* 16 (April 1985): 133–46.

Sussman, Robert Wald. *The Myth of Race: The Troubled Persistence of an Unscientific Idea.* Cambridge, Mass.: Harvard University Press, 2014.
Swett, Morris. "Sergeant I-See-O, Kiowa Indian Scout." *Chronicles of Oklahoma* 13 (September 1935): 341–56.
Tate, Michael. "From Scout to Doughboy: The National Debate over Integrating American Indians into the Military, 1891–1918." *Western Historical Quarterly* 17 (1986): 417–37.
———. *The Frontier Army in the Settlement of the West.* Norman: University of Oklahoma Press, 1999.
———. "Soldiers of the Line: Apache Companies in the U.S. Army, 1891–1897." *Arizona and the West* 16 (Winter 1974): 343–64.
Thomas, Evan. *The War Lovers: Roosevelt, Lodge, Hearst, and the Rush to Empire, 1898.* New York: Little, Brown, 2010.
Thornton, Russell. *American Indian Holocaust and Survival: A Population History since 1492.* Norman: University of Oklahoma Press, 1987.
Tomkins, Frank. *Chasing Villa: The Last Campaign of the U.S. Cavalry.* Silver City, N.Mex.: High Lonesome Books, 1996.
Tomkins, William. *Indian Sign Language.* New York: Dover Publications, 1969.
Turcheneske, John A., Jr. *The Chiricahua Apache Prisoners of War: Fort Sill, 1894–1914.* Niwot: University of Colorado Press, 1997.
Utley, Robert. *Frontier Regulars: The United States Army and the Indian, 1866–1891.* Lincoln: University of Nebraska Press, 1993.
———. *Geronimo.* New Haven, Conn.: Yale University Press, 2012.
———. *The Indian Frontier of the American West, 1846–1890.* Albuquerque: University of New Mexico Press, 1984.
Vandiver, Frank. *Black Jack: The Life and Times of John J. Pershing.* 2 vols. College Station: Texas A&M University Press, 1977.
Viola, Herman. *Diplomats in Buckskin: A History of Indian Delegations in Washington City.* Bluffton, S.C.: Rivilo Books, 1995.
Walker, James. "Communal Chase of the Buffalo." In *Lakota Society,* ed. Raymond DeMallie, 74–94. Lincoln: University of Nebraska Press, 1982.
Walker, Jerrell. "The Sign Language of the Plains Indians of North America." *Chronicles of Oklahoma* 31 (1953): 168–77.
———. "War Chiefs of the Army." *World's Work Magazine* 31 (November 1915): 652–72.
War Department Reports. Washington, D.C.: U.S. Department of War, 1916.
Washburn, Wilcomb. *The Assault on Indian Tribalism.* Malabar, Fla.: Krieger, 1986.
Weigley, Russell. *History of the United States Army.* New York: Macmillan, 1967.
Welsome, Eileen. *The General and the Jaguar: Pershing's Hunt for Pancho Villa; a True Story of Revolution and Revenge.* New York: Little, Brown, 2006.
West, Elliott. *Contested Plains: Indians, Goldseekers, and the Rush to Colorado.* Lawrence: University Press of Kansas, 1998.
Williams, Walter, L. "United States Indian Policy and the Debate over Philippine Annexation: Implications for the Origins of American Imperialism." *Journal of American History* 66 (March 1980): 810–31.

Wooster, Robert. *The Military and United States Indian Policy, 1865–1903*. New Haven, Conn.: Yale University Press, 1988.

———. *Nelson A. Miles and the Twilight of the Frontier Army*. Lincoln: University of Nebraska Press, 1993.

———. "Brigadier General Scott: Pacificator." *Outlook* 105 (December 20, 1913): 823.

———. "General Scott on Turtle Mountain History." *Indian's Friend* 42 (March 1930): 4.

———. "General Scott, Practical Peacemaker." *Literary Digest* 50 (February 13, 1915): 328.

———. "How General Scott Smoked the Peace Pipe." *Literary Digest* 50 (April 3, 1915): 762.

———. "Persons in the Foreground: The American General Who Hypnotizes Piutes, Moros, and Mexican Bandits into Good Behavior." *Current Opinion* 58 (May 1915): 322–24.

———. "Portrait." *Outlook* 105 (December 20, 1913): 836.

———. "Portrait." *World's Work Magazine* 28 (July 1914): 278.

———. "War Chiefs of the Army." *World's Work Magazine* 31 (November 1915): 652–72.

Zimmermann, Evan. *First Great Triumph: How Five Americans Made Their Country a World Power*. New York: Farrar, Straus and Giroux, 2002.

▼ ▼ ▼

INDEX

Adjutant-General's Office. *See under* United States Army
Ah-pia-ton (Wooden Lance), Kiowa, 59–60, 68, 217n8
Ainsworth, Fred C., 160, 161, 164
Alger, Russell, 113, 224n11
American Anthropologist, articles by Scott in, 189, 244n42
American Indian Defense Association. *See* Collier, John
Anadarko, Okla., 57, 60, 62, 66, 68, 70, 80, 177
Anadarko Agency, 56
Anadarko Tribal Council, 221n32
Apaches. *See* Chiricahua Apaches; Mescalero Apache reservation
Arapahos, 59, 71, 244n42
Arlington National Cemetery, 206n1
army. *See* United States Army
Army Corps of Engineers. *See* United States Army
assimilationists, 181–82, 183
Ayer, Edward, 102, 168

Baker, Newton D., 98, 163, 164, 165, 194. *See also* Scott, Hugh L.
Baldwin, Frank D., 79–80
Bates, John C. *See* Bates Agreement
Bates Agreement, 81–82, 124, 125, 128–29, 139

Battle of Little Big Horn, 1, 20, 24, 25, 29, 45, 209n31
Battle of Muddy Creek, 27
Battle of San Juan Hill, 113
Beach, Francis, 81
Bears Paw Mountains, 25, 33, 44, 45, 48, 49
Bell, J. Franklin, 233n5
Benteen, Frederick, 21
Biographical Register, 58
Biroa. *See* Moros
Bismarck, N.Dak., 19, 21, 29, 33, 44
Blackfeet Agency, 178, 186, 191
Blackfeet tribe, 194
Black Hills, 23, 24, 26, 40, 43, 48, 152; Custer's attempt to conquer, 24, 37; discovery of gold, 22; sacredness to Sioux, 22
Bliss, Tasker, 100, 116–17, 120, 121, 157. *See also* Scott, Hugh L.
Board of Indian Commissioners, 64, 87, 102, 168, 169, 172, 174, 181, 182, 186, 187; criticism of Scott, 177, 179–80, 180–81; Scott's administrative reform plan for Bureau of Indian Affairs submitted to, 180, 183–84, 240n19; Scott's role on, 1–2, 168–69, 172, 173, 174, 175, 176, 178, 179, 180, 181, 182, 186, 188, 191, 192, 194; termination of, 186–87. *See also* Scott, Hugh L.

259

"Boomers," 64, 65
Booz, Oscar, 148
Boxer Rebellion, 120
Bozeman Trail, 22
Breckenridge, Joseph, 113
Brookings Institute, 184
Brown, Dudley, 80
Browning, Daniel, 69
Browning, Mont., sign language conference in, 178, 191
Brule. *See* Sioux
Bud Bagsak. *See* Moros
Budd, Ralph, 193
Bud Dago Massacre, 143, 200, 231–32n71
buffalo, 19, 23, 32, 36, 39; commercial use of hides, 36, 54; cultural significance to tribes, 27, 36; extinction of, 24, 27, 35, 46, 55, 56, 58, 202; Indian hunting of, 22, 23, 24, 35, 55
Buntin, John, 186
Bureau of Ethnology. *See* Smithsonian Institution
Bureau of Indian Affairs (BIA), 3–4, 23, 27, 34, 40, 46, 82, 84, 150, 175, 179, 184, 198; and agency supervisors, 26, 27, 78, 178, 179, 184, 189; and Board of Indian Commissioners, 180, 181, 182, 240n19; and Charles Burke, 182; and Charles Rhoads, 184; corruption in, 3–4, 27, 175, 177; Lewis Meriam and *The Problem of Indian Administration*, 185; Scott's criticism of, 46, 78, 79, 170, 174, 179, 180–81, 184, 240n23; Scott's plan to reform the administration of, 178–79, 180; and turnover in field personnel, 78
Burke, Charles, 180, 182
Bursum, Holm, 176, 182
Bursum Indian Land Bill, 181, 182

Cameron, J. Donald, 50
Camp, Walter, 49
Campbell, Fred C. 173, 186, 198
Camp Dix, N.J., 101, 166, 167, 194
Camp Hamilton, Ky., 113
Camp Thomas, Ga., 112
Capron, Allyn K., Jr., 76, 80
Carlisle Indian Industrial School, 85
Carranza, Venustiano, 153, 154, 155
Carlton, C. A., 71
Cedula Tax. *See* Moros
Centralia College, Ky., 7, 113
Century of Dishonor (Jackson), 3
Charles, Oscar J., 137, 147, 229n57, 230n60
Cherokee Commission. *See* Jerome Commission
Cheyenne River Agency, 25, 26, 45
Cheyennes, 23, 24, 26, 27, 32, 33
Chief Joseph, 32, 33, 44, 47, 48, 194, 34, 39, 47, 57, 59, 71, 108, 190; friendship with Scott, 32, 33, 44, 47, 48, 51; Scott's role in capture, 44, 48, 48–49, 108, 215n41. *See also* Nez Percés
chief of staff. *See under* United States Army
Chiricahua Apaches: arrival at Fort Sill, 1, 71, 72; challenges confronting, 72, 73, 74, 81, 82, 84, 85, 86; duties on reservation, 74, 74–75, 77, 81; excellent conduct of staff noted, 76, 77, 81; prisoners of war, 76, 77, 78, 81–82, 190; removal to New Mexico, 82, 83, 85, 86, 87, 157, 174; Scott's advocacy on behalf of, 72, 73, 74, 75, 75–76, 77, 83, 84, 87, 88, 89, 150, 169, 198, 199; status as prisoners of war, 76, 77, 78, 81–82, 190. *See also* Scott, Hugh L.
Cienfuegos, Cuba, 119
Civil War, 11, 40, 41, 55, 109, 112, 153, 159, 190
Clark, Benjamin H. "Ben," 190
Cleveland, Grover, 69, 72
Collier, John, 104, 182, 186, 241n26; and American Indian Defense Association, assimilationists view of, 182, 187; as a cultural pluralist, 182–83. *See also* Scott, Hugh L.
Columbian Exposition, 189

Comancheria. *See* Comanches
Comanches, 1, 25, 40, 53, 54, 55–56, 56–57, 58–59, 59–60, 61–62, 64, 65, 70, 72, 73, 74, 75, 76, 77, 78, 79, 80, 82, 83, 86, 87, 88, 133, 176–77, 187, 198
Company E, Seventh Cavalry, 48
Company I, Twelfth Infantry, 76
conscription, Scott's plan for. *See* Scott, Hugh L.
Conspiracy of Pontiac (Pontiac), 21
Corbin, Henry C., 138
cotta. See Moros
Council of One Hundred, 183, 184
Crane, Leo, 173, 198
Crazy Horse, 30, 37, 45, 108
Crook, George, 24, 27
Crower, Enoch, 161, 163, 164
Crows, 32, 35, 38, 211n11
Cuban insurrectionists, 107
cultural pluralists. *See* Collier, John
Current Opinion, 194
Curtis, Charles, 175, 176
Custer, George A., 1, 20, 23, 24, 27, 29, 33, 37, 38, 60, 190; avengers of, 26. *See also* Battle of Little Big Horn

Dakota Territory, 19, 20–21, 22, 29–30, 32, 33, 34, 38, 39, 40–41, 44, 45, 118, 150, 151
Danville, Ky., 7, 113
dato. *See* Moros
Davis, George W., 83
Dawes Severalty Act, 63, 63–64, 65, 187; consequences of, 3, 62, 68, 87, 171, 187; criticism of, 65, 69; enforcement of, 89; passage of, 57–58
Day, George, 66, 68
Department of Mindanao, 124
Department of the Interior, 27, 46, 46–47, 56, 68–69, 72, 78, 79, 81–82, 84, 86, 88, 219n21
Department of War, 20, 27, 34, 53, 58, 69, 72, 77, 78, 81, 82, 83, 84, 85, 84–85, 86, 88, 100, 106, 107, 110, 111, 115, 219n21

Devil's Lake, N.Dak., 32, 38, 151
Dewey, George, 107
Diaz, Porfirio, 153
Division of the Missouri, 27, 71, 71–72, 76
Doane, Gustavus, 48
Dod, Robert, 10, 14
Dunbar, John B., 190
Dutch Reformed Missionaries, 87

Eagle Pipe, 26
El Paso, Texas, 25, 156, 157, 165
Eliot, Samuel, 169, 186
Engagement of American Forces with Moros on Mount Dago, 176, 177, 178, 183, 231n68

Fall, Albert, 99, 174, 174–75
federal wardship, 87, 169, 170, 171, 172, 179, 184–85, 187, 194–95. *See also* Scott, Hugh L.
Ferris, Scott, 86
Fetterman, William, 55
Field Museum, 168
Fort Abraham Lincoln, N.Dak., 19, 20–21, 25, 29, 45, 108, 150
Fort Benton, Mont., 25, 32
Fort Berthold, N.Dak., 33, 21, 25, 29, 45, 108, 150
Fort Davis, Texas, 19
Fort Huachuca, Ariz., 25, 11
Fort Keogh, Mont., 25, 44
Fort Laramie, Treaty of, 22, 23, 23–24, 26, 37
Fort Leavenworth, Kans., 47, 48
Fort Meade, S.Dak., 40, 48, 109, 162
Fort Sam Houston, Texas, 153
Fort Sill, Okla., 1, 25, 50, 52, 53; arrival of Chiricahua Apaches, 71–72, 74, 76, 77; problems at, 57, 58, 62, 66, 68, 78, 79, 83, 85, 87, 96; termination of Chiricahua Apaches at, 82, 83, 84, 85, 86, 88, 89, 157, 199, 221–22n37

Fort Totten, N.Dak.: Scott's married life at, 39; Scott's posting at, 38, 47, 49–50, 89, 109, 118, 150, 162; Scott's return to, 151, 176
Fort Yates, S.Dak., 25, 39
Fourteenth U.S. Cavalry, 122, 152
Fourth U.S. Cavalry, 20
Frazier, Lyman, 186
Friends of the Indian, 80, 89, 181; eclectic group of reformers, 63; Scott's relationship to, 89, 170, 67–68

Garlington, Ernest, 20, 209n31
General Staff. *See* United States Army
Geronimo, 71, 72, 81, 113
Ghost Dance religion, 57, 58, 59, 60, 69, 79, 88; end of, 33, 48; Jack Wilson and, 58; name Wovoka, 58, 59, role of I-See-O in preventing violence from, 4, 6, 60, 61, 76–77, 190, 198. *See also* Scott, Hugh L.
Glacier National Park, 195
Grant's Peace Policy, 64, 169
"grass" money, 75, 80
Great Northern Railway, 193
Great Sioux War, 24, 27, 29, 33, 41
Grinnell, George, 243n40
Gros Ventres tribe, 33

Hall, J. Lee, 57, 66
Harding, Warren, 176, 177
Harrison, Benjamin, 43, 57
Haskell Institute, 195
Hatch, 181
Hayden, Carl, 176
Hayes, Rutherford, 34
hazing. *See* United States Military Academy
Helena, Mont., 25, 32
Henderson, Earl, 187
Hodge, Charles, 7–8, 8, 11, 16, 188; death of, 39; influence of on Scott, 8–9, 10–11, 14, 17, 28, 51, 148; reputation as theologian, 7, 8, 42, 52, 170. *See also* Scott, Hugh L
Hodge, Mary Elizabeth. *See* Scott, Hugh L.
Hoover, Herbert, 184, 185
Hopis, 157; difficulties with, 157, 173; educational difficulties, 173
Hotevilla (Hopi village), 173
House Committee on Indian Affairs. *See* United States Congress
Howard, Oliver O., 48
Huerta, Victoriano, 153
Hunkpapa Sioux, 23
Hunter, David, 11, 14, 39

Ickes, Harold, 183, 187
Illustrated World, 194
Indian Department. *See* Bureau of Indian Affairs (BIA)
Indian Office. *See* Bureau of Indian Affairs (BIA)
Indian Re-organization Act, 187
Indian Rights Association, 64, 86, 175, 184, 185
Indians: and Dawes Act, consequences of, 63, 63–64, 65, 68, 69, 87, 89, 171, 187; efficacy of farming and ranching, 74, 85, 171–72, 187, 188, 203; and Ghost Dance religion, 57, 59, 60, 61, 69, 87–88, 190, 198; graft against, 56, 57, 78, 80; and tribal devastation, 206n3; and value of buffalo, 23, 35, 36, 39, 46, 54, 55, 56, 58, 202, 212n16. *See also names of specific tribes*
Indian scouts, 30, 59, 69, 72, 88, 190
Indian Service. *See* Bureau of Indian Affairs (BIA)
Indian sign language. *See* Plains Indian sign language
Isatai, 80
I-See-O, 93, 219n24; early life of, 60–61; relationship with, 61, 62, 70, 88, 154, 156, 176–77, 190, 198

Jackson, Helen Hunt, 3
Jamal ul Kiram II. *See* Moros
Jenkins, J., 178
Jerome, David H., 63,-64, 66
Jerome Agreement, 67, 73, 82, 83
Jerome Commission, 63–64, 68, 79, 87, 89; corruptive practices of, 65, 79; created to implement Dawes Severalty Act, 63–64, 89, 63–64, 66, Scott's role in, 87, 89; visit to Fort Sill, 64
Jolo, 124, 127, 129, 131, 133, 133–34
Jones, Andrieus, 176
Juarez, Mexico. *See* Villa, Francisco "Pancho"
juramentado, 134–35, 140, 141, 142, 143, 143–44, 198

kāfir. *See* Moros
Keams Canyon, Ariz., 173
Kickapoos, 172
Kingston, N.J., 166–67, 188
Kiowa-Apaches, 57, 61, 65, 70, 79, 88
Kiowa-Comanche Reservation, 25, 58, 59, 72, 74, 86, 88
Kiowa-Comanches, 74; consequences of Treaty of Medicine Lodge, 55; exposure to graft, 56, 57, 68; growing dependence on federal annuities, 56; incursions from Anglo settlement and disease, 61–62, 64, 82, 83; loss of buffalo 54, 55–56; use of horse, 54
Kiowa-Comanche Tribal Council, 73, 83, 86
Kiowas, 1, 17, 25, 41, 53, 55, 58–59, 60–61, 62, 65, 68, 69, 70, 71, 73, 74, 75, 76, 78, 80, 81, 83, 84, 86, 87, 88, 133, 154, 176–77, 186, 187, 190, 198
Koran. *See* Moros

Lake Lanao, 25, 126, 131, 165
Lake Lanao campaign, 126, 142

Lake Mohonk Conference, 4, 64, 180; Albert Smiley, 64; Daniel Smiley, 4; Scott's contribution to, 180
Lane, Frank, 175
Langhorne, George T., 138, 141–42
Lawrence, Kans., 195, 142, 143, 144
Leavitt, Scott, 191, 192
Lenroot, Bill, 182
Leupp, Francis, 80
Lexington, Ky., 113
Literary Digest, 194
Little Big Horn. *See* Battle of Little Big Horn
Little Wolf, 26
Lone Wolf, 65, 68; opposition to Dawes Act, 65, 66
Lone Wolf v. Hitchcock, 3
Lord, Herbert, 176
Los Moros. *See* Moros
Ludlow, William, 114, 115, 116

Madero, Francisco, 153
Maine, 107
March, Payton C., 157
Maus, Marion, 72
Maytorena, Jose, 155
McCoy, Frank, 116, 121, 137. *See also* Scott, Hugh L.
McDowell, Malcom, 169, 176, 179–80, 184, 191
McGee, John F., 43, 151, 151–52
McKinley, William, 83, 107, 111, 121
McLaughlin, James, 173
Medicine Lodge, Treaty of, 55, 56, 65; objectives, 55; used by tribal groups to thwart implementation of the Dawes act, 66, 67
Memorandum to the Secretary of War, 143, 144, 145. *See also* Scott, Hugh L.
Mentor (periodical), 194
Meriam, Lewis, 39, 41, 42, 43, 50, 184–85; report by, 184, 186; Scott's criticism of

Meriam, Lewis *(continued)*
184. *See also* Bureau of Indian Affairs (BIA)
Merrill, Mary. *See* Scott, Mary Merrill (wife)
Mescalero Agency, 175, 177
Mescalero Apache Reservation 25, 85, 174–75, 176, 177, 179; Chiricahua Apaches on, 84–85, 85–86, 87
Messiah Dance. *See* Ghost Dance religion
Mexican border campaign, 153, 155, 156, 164, 165. *See also* Villa, Francisco "Poncho"
Mexican Revolution, 156
Miles, Nelson A., 32, 44, 47, 48, 49; assistance to Scott, 43–44, 47, 48, 49, 71, 72; first encounter with Scott, 3, 44; growing alienation from executive branch, 112
Military Reorganization Act, 108–9
Mills, Albert, 147, 149
Mindanao, province of, 120, 121, 122, 123–24, 127, 131, 138, 165
Miniconjou. *See* Sioux
Missouri River, 21, 22, 29, 32, 34, 45
Montezuma, Carlos, 4
Mooney, James, 110; and Ghost Dance religion, 217n7; Scott's association with, 110; Scott's criticism of, 238n6
Morehead, Warren K., 169
Moqui Indian Agency, 173
Morgan, Fred C. 176
Moros: Bates Agreement and, 124, 125, 128–29, 129, 139; Biroa, 128, 129, 129–30, 133; Bud Bagsak, 136; Bud Dago Massacre, 143, 200, 231–32n71; cedula tax, 124, 125, 126, 131, 139, 140, 141, 200; dato, 123, 125, 128, 129, 130, 131, 132, 133, 135, 135–36, 140, 142, 143, 162, 198, 203; Jamal ul Kiram II, 95, 124; *juramentado*, 123, 128, 135, 136; *kāfirs*, 123; Koran, 123; Muhammad, 202; Pala, 140; Panglima Hassan, 129, 130, 133–34, 134, 135, 136, 36–37; Panglima Indinan, 129; Raja Muda, 130, 154; sharia law, 123, 130; and Spanish authority, 122–23, 124, 126, 139; Sulu region, 1, 95, 105, 122, 123, 124, 125, 128, 129, 130, 131, 132, 135, 136, 137, 138, 139, 165, 200
"Moros of Jolo Island, The" (Scott)
Muhammad, 202
Muslims. *See* Moros

Naco, Ariz. *See* Villa, Francisco "Pancho"
Naco, Sonora, 155
Natalish, Vincent, 85
Nation, The, 194
National Defense Act. *See* United States Army
National Guard (state militia), 110, 165; McKinley's use of, 107, 109, 112; Scott's criticism of, 109
New Jersey Highway Commission, 179, 193
New York Times, 143
Nez Percés, 32, 32–33, 44, 45, 48, 49, 72, 79
Nez Percé War, 44, 45, 49, 72, 79, 215
Ninth U.S. Cavalry, 215–16n41
Northern Cheyennes. *See* Cheyennes
Northern Pacific Railway, 21, 23, 29, 41

Obregon, Alvaro, 153, 153–54
Office of Adjutant General. *See* United States Army
Office of Indian Affairs. *See* Bureau of Indian Affairs (BIA)
Office of the Surgeon General. *See* United States Army
Oglala Lakotas. *See* Sioux
Ordinance Department. *See* United States Army
Organic Act, 159, 161
Otis, Elwell, 40
Outlook (periodical), 194

Paiutes, 180–81, 240n23
"Paiute 'Uprising'" (Scott), 181, 240n23
Pala. *See* Moros

Index

Panglima, Hassan, 129; capture of, 135–36; conference with, 129–30, 130; death of, 136; war in Sulu, 133, 133–34, 135. *See also* Moros
Panglima, Indinan. *See* Moros
Parker, Quanah, and Jerome Commission, 68, 65, 65–66, 70, 79–80
Peace Policy, 64, 169
Pendleton Civil Service Act, 78
Pershing, John J., 103; appointed as general of American Expeditionary Force, 165; Mexican campaign, 165; Philippine campaign, 126, 131, 165. *See also* Scott, Hugh L.
Philadelphia, Pa., 7, 39, 50, 89, 110, 169
Philippine Commission, 125, 125–26, 131, 132, 157, 198. *See also* Scott, Hugh L.
Philippine Service. *See* Scott, Hugh L.
Pinar del Rio, 115–16
Pine Ridge Agency, 25
Plains Indian sign language, 33, 35, 44, 74, 202–3; movie on, 191, 244n45; Scott's initial interest in, 1, 189, 200, 211n10; Scott's speeches on, 192–93, 193; Scott's study of, 31, 35, 167, 168, 171, 189, 190, 191, 243n40; value as a negotiating tool, 31, 43, 44, 51, 52, 110, 127–28, 171, 194, 199, 200–201
port of Cienfuegos, 119
port of Tampa, Fla., 112
Pratt, Richard H., 85
preparedness campaign, 162, 163, 165, 193. *See also* Scott, Hugh L.
Presbyterian Church. *See* Danville, Ky.; Princeton Theological Seminary
Presbyterian faith, 4, 7, 8, 170, 202
Princeton, N.J., 4, 7, 9, 12, 21, 29–30, 39, 50, 51, 89, 110, 167, 188
Princeton Review, 8
Princeton Theological Seminary, 4, 7, 8, 42
Princeton University, 9, 50, 162, 162–63
Problem of Indian Administration, The (Meriam Report), 184

Proctor, Redfield, 223n8
Pueblo peoples, 181, 182
Puerto Rico, 112

Quartermaster's Corps. *See* United States Army
Quay, Alexander, 42
Quay, Andrew Greg Curtin, 71
Quay, Matthew S., 42–43, 43, 50, 69, 92
Quinette, William H., 75; assistance to Scott, 75; at Fort Sill, 75

Raja Muda. *See* Moros
Rankin, Edward P., 14
Red Cloud, 26, 32, 33–35, 51
Red Cloud Agency, 26, 34
Red Cloud's War, 33, 34
Red Horse, 26
Red Man, The (periodical), 194
Red River War, 48
Reeves, James, 142, 144
Republican National Committee, 43
Rhoads, Charles, 184, 185, 186
Ricketts, Palmer, 7, 207–8n16
Ripley, Henry, 82
Roe Cloud, Henry, 4
Roosevelt, Franklin, 2, 186–87, 192
Roosevelt, Theodore, 43, 148, 162; appoints Scott superintendent at West Point, 137, 149; assistance provided to Scott, 121, 121–22, 137, 138, 144, 149, 150, 151, 152, 163, 200; relationship to Leonard Wood, 113, 114, 121, 125, 126, 149, 160, 200. *See also* Scott, Hugh L.
Root, Elihu: and Jerome Commission, 68; Scott and Root commission, 193; as secretary of war, 2, 84, 121, 158, 160, 223n2
Rushmore, Charles, 43, 151, 152

San Antonio, Texas, 153–54, 156
San Carlos Agency. *See* San Carlos Reservation

San Carlos reservation, 25, 177
San Francisco earthquake (1906), 145
Sans Arcs, 26
Sayre, Ferdinand, 81, 82, 105
Schofield, John, 46, 69, 69–70
"scientific" racism, 5
Scott, Anna Merrill (daughter), 213n24
Scott, Blanchard (daughter), 167, 213n24
Scott, Charles Hodge (brother), 7, 9, 11, 14, 20–21, 39, 41, 50
Scott, David Hunter (son), 49–50, 116, 118, 139, 167, 176, 213n24
Scott, Hugh Lenox; and adventure, desire for, 9, 11, 18, 20, 29, 30, 31, 32, 44, 51, 189, 192, 200; admission to the United States Military Academy, 11; and African Americans, 18–19, 203; ambivalence in use of overt military force, 106, 130, 131, 132–33, 134, 135, 136, 142, 143, 144–45, 147, 162, 165; on American Indians, 1, 5, 30, 31, 32, 35, 36, 37, 43, 34, 46, 47, 53, 57, 60, 61, 77, 85, 89, 118–19, 133, 145, 157, 168, 170, 172, 175, 176, 177, 178, 180, 182–83, 193–94, 198, 201, 202, 211n11, 244n47; and Apache prisoners of war, 1, 71, 73, 76, 77, 81, 85–86, 190; and Apaches, 87, 199; and apologies to the Chiricahua Apaches, 87, 199; articles about, 194, 204; articles by, 189, 190, 191, 194, 203, 204, 244n42; autobiography of, 193, 194; and Ben Clark, 190; birth of, 7, 8; and Board of Indian Commissioners, 1–2, 87, 102, 168–69, 174, 179, 180, 187, 188, 194; and Bud Dago massacre, 141–42, 143–44, 145, 200, 231n67; and Bureau of Indian Affairs, 46–47, 78, 79, 84, 174, 175, 177, 178, 179, 180, 181, 182, 184, 185, 198, 240n23; as cadet at United States Military Academy, 12, 13, 14, 15, 16, 17, 18, 20, 28; and Charles Hodge, 7, 11, 28, 39, 148, 188; and Chief Joseph, 32–33, 44, 47, 48–49, 51, 108, 194–95; 215–16n41; as chief of staff, 1, 100, 115, 117, 157–58, 160, 161, 162, 163, 165, 166, 179, 181, 193, 194, 197, 200, 236n23; childhood of, 7, 9; and Chiricahua Apaches, 1, 71, 72, 73, 74, 75, 76, 77, 78, 81, 83, 84, 85, 86–87, 88, 150, 157, 169, 190, 198, 199; on Columbus, N.Mex., raid, 156–57; and conscription proposal, 163–64, 165, 197, 236–37n26; and Cuban service, 1, 57, 112, 114, 115, 116, 117, 118, 119, 120, 126, 139, 150–51, 157–58, 197; and David Hunter Scott, 49–50, 116, 118, 139, 167, 176; death of, 1, 195; described by others, 42, 43, 46, 47, 72, 115, 133, 137, 154, 157–58, 163, 84, 185, 189, 191, 192–93, 193–94, 194–95, 198, 204, 229n57; and early life in Princeton, N.J., 7, 9, 12, 21, 29–30; and failure of appointment to Office of the Adjutant-General, 111; and family support, 4, 10–11, 14, 15, 16, 19–20, 28, 39, 110, 117, 148, 150–51; farm purchase, 188; and federal wardship, 87, 169, 170, 171, 172, 179, 185, 242n36; financial challenges, 40, 89, 117, 188; first view of northern Great Plains, 21, 22, 30; at Fort Abraham Lincoln, 19, 20–21, 25, 29, 45, 108, 150; at Fort Meade, 40, 48, 109, 162; at Fort Sill, 1, 25, 50, 52, 53, 56, 57, 58, 61, 62, 64, 66, 68, 70, 71, 72, 74, 75, 76, 77, 78, 79, 80, 81, 82, 83, 84, 85–86, 87, 88, 89, 105, 110, 133, 146, 150, 157, 161, 162, 169, 172, 174, 176, 177, 198, 199; at Fort Totten, 38, 39, 47, 49–50, 89, 109, 118, 150, 151, 162, 176; and Francisco "Poncho" Villa, 97, 153–55, 156–57, 234n11; and Frank McCoy, 116, 121, 137; and "frontier" diplomacy, 5; and Ghost Dance religion, 58–59, 60, 61, 69–70, 88, 176–77, 190, 198, 217n8; and I-See-O, 60–61, 62, 70, 88, 93, 153–54, 156, 176–77, 190, 198; and John Collier, 104, 182, 183, 241n26; and

John J. Pershing, 103, 131, 165; and Leonard Wood, 94, 105–6, 115, 116–17, 118, 120–21, 122, 127, 128, 129, 131, 134, 135, 137, 139, 141, 142, 143, 144, 145, 146, 149, 151, 152, 157–58, 160, 162, 163, 200, 232n73; and Little Big Horn battlefield, 45; loneliness of, 38, 89, 110, 139, 230–31n64; and marriage to Mary Merrill, 39; and Mary Elizabeth Hodge (née Scott), 11, 14, 15, 16, 17, 19–20, 28, 39, 114, 212n21, 212n22; and *Memorandum to the Secretary of War*, 143, 144, 145; and Mexican border conflict, 153, 154, 156, 164, 165; and Moros, 5, 105–6, 120–21, 122, 126, 128–29, 130, 131–32, 132–33, 134, 135, 136, 138–39, 140, 141–42, 143, 144, 145, 154, 165, 200, 201, 202, 203; and *The Moros of Jolo Island*, 143; motion pictures made, 191, 192, 244n45; and Nelson Miles, 32, 33, 43, 44, 45, 47, 48, 49, 52, 69, 71, 72, 80, 91, 112, 113, 115; and Newton D. Baker, 98, 163, 165, 194; and Nez Percés, 32–33, 44, 45, 48, 49, 72, 79, 215n41; and *On Indian Bureau Re-organization*, 183–84, 241n28; and organization of Troop L, 71, 75, 77, 78, 80–81, 87, 190, 198, 220n25; and Panglima Hassan, 129, 130, 133, 134, 135, 136; and Panglima Indinan, 129; and the Philippine Commission, 131-2, 157, 198; and Philip Sheridan, 33, 43, 44, 46, 47; and Plains Indian sign language, 35, 43, 110, 168, 171, 189, 190, 191, 183, 194, 199, 202–3, 243n40, 243–44n41; and preparedness campaign, 162, 164–64, 165, 193; promotions of, 1, 43, 48, 50, 52, 89, 106, 107, 109, 110, 111, 112, 115, 116, 118, 119, 120, 121–22, 138, 149, 150, 151, 152–53, 157, 161; and racial marginalization, 4, 5, 6, 19, 145, 201, 203; and Red Cloud, 34–35, 51; and sense of loyalty, 61, 106, 111–12, 117, 122, 131, 132, 133, 156–57, 197, 198, 200, 202; in settling disputes with tribal groups, 32, 33, 34–35, 51, 157, 173, 203; Seventh U.S. Calvary, 3, 19, 20–21, 29, 34, 38, 48, 50, 150, 177, 209n31; Spanish American War, 1, 108, 158, 164, 166, 183, 189; staff assignments, 1, 47, 48, 49, 52, 80, 199, 108, 109, 119, 111, 115–16, 117, 120, 150, 152, 157–58, 159–60, 161, 162, 163, 165, 166, 179, 181, 193, 194, 197, 200; as superintendent at United States Military Academy, 17, 84, 145, 147, 148, 151, 152, 161, 193; support from friends, 137, 150–52, 216n43; and Tasker Bliss, 100, 116–17, 120, 121; and Theodore Roosevelt, 121–22, 137, 138, 144, 148, 149, 150, 151, 152, 162, 163, 200, 234n8; and Woodrow Wilson, 162-63; wounded in action, 134, 135, 195

Scott, Hunter. *See* Scott, David Hunter (son)

Scott, Louis Merrill "Pudd" (son), 154, 167

Scott, Mary Blanchard (daughter), 167

Scott, Mary Elizabeth Hodge (mother), 4, 9, 11, 15, 16, 17, 19–20, 28, 39, 41, 49–50, 114, 170

Scott, Mary Merrill (wife), 39, 49–50, 89, 110, 114, 118, 120, 134, 139, 152–53, 166–67, 188, 195; assistance in husband's promotion, 110, 120, 150–51, 223n4; health of, 89

Scott, Sarah Houston "Houty" (daughter), 139

Scott, William Berryman "Wick" (brother), 9, 17, 39, 50

Scott, William McKendree (father), 4, 7, 8, 9–10

Second U.S. Cavalry, 157

Sells, Cato, 175, 176

Senate Committee on Indian Affairs. *See* United States Congress

Senate Committee on Military Affairs. *See* United States Congress

Senate Indian Investigation Committee.
  See United States Congress
Seton, Ernest Thompson, 243n40
Seventh U.S. Cavalry, 3, 19, 20, 34, 38, 48,
  50, 150, 177; Indian troop in, 71, 75,
  7, 78, 80–81, 87, 190, 198; at Little Big
  Horn, 20, 21, 29, 150, 209n31
Seventy-Eighth Division, 166
Seymour, Flora Warren, 102, 169
sharia law. *See* Moros
Shawnee, Okla. 172
Shawnee Agency, 172
Sheridan, Philip, 12, 27, 33, 34, 43, 44, 46,
  47, 48
Sherman, William T., 12, 33, 34, 46, 48
sign language. *See* Plains Indian sign
  language
Sioux, 23–24, 25–26, 27–28, 30, 31, 32, 33,
  34–35, 36–37, 39, 41, 45, 48, 53, 55, 57,
  58, 59, 69, 79, 88, 108
Sitting Bull (Arapaho), 59
Sitting Bull (Lakota), 23, 24, 26, 30, 32, 33,
  34, 44, 45, 48, 49, 59, 108
Slocum, Horace, 20, 168
Smiley, Albert. *See* Lake Mohonk
  Conference
Smithsonian Institution, 110, 189, 192
Snyder, Homer, 175
Some Memories of a Soldier (Scott), 193,
  194
Sonora, Mexico, 25, 153, 154, 155, 156, 172
Spanish-American War, 1, 108, 158, 166,
  183, 189; lack of preparation for, 106,
  110; use of National Guard and state
  militia units in, 107, 109–10, 164
Spencer, Seldon, 176
spoilers, 26
Spotted Elk, 26
Spotted Tail Agency, 26
"squaw men," 57, 67, 79
Standing Rock Agency, 26
Stecker, Ernest, 80, 84, 177, 198;
  difficulties with government

personnel, 175, 176, 177, 178; as
  reservation agent, 80, 173, 175, 177;
  Troop L commander, 71, 80
Stockton, Mary Hunter, 11, 39, 42, 52
Stockton, Samuel, 14, 20, 42, 52
Sturgis, Samuel D., 40–41, 45, 47, 50
sultan of Sulu, 95, 123, 124, 125, 128, 129,
  130, 132, 156
Sulu Archipelago, 1, 95, 122, 123, 124, 129,
  130, 135, 136, 200
Sulu Province. *See* Moros
Systematic Theology (Hodge), 8

Taft, William Howard, 153, 160, 162;
  as governor-general of Philippine
  Commission, 126, 157; Scott's
  relationship with, 138, 143, 144, 157;
  secretary of war, 138, 143
Tampa, Fla., 112, 114, 115
Terry, Alfred, 27, 29, 33–34
Thackery, Frank, 172, 173, 198
Third Division, First Army Corps, 112, 113
Third U.S. Cavalry, 153–54
Thomas Training Camp. *See* Camp
  Thomas
treaties, 3, 27, 32, 34, 55, 56, 64, 68, 123,
  124, 139; Fort Laramie, 22, 23–24,
  25–26, 34, 37; Medicine Lodge, 34, 55,
  56, 65, 66, 67
Troop K, 48
Troop L, 71, 78, 80–81, 190; defended by
  Scott, 77, 198; organized by Scott, 75,
  87. *See also* Scott, Hugh L.
Troop M, 50
tuberculosis, 87, 89
Two Kettles, 26

United States Army: Adjutant General's
  Office, 111, 112, 114, 116, 117, 158, 160,
  165–66; Army Corps of Engineers,
  158; Bates Agreement, 124, 125, 128–29,
  139; Commissary Department, 47, 50,
  109, 116–17; conflict with Department

of the Interior over administration of Indian affairs, 68–69, 219n21, 219n22; conscription in, 163, 164, 165, 197; creation of general staff, 158, 159, 160, 161, 162, 236n23; criteria for advancement in, 107, 110; difficulty in embracing change, 106; Elihu Root and, 2, 84, 121, 158, 160; enforcement of treaties by, 22–23, 23–24, 27, 32, 55, 56, 64, 65, 66, 68; expansion of, 158–59, 161; increased professionalism in training, 2, 70, 83, 89, 106–7, 112, 132–33, 159, 164–65, 166; limited advancement in, 2, 41, 42, 105, 106, 111, 113, 150, 152, 105, 106, 111, 113, 150, 152, 179, 199; line versus staff, 108, 109, 159, 162; National Defense Act, 161, 163, 166; occupation of Cuba, 117, 119, 124, 125, 139, 197; occupation of Philippines, 95, 120, 121–22, 124, 125, 127, 133, 138, 139, 165, 197, 198, 200; Office of the Chief of Staff, 1, 100, 152, 157–58, 159, 160, 161, 162, 163, 165, 166, 179, 181, 193, 194, 197, 200, 236n23; Office of the Surgeon General, 158; Ordinance Department, 158; Organic Act, 159, 161; and parsimonious Congress, 2, 41, 141, 126; promotion in, 50, 105, 107, 108, 109, 115, 122, 151, 153; and Quartermaster's Corps 158; racial bias among officers, 18–19; regimental rule and, 41, 108; relinquishes control of Indian affairs, 81, 82; and Reorganization Act, 108–9; Scott's use of influence to gain promotion in, 42–43, 43–44, 50, 52, 69, 71, 108, 110, 111–12, 114, 115, 119, 121–22, 151–52; Scott's view of volunteers in, 109–10, 164, 224n1; Spanish American War, 106, 107, 158–59, 183; static retirement system, 50, 106; training volunteers for, 107, 109–10
United States Congress: *Congressional Record*, 143, 144; House Committee on Indian Affairs, 67, 175, 176, 191; Senate Committee on Indian Affairs, 186; Senate Committee on Military Affairs, 143, 150, 151, 152; Senate Indian Investigating Committee, 186
United States Military Academy, 12, 13, 14, 17, 18, 20, 139, 149, 151; curriculum at, 12, 28; discipline at, 12, 13, 17; hazing at, 15, 16, 17, 148; Scott as cadet, 11–17, 19, 20, 38, 39, 150; Scott as superintendent, 1, 17, 151, 152, 193
Upton, Emory, 17

Vaux, George, Jr., 180
Villa, Francisco "Pancho," 97, 153, 154, 155, 156; friendship with Scott, 97, 153–54, 155, 156, 157, 234n11; and Mexican border campaign; raid (1916) led by, 156–57. *See also* Scott, Hugh L.
Villistas, 155, 156

Wagner, Arthur L., 223n2
Walter Reed General Hospital, 1, 195
Wanamaker, John, 216n43
War College Board, 83
War Department, 20, 27, 34, 53, 58, 69, 72, 77, 78, 81, 82, 83, 84–85, 86, 88, 100, 106, 107, 110, 111, 115, 144, 150, 152, 158, 159, 160, 200
Warren Francis E., 151
Washington, D.C., 1, 44, 52, 56, 134, 143, 152–53, 154, 156, 157, 158, 173, 174, 178, 179, 183, 184, 189, 194, 195, 197
Washington National Cathedral, 195
West Point. *See* United States Military Academy
Wheeler, Burton K., 186
Wheeler-Howard Act, 187
White Eagle, 26
White House, 57, 163
Whitetail District. *See* Mescalero Apache reservation
Wilber, R. Lyman, 185

Wilson, Jack. *See* Ghost Dance religion
Wilson, James, 112, 114
Wilson, Woodrow, 162–63, 164, 165
Wood, Leonard, 94, 113, 124, 126; and Bud Dago massacre, 143, 145, 200, 231–32n71; and Fred Ainsworth, 160, 161, 235–36n21; and Lake Lanao campaign, 126, 134, 143, 152–53, 154, 156; and Philippine Campaign, 120, 122, 126, 131, 134, 135, 138, 139; and Santiago (Cuba) campaign, 116–17, 125, 165; Scott's help from, 106, 115, 116, 117, 118, 120–21, 122, 137, 138, 145, 146, 149, 151, 152, 157, 200; Scott's initial reluctance to work with, 115; Scott's loyalty to, 106, 117, 122, 134, 138, 144, 145, 157; Scott's problems with, 105–6, 160, 161, 163, 165, 200; and Theodore Roosevelt, 113–14, 121, 122, 125–26, 149, 160, 200

Work, Hubert, 183, 184
World Publishing Company, 194
World's Work, 194
World War I, 187, 193, 204
Wotherspoon, William, 157
Wovoka. *See* Ghost Dance religion
Wrattan, George, 74–75

Yankton, S.Dak., 25
Yellow Bull, 49
Yellowstone District, 48
Yellowstone River, 21, 23, 32, 45, 49
Yellowstone Valley, 49
Yukeoma (Hopi), 173

Zamboanga, 127

www.ingramcontent.com/pod-product-compliance
Lightning Source LLC
Chambersburg PA
CBHW020833160426
43192CB00007B/629